# LOCUTIONS
## TO THE
## WORLD

### VOLUME 1

# LOCUTIONS TO THE WORLD

## VOLUME 1

LOCUTIONS TO AN ANONYMOUS MYSTIC
UNDER THE
DISCERNMENT OF
MSGR. JOHN ESSEFF

DECEMBER 10, 2010 THROUGH DECEMBER 17, 2011
(as recorded on www.locutions.org)

LOCUTIONS TO THE WORLD: VOLUME ONE

The Cover Icon

The icon on the cover bears the title *Göttesmutter Hodegetria.* The icon depicts the *Mother of God* (*Göttesmutter*) holding the Child Jesus at her side while pointing to Him as the source of salvation for mankind. *Hodegetria* (Greek: Ὁδηγήτρια) means literally: "She who shows the Way." In the Western Church this type of icon is sometimes called *Our Lady of the Way.*

The image of this icon was obtained from its iconographer, Eva-Maria Steidel and is used with her gracious permission. Ms. Steidel's iconographic work may be seen at http://www.graphicon-online.de

Volume One
*Locutions to the World: Let the Word Go Forth*
December 10, 2010 to December 17, 2011
ISBN-13  978-1495299834
ISBN-10  149529983X

Volume Two
*Locutions to the World: Let the Word Go Forth*
December 18, 2011 to October 28, 2012
ISBN-13  978-1496089717
ISBN-10  1496089715

Volume Three
*Locutions to the World: The Two Hearts Speak to the World*
July 14, 2012 to January 30, 2014
ISBN-13  978-1495350597
ISBN-10  1495350592

Published by SERVANTS PRESS
in cooperation with Msgr. John Esseff

# EDITOR'S INTRODUCTION

*The following locutions, covering the period from Dec. 10, 2010 to December 17, 2011are taken from (and can be currently found on) the website www.locutions.org*

*The background to these locutions is as follows:*

Let me introduce myself; I am Monsignor John Esseff, a diocesan priest of Scranton, Pa., ordained in 1953. In 1959, Padre Pio became my spiritual director. For many years, I was the spiritual director for Mother Teresa of Calcutta. As a favor to her, I traveled all over the world, giving retreats, to her sisters. Above all, I am privileged to be spiritual director for hundreds of souls, at every stage of the spiritual life. Some are beginners, others are advanced and some are mystics.

For many years, I have been director for a special soul. Five years ago, Jesus and Mary began to speak to this soul through the gift of locutions (as described by John of the Cross). These locutions now total over 800. I have discerned the validity of these locutions. Until now, these locutions were personal teachings given for the small community that gathered in prayer. Beginning on December 10, 2010, a new phase began, namely, some locutions were to be told to the whole world.

The beginning locutions are very special; focusing on the Fatima Vision (revealed by the Vatican (June 2000).

*Monsignor John Esseff*
December 11, 2010

## Concerning private revelation

*These are private revelations and there is no need to believe them. If these revelations help your faith, then receive them. If not, you can set them aside. We are called to believe only public revelations.*

Volumes Two and Three of these locutions are published separately. Volume Two covers the period from December 18, 2011, October 28, 2012. Volume Three covers the period from July 14, 2012 to January 30, 2014. On-going locutions may be read at www.locutions.org

December 10th, 2010
# LET THE WORD GO FORTH

## Mary

I will soon begin to speak to you for the whole world. You will receive these words as you have received all the other words. You will write the words down and record the proper dates. You will take these words to Monsignor Esseff, for his discernment. If his heart discerns that these messages should be released to the whole world they will go forth. He will correctly say that these are being given to one of his directees. The time is short and that is why I have moved you so quickly.

# LOCUTIONS TO THE WORLD
## PART 1

## FEBRUARY 4, 2011 TO JULY 6, 2011

# TABLE OF CONTENTS
# PART 1

## LUCY'S FATIMA VISION

*Since the messages that follow concern the effects of the Pope's dream which Mary revealed to the three children of Fatima (July 13, 1917), I will put here Lucy's description of that vision as released by the Vatican (June 2000).*

We saw in an immense light that is God: "something similar to how people appear in a mirror when they pass in front of it," a Bishop dressed in white. We had the impression that it was the Holy Father. Other bishops, priests, men and women religious going up a steep mountain, at the top of which there was a big Cross of rough-hewn trunks, as of a cork-tree with the bark; before reaching there, the Holy Father passed through a big city half in ruins, and half trembling with halting step, afflicted with pain and sorrow, he prayed for the souls of the corpses he met on his way; having reached the top of the mountain on his knees at the foot of the big Cross, he was killed by a group of soldiers who fired bullets and arrows at him, and in the same way, there died one after another, the other bishops, priests, men and women religious, and various lay people of different ranks and positions. Beneath the two arms of the Cross, there were two angels each with a crystal aspersorium in his hand, in which they gathered up the blood of the martyrs and with it sprinkled the souls that were making their way to God.

February 4, 2011
## 1. Keep Your Eye on Israel

## Jesus

How long will it be? Keep your eye on Israel. This is the center. By keeping your eye on Israel you will get to know the time. Not exactly, but you will see it coming closer. The more danger there is to Israel, the closer the time will be.

I love Israel and I love Jerusalem. In Jerusalem, I shed my blood, redeemed the world and rose from the dead. It is a sealed city, sealed in my blood and in my Holy Spirit. Even more than geography, I love the Jewish people. They are my people. But Jewish lips do not call out, "Jesus is our Messiah." I like to hear these words from anyone's lips. But I have my greatest joy when I hear those words from the lips of a Jew and from the lips of Israel. This is the deepest hope of my heart.

### Comment
*In these locutions, Israel takes center stage, both in the time frame*
*of events and in Jesus' heart.*

## Mary

I am a daughter of Israel and I dreamed of Israel gathered around the Messiah, for whom they had waited so long.

But then, what did I experience? I saw Israel reject my Son, call him a false Messiah, reject his claims and nail him to the cross.   But that was only my first sorrow as a daughter of Israel. After He rose from the dead and the apostles began to preach, I held new hopes. Certainly now, Israel would accept my Son as Messiah. Instead, I experienced a second rejection. My own people did not accept Him as their Messiah. Twice, I have been broken in heart. Twice, they have rejected Jesus as Messiah. But it will not happen a third time. I look forward to the day when all of Israel will proclaim my Son as Messiah.

The moment of the greatest darkness is the moment before the greatest light. The very moment when it seems that Israel will be destroyed is the moment when I will save Israel and all will proclaim that Jesus is the Messiah. I have revealed the deepest sorrow of my heart.

### Comment
*Mary's two-fold sorrow brings forth a promise that this time the result will be*
*different. Israel's moment of greatest darkness will be the moment when*
*Mary rescues Israel.*

February 7, 2011
## 2. Seeing the Future of Israel

### Jesus

As I stood at the table of the Last Supper, I saw Israel. All its future history unfolded before me, the destruction of the city by the Romans, the dispersal of Israel all over the world and the moment when the Jewish people would be invited to return, as the State of Israel was formed. As they returned, all rejoiced. However, they put their trust in their own strength, as their forefathers had done. They built weapons of war and rejoiced in these weapons. They were on the wrong road, being led down a path that led into the hands of their enemies, instead of withdrawing into the safety of my arms. Now, their enemies gather arms and the tide is shifting. Their protection drops away from them. There is terror on every side and still they do not turn to me.

Centuries ago, the Father intervened on their behalf and sent me, hoping that all Israel would proclaim me as Messiah. But they killed me. What will the Father do now? He cannot send me again to die. So, He will send my Vicar, the Pope.

The Pope will enter Jerusalem as I entered it. The city will already have suffered much and Israel will begin to despair, wondering what can be done. Then this figure clothed in white will come, sent by the Father just as He sent me. He will come to save Israel, just as I came. He, too, will die in Jerusalem but his death will have a profound effect upon the whole world. For the whole world will weep at his death and his death will bless Israel. Why do I reveal these things now? Why do I bring you to the center of the mystery so quickly? Because the time is short. The events are near. They are not far away.

*Comment*

*Jesus describes what has happened since the State of Israel was formed and why it is now prey to so many enemies. Most important, the Holy Father goes to Jerusalem, dies there, and a series of events begin that save Israel.*

February 9, 2011
## 3. The Pope Dies in Jerusalem

### Jesus

The Church came forth from Israel, like a child begotten by a mother, but Israel began to reject her own child. The soil rejected the fruit it had brought forth. Then came the saddest time of all. Israel and the Church were separated. Now they stand as distinct groups. The mother has rejected her child and the soil has rejected the roots that should have stayed within it.

Peter was the apostle to the Jews and Paul always preached first in the synagogues. The word was preached and the roots tried to enter more deeply into the soil. However, they could not pierce its resistance. Without deeper roots, the plant could not stay long in its original soil.

However, when the darkness comes and Israel is in distress, there will be a new moment. The Pope, the head of the Catholic Church, will go to Israel in its darkest hour and lay down his life for Israel. The eyes of many Jewish people will be opened. They will say, "We have been saved by the Catholic Church." The soil will be open and receptive again to the original seed. My Church and my Jewish people will be joined as I have wanted them to be for centuries.

As the Church's roots are placed once more into its original Jewish soil, the other divisions of the churches will be healed because they happened due to this first division of the Church from the Synagogue.

It will be clear to all the Christian Churches that there is a new call to unity, a call to unity at the roots and in the heart.

Churches will see what they have never seen and do what they thought they would never do. Seeing the union of Israel and the Catholic Church, they will say, "We must be one." All the barriers to unity, put up over the many centuries, will be swept away in one breath of the Spirit.

There will be the ingathering prophesied by Isaiah. All the riches of the nations will come to Israel. This will be true wealth, the spiritual wealth of all the Churches gathering as one in Jerusalem with Israel and the Catholic Church. My prayer will be fulfilled, that all would be one as the Father and I are one.

Also, the world will see something quite different, what they have never seen. They will see the Churches united and all the Churches united with Israel. The world will experience a powerful call to come out of darkness. The Church and Israel will be a light to all nations. The light will not be lessened or covered over by divisions of the Churches or divisions between the Churches and Israel. The world will not be able to escape the invitation. The unity will stand before them inviting them to accept Me as Lord.

### Comment

*This is extraordinary. The sacrificial death of the Pope leads to a full union between Israel and the Catholic Church which leads to a reunion of all of Christianity, planted again in the soil of Israel. This greater witness will confront the world with a more powerful invitation to accept Jesus Christ as Lord.*

## Mary

A moment will come when I will take my beloved son, the Pope. I will walk with him to Jerusalem. For the second time I will go to Jerusalem to witness the death of a son.

When this happens the eyes of the Jewish people will see for the first time. They will see in the Pope's death what the Catholic Church has done for them. There will be no mistake about which Church has blessed them, because it will have been done by the head of the Church and by the greatest of sacrifices. Israel will embrace the Catholic Church.

All Catholics will welcome Israel because all will have seen the decision of the Holy Father (the bishop dressed in white) to offer his life for Israel. The union between the Catholic Church and Israel will be a union of hearts brought about by the events that the whole world will have has seen and can never forget.

### Comment

*By the Pope's death, Israel's eyes will be opened to the Catholic Church and how Catholic hearts will be opened to Israel. Both happen from the same event.*

February 11, 2011
## 4. The Valley of Decision

## Jesus

After the events of Jerusalem and the unifying of the Church with Israel, I will call all the nations into the Valley of Decision. It does not need to be a physical valley because all the nations are already linked by communications. This Valley of Decisions will be a special moment in history.

Just as Israel was in the moment of distress, so the world itself will be in a moment of complete helplessness. But I will gather the nations and there will be a new breath in the air, a new opportunity, when all the nations will be united into the light. Some nations will leave the Valley and return to darkness, but most will stay in the light. Armaments will be limited. Money will be spent on food. There will be international cooperation that has been sought by many but never brought about.

I will give these blessings to all the nations in the Valley of Decision as a free gift from my hands. There will be peace and a new springtime.

### Comment

*This shows the effects of these events upon world leaders at a moment when all the world is in distress. The crises are solved by heaven changing hearts of world leaders.*

8

*All of these locutions, extraordinary as they are, merely reveal the full effects of Lucy's vision of the death of the Holy Father (July 13, 1917).*

February 11, 2011
## 5. The Holy Spirit and the Immaculate Heart of Mary

### Mary

Why does the heavenly Father want to establish devotion to my Immaculate Heart? Only in this way can there be an Age of the Spirit.

The easiest way to understand the Holy Spirit is through my Immaculate Heart. My Heart is the way of entering the Age of the Spirit. This will not be a final Age but will prepare for the Second Coming.

February 18, 2011
## 6. The Problem of Russia

### Jesus

The problem is Russia. She is the mother of iniquity. She loves neither America nor Israel. That is why my mother asked that Russia be consecrated to her Immaculate Heart. When Russia is consecrated all will be drawn together. For now she spreads her iniquity. All the other evil is nourished by her, for she still wants to be the first among the nations. She uses others for her goals, finding partners in evils.

February 18, 2011
## 7. The Demonstrations in the Street

### Jesus

The media covers the rioting of the people on the streets but the people with real power are not on the streets. They are in hiding. The real evil lies not in the demonstrations that all can see, but in the evil which no one can see. They are like bombs planted to go off. When they explode, they will not hit the center, Israel. I know the timetable of darkness. When they do hit the center (Israel), my plan for the Holy Father will be ready to be implanted.

9

February 21, 2011
## 8. The Earth Tilts towards Evil

## Jesus

Everything is tilting towards evil and darkness. This has been going on for some time but there is no longer any balance. All has shifted and there will be a quickening of events. All will culminate in the events that I will describe.

At this point, no one can quell the uprisings. They are fires that will continue until all the wood is consumed. Then, like any fire, they will burn themselves out. However, Satan never intended these fires to accomplish his final goal, the destruction of Israel. The purpose of these fires was to weaken all the protection, all the buffers around Israel. This is what is happening but this is not meant to be Satan's final attack.

February 21, 2011
## 9. Significance of the Egyptian Uprising

## Mary

The forces of evil have passed the point of no return. The ultimate clash between good and evil is inevitable. Many view the uprising in Egypt in a positive way. They see that a dictator has been removed. However, you must see it in another way, that a war has broken out. Many see the uprising as good but this is the way Satan acts. He get people to do his work by making them think that they are pursuing their own goals. Later, when they have done his work, he reveals himself. Then it is too late to do anything. See this clearly. Egypt is the first step towards the ultimate confrontation.

February 27, 2011
## 10. The Holy Spirit's Words

## Mary

You must not think that I speak on my own. I conceived the Eternal Word by the power of the Holy Spirit and I conceive these living words only through the Spirit's light. The Holy Spirit made me the Mother of God and Mother of the Church. He abides in me and through these words he will bring forth new children of the Father.

*Comment*
*Mary gives these locutions but the Holy Spirit, her spouse, is their source.*

## The Encourager

In the Gospels, I said little because my Son's voice had to be heard. However, the world did not listen because he spoke words of judgment and repentance, which the world did not want to hear. I am the encourager, inviting the world to listen more carefully to his words.

*Comment*
*Mary assumes a mother's role of explaining the difficult sayings of Jesus.*

## Darkened Minds

Jesus' words are light but minds are often darkened. I will explain his words, and give everyone a chance to hear his words a second time. Listened to afresh, his invitation to the kingdom will be heard anew. I will explain his most difficult sayings, which Satan twists to create obstacles. When these obstacles are removed, the sheep will follow the Shepherd's voice.

*Comment*
*Mary overcomes Satan's strategy of using Jesus' words as stumbling blocks.*

*"If anyone does not take up his cross and follow me, he cannot be my disciple."*
The cross forces each soul to ask, "What are my motives? Do I really love Jesus?" This saying forces the soul to look within. If it finds love, then it will follow. If it does not find love, then it must search for it. Without love, the soul will begin the journey but will never complete it. The soul will overcome trials only by some inner love for Jesus that forces it to go on.

*"Whoever looks at a woman with lust has already committed adultery*
*with her in his heart."*
These words challenge the soul to greatness, to conquer their own heart and the passions that flow within. Only a purified heart can receive God's gifts, so these words protect the soul from shameless ventures that would defile the soul.

*Comment*
*It is easier to conquer the world than to conquer your own heart.*
*"If your eye is a scandal, then pluck it out."*

11

These words contain a hidden wisdom which is needed because this world is not perfect. These words are needed for this time on earth, until that which is perfect comes. Just a little while. That is all Jesus asks. Discipline your eyes.

*"Unless a man deny himself, he cannot be my disciple."*
My Son came to gain divine life for you. Can you receive the new if you cling to the old?
<u>Comment</u>
*Denying self-love opens you to God's love.*

*"Seek first the Kingdom of God."*
What else should you seek? Does my Son offer you half a loaf? Or give you bread that perishes? He gives you a noble task, worthy of the human person. He created you for the kingdom.
<u>Comment</u>
*The kingdom is man's highest calling.*

*"The seed falling into the ground must die, or it remains alone."*
Jesus has placed great treasures within you. Will you take these to your grave still unopened? A seed that does not die is an unopened treasure, worthy only to be cast out. Its existence has served no purpose.
<u>Comment</u>
*An unopened treasure is useless.*

*"It would be better for that man if he had never been born."*
When Jesus said these words, his heart was sorrowful and broken. He had done all he could to save Judas. However, Judas had made his decision and had departed the Last Supper.

## 10a. The Holy Spirit's Words

More grace was fruitless. No one enters the kingdom just because they have received much grace (as Judas had). The free will must speak its "yes" to God's grace.
<u>Comment</u>
*God has given you the great gift of existence. He also offers you graces to gain a heavenly existence. To these you must say yes.*

12

March 2, 2011
## 11. The Holy Spirit

## Mary

Often you invoke spirits whom you fear and do not really know. I will tell you about a Spirit whom you need not fear. He is the Holy Spirit, the Spirit of my Son. This is what happened.

When my Son rose from the dead, he came to his disciples, those whom he had trained from the beginning. They were in deep darkness and feared for their lives.

He came into the room without opening the locked doors. When he said, "Peace I leave with you," all their fears vanished. He showed himself alive in a real body, but transformed by heavenly glory. He breathed upon the disciples and said, "Receive the Holy Spirit."

For forty days he appeared to them in this way, telling them to wait in Jerusalem for a full outpouring of this Holy Spirit. He was taken up to heaven and they all saw him go up. This happened right before their very eyes.

They obediently returned to Jerusalem, to that same upper room, and they waited for this Holy Spirit that I want to teach you about.

On a day we call Pentecost (meaning fifty) the heavenly Father and Jesus, His only-begotten Son, sent their Holy Spirit. He came with many signs – a mighty wind and tongues as of fire which parted and rested on each one of us. We were all filled with the Holy Spirit. As a proof of the new gift, we all began to praise God in strange languages which we did not understand.

The sounds created by the Holy Spirit were heard all over Jerusalem, and people who were there for the feast gathered around this upper room. When they heard us speaking in their own language, they were amazed. This leads to the next part of our story.

*Comment*
*Many people fear and worship false spirits. Mary wants them to know the Spirit of her Son, the Holy Spirit, the source of eternal life.*


March 2, 2011
## 12. Mary Sets You Free

## Mary

Peter in Jail (Acts 12:6-10)
The soul has two chains, its passions within and its culture without. It feels alone, as

if in prison but dreaming of its freedom. The faintest light of hope still burns within. But, for how long can this last before the passions and the culture snuff it out.

O soul, you have read my words this far. I promise that I will do more than break these chains. Like Peter, you will see them "fall from your wrists" (12:7). I will lead you out. All the doors will open. Just follow me. Read on. My words will lead you, touch your heart and convince you that your heavenly mother spoke them.

*Comment*
*To the soul who has entered her heart, Mary promises total freedom.*
*Continue to read on.*

## The Means to Freedom

What chains bind you? Review your life. Untangle the past. Recall the events, the circumstances, the decisions and the mistakes. Omit nothing. Then, speak to me of all that has happened. Your own words, spoken in my presence, will heal you. The pain will be removed. The light will enter and you will breathe the air of truth.

## Find a Priest

Now, go find a priest. Do not wait. You have told your sins to me. Now, tell them to a priest. He will say, "I absolve you from your sins." The chains will be permanently loosed. Then return to me and we will talk some more.

*Comment*
*Mary's path to freedom is quite clear. Identify the chains of your sins. Tell them*
*privately to Mary. Then, go to confession.*
*After that you will hear more of Mary's words.*

## The Source of Freedom – Jesus' Blood

Did you ever think that the past could be set aside so quickly and with such little effort? Just a few steps took you out of prison. Now I can help you. First, let us thank my Son. Reflect, "What power set you free? Why do you experience freedom, with your mind turned away from the past? Your freedom was purchased at a price. Come I will show you how it happened.

One day, an angel announced the mystery, that I would conceive a child by the Holy Spirit. He would be the world's Savior by the shedding of his blood. This was holy blood, blood taken from my womb. This is what God asked – that I would give His Son a body and blood. Then I was to be with him when his body was nailed to a cross and his blood was shed.

14

At the cross, Jesus gave me his blood until the end of time. This is why you are free. I have touched you with one drop of his blood.

### Comment
*The personal freedom, so quickly given in confession, does not come from psychological causes. In every confession, the blood of Jesus purifies the inner heart of the person.*

March 5, 2011
# 13. Mary, Mother of the Church
*In these lengthy locutions, Mary acts as Mother of the Church.*
*First, she speaks about the Popes.*

## The Pope Consecrating Russia

The secret of the First Pentecost was that Peter gathered with me and I was able to prepare him to receive the Holy Spirit, my spouse. I was God's lowly handmaid, but I was instructed by the most high God and knew the secrets of the king.

The crowds at Pentecost did not overwhelm Peter. His clear words invited the people to do what he had done, to repent and to receive the Holy Spirit.

I took great hope that day. I saw that my Son's message would be preached until the end of time. I saw all of Peter's successors, the long line of popes. They were all placed in my heart. As Mother of the Church I accepted them all. How I have watched over them, even those whose personal lives were not in order, making sure that they did not err in faith and morals. And the holy popes, I have used to enlighten the world.

What should I say of the recent popes? They have all blessed my Church, opening doors to the Holy Spirit encouraging vast works and inviting all to participate in Church life.

But the great work is still to be done, left to the last minute, so to speak, the work I spoke about at Fatima and which I later commanded to be done – the consecration of Russia to my Immaculate Heart and devotion to the five First Saturdays. These two are joined together, the mutual work of the Pope and the faithful. Do not ask why the Pope delays. That is in my hands. My desire is that the faithful do not delay. No one holds them back. They must begin to practice the Five First Saturdays immediately. The power will build and sweep the Holy Father along, then both head and members will be ready with full heart to consecrate Russia to my Immaculate Heart.

### Comment
*Although these words center on the popes, the real message is for you, the reader.*
*Begin now to practice the Fire First Saturdays. You will be hastening the*
*papal consecration of Russia to the Immaculate Heart.*

The Five First Saturdays

To fulfill Mary's request, you must do four things on the First Saturday of five consecutive months.

1.  Receive Holy Communion (If this is not possible on Saturday, then the Sunday following)
2.  Receive the sacrament of Reconciliation (a week before or a week after)
3.  Say a rosary (5 decades)
4.  Meditate for fifteen minutes on a mystery of the rosary.

Your motive for doing these must be to make reparation for sins against Mary's Immaculate Heart.


Mary and the Priests

I see my priests. Some are worthy. Some are unworthy. Some bless the Church and some disgrace the Church. But they are all my priests and for each I have a word that they need to hear, a word that comes from a mother's heart.


To My Sinful Priests

These priests hear many words from their consciences which reprove them, but they do not respond. Their emotions are empty and they are helpless.

So, to you my sinful priests, I speak no word of rebuke. I speak a mother's word. Do not act upon my word immediately for you are in too much pain. First, let my word heal you. Then, arise from your sickness and walk to your brother priest in sorrow and repentance. I will greet you there in the sacrament of penance.

Oh, you have been to confession often but without the repentance needed to rise from your sins. Notice, I will have you rise first. You will already have repentance before you confess your sins. When the sacrament is over, we will walk together. This, too, you have lacked in previous confessions. You had no one to guide you after you confessed.

The secret lies in my words. Listen to these words and let them surround your heart. Do not dismiss them. They are my messages of hope and healing. If you take my words into your heart, recalling them and remembering them frequently, I promise that you will arise from your sins. If this does not happen immediately, remember that these are words of grace which must first permeate you and attract you into the light.

I speak these words to you, yes, to you my sinful priests, who have done unspeakable things which cling to your memory and weigh upon your heart. These deeds are like an anchor which does not allow you to come to Jesus, even though you are invited so often during the liturgical year. The following are your heavenly mother's words. They come from my heart, so listen carefully.

I know your name. In your heart right now, I am speaking your name. Listen to your name spoken by the Queen of Heaven. How do I know you? Of course, I know you. A mother never forgets her priest son.

Why did you stray? What took you so far away from your priestly life? Who led you down the wrong road? These questions have answers but does it really matter now? Why pull up those memories? Why recall your mistakes? What good does it do? That road is too long and you will never come to the end. You must turn around. You have wandered because of human love – for things or for others.

By these words, I reveal my human love for you. Yes, my human love, a mother's love. I do not want you to perish in hell. A priest in hell is a special trophy for the Evil One, a splendid victory that he marches around because it displays his craftiness. Also, I do not want your remaining years on earth to be filled with remorse, emptiness and darkness. Satan will claim you as early as he can, dragging you into his darkness long before your death. In this way, you are his and his victory is sealed, many years before you actually die.

I want you to come into my light and into a new fruitfulness in your priestly ministry. I want to give you spiritual children whom you bring into the light. I have waiting for you a happy priesthood, filled with those who love you and will walk with you into eternal life.

Which life do you want for yourself? Do you want years lived in your sins, filled with indescribable loneliness which lead only to the grave and to hell? Or a new life, filled with people who need your priestly powers, who will pray for you and be with you. Yes, I will send them, but you must repent. These final years can lead to a happy death and to life everlasting.

Look at the two roads! Look at the two roads!!

Right now you are on the wrong one and are unable to choose the right one. Your only hope is in my words. Read them again and again until the tears stream down your face. Then, go and find your brother priest. He will be a fountain of God's mercy. I will wait for you there.

## Comment

*Mary knows that the sinful heart is anchored, hopeless and unable to repent. Even her loving powerful words do not have instant results. Slowly they permeate. Although the process is long, the results are true and lasting – a priest restored to grace, a true pastor of his people.*

To My Discouraged Priests

You experience a pervasive darkness, thinking that you are a failure. You do not say this aloud nor proclaim it to others, but the feeling gnaws away. It is a truth that confronts you at every turn, in the poor response of your people, in your small harvest and in your loss of enthusiasm.

You try so many remedies! Sometimes you lose yourself in entertainments. Sometimes you see new ministries. O you discouraged priests, return to the initial spring of your call. Those waters still flow. You drank from them in your youth but you think that they are no more. I promise you that I will release them afresh within you.

I ask these questions. Did I not call you to your priesthood, saying, "Come on this path. Do not walk another. Give up wife and children, home and family." In those early days, did you not hear my voice? Did you not turn away from all that your human nature so powerfully sought?

Now answer me this question, "Did I stop speaking to you? Did I lead you into the priesthood and then abandon you? Is it my joy to see you overwhelmed with failure, your years spent in darkness? Go back. Recall how you heard my voice, the spring of your priestly call. This voice still flows within you. Do not plunge into your recreations or into your empty works. Go back and plunge into the power of my words that brought you to the priesthood. We will begin again and search together. As your mother I will lead you by my words.

You have looked outside of yourself but you have not looked inside of yourself to the voice of your mother who led you to the priesthood.

*Comment*

*The priesthood is an inner call, and Mary highlights this mystical inner spring of her voice that led the young man to embrace his priestly call.*

*Now, she calls him back to her voice and her words.*


March 6, 2011

# 14. Cleansing the Heavenly Stream


# Mary

The world is grasped by a whirlpool of destruction. It tried to delay the inevitable but with little success, It does not understand the stream of heaven which purifies and awakens people to God. However, when sin is committed and there is no repentance, this stream becomes polluted and unable to awaken people to God.

Only repentance and reparation can cleanse this stream and keep it a vital force in human history, bringing forth a goodness in people that pleases the Father.

When unrepented sin enters, this stream loses its power and the Father must cleanse the world by chastisements. This is the only option unless man turns back to God.

### Comment
*The image is very clear, a stream coming from heaven which awakens man to heavenly things. Sin destroys the power of this stream. So, either man repents or God chastises, the only two ways of keeping the stream powerful.*

March 7, 2011
## 15. Rome and Jerusalem

### Jesus
Great vision is needed because the devil believes that he is finally able to destroy the Church. He has almost all of his people in place to attack the Church of Rome. However, the heart of my Church is not in Rome, but in Jerusalem. The Church was transplanted to Rome because Jerusalem would not survive. So, the move of Peter and Paul to Rome was my will.

Rome is not Jerusalem. All the churches see the uniqueness of Jerusalem. After the Pope is killed, there will be a question. Will the papacy stay in Jerusalem or return to Rome? The deceased Pope will have instructed his followers clearly. Some people will remember the splendor of Rome and will want to return. They will return but those who are faithful will elect a new Pope and the world will know that the soul of the Church is in Jerusalem. This small seed will grow strong in Jerusalem and the gift will take root.

## 16. Attacks on the Worldwide Church

### Jesus
Satan will attack the Church, in its external form throughout the world. How can this be, since the Church exists everywhere, with places of worship in many cultures? You will see surprising things. The Church is different in each country, and has a different relationship with the government and with the people. Satan will know the weakness of the Church and how it can be attacked and destroyed in each culture. However, he does not see that I am building a Church of faith and belief.

March 15, 2011
## 17. Heaven's Moments of Opportunity

## Jesus

This is a time of heavenly blessings because the problems are so great and man has no solutions. Before, man could look to his own resources. Now, Satan has released so many problems of such great magnitude, that man can no longer respond. There is a growing despair.

Yet, this is a moment of opportunity, and heaven will respond. Then, all will know that man did not solve the problems. The heavenly Father intervened. Not just with one gift, but with many gifts. Not just with small gifts, but with large gifts. Those with faith must lift up their eyes and open wide their arms.

March 15, 2011
## 18. Mary's Words of Advice

## Mary

### To the Confused Person

How did things get to this point? Why is the world in such dire straits? Mankind has gone in the wrong direction for centuries, unable to cope with the rapid speed of technology. Quick, so quick. Everything is quick, with no sense of direction.

So stop. Do not rush headlong. Pause, be still. Ask yourself, "Where am I going? What is my goal?" In this stillness, I will whisper to your heart, "Come this way." It will be a surprising direction. One you would never have thought of. It is your Mother who leads you. Follow me."

*Comment*

*Mary's command is so needed, "Pause. Be still. Examine your goals. Listen." Her promise is even greater, to lead you in a surprising direction.*

### To the Discouraged Person

As the tribulation continues, the faith of many will be shaken because they have built their house upon sand. But, is it too late? Will they collapse? All things are possible to God. This is my promise. Even those whose faith has not been built on solid ground I will receive into the Ark of my Immaculate Heart.

That is why this word must go forth. No one is rejected. It is never too late. The door of my heart will only close at the last minute, when all have had a chance to enter.

20

Never, never say, "It is too late." My word is a constant stream of hope. Wherever it reaches, hope enters, saving hope.

You, discouraged soul. You, frightened soul. Get up from your bed of despair and walk to the Ark. Just use my name, Mary. Suddenly, the Ark will be in front of you and the door will be open. I will await you there.

### Comment
*This is a beautiful message because people who have not lived a life of faith feel they have no chance in these tribulations. They must act now. Tomorrow might be too late.*

## To the Overwhelmed Modern Person

Everything swirls around with no sense of purpose. Each minute cries out, "Take care of me because the future has no hope."

So, you plunge into what is at hand. Why ask? Why search? Why look for more than what the present holds?

The whirlpool gets greater. The helplessness grows. O child, you get carried away by forces that are greater than you. So, I stretch out my hand. My strength is enough. I am the saving Mother who searches endlessly for my children, finding them in back alleys and deep valleys. Wherever you are right now, I am with you. Just stretch out your hand. I do not say, "Grasp my hand," because you do not have the strength. I do not say, "Hold on to me." I will hold on to you. I do not say, "Follow me." I will lift you up.

Just one act of your will is enough. Use my name, "Mary." It opens the door of my heart.

### Comment
*The modern person is so overwhelmed and the way back to God seems too complex. With these words, Mary provides and easier solution.*

## To Lost Souls

I am the Mother of Sorrows whose woes will not come to an end until all the events written in the Book of Life are fulfilled. I am the Mother of Life. Where there is life there are also sorrows until all my children are gathered into the kingdom. I am not condemned to sorrows because they are not the final word.

These days, however, are days of travail, of bringing to new life, and of restoring life that has been lost. Yes, many of my children have lost the life I gave to them in Baptism. Many have cast aside the life I suffered to give them. They chose their own life. Others were carried away from a life of devotion. So many causes. So many

21

snares. So many had roots with no depth. This is the state of the Church and my deepest sorrow.

Yet, I do not cast them out of my heart. I take them deeper into my heart, allowing them to cause me even greater sorrows. I let them surround my heart, hoping that just one might understand, "I am causing sorrow to my mother."

Dear reader, think of your earthly mother. Think of her faith and what she taught you. Did she not teach you my name and to fold your hands in prayer, and to say the Hail Mary? I ask you, "How does she see you now? Do you not cause her sorrow even though she is in heaven? Think of your earthly mother and turn back to the ways which she taught you. I will be waiting there for you.

Comment

*Mary, like a true mother, is willing to experience even greater sorrow to save her child. How powerful to recall the devotion of your earthly mother.*

## Inviting Souls to Return

Little by little. Step by step. No need for great efforts. One step after another, like two feet on a journey.

You have so many questions. "What will others think? Am I able to return? What will it be like?" Do not ask these questions. They are of no help. They are not the way back.

Here are the steps you must take. First, leave behind what is sinful. You believe that sin's grasp upon you cannot be broken. This is not true. Just remove your desires for the sinful. Once you let go, I will take what is sinful from your hand. Easily, quickly and with little effort, your hand will be empty, easily able to select the good.

Second, search your heart. It will be able to choose what is above, the gifts which heaven offers. This is what you have always wanted and it is yours because sin's power is broken.

Thirdly, seek out others who also want heaven's favors. All your hands will be lifted high, freed from what is below you and receiving what is above.

Comment

*Mary describes the steps to a solid conversion in the easiest of terms.*

## To the Fallen Away Catholic

These are not mere words. They are gifts from a mother's heart, filled with enticements. I place the needed medicine in a candy so you will eat. As you chew on my words, a power will enter your hearts. You will taste a new hope. What you thought was impossible is suddenly within your grasp, like a lifeboat in a dark ocean.

I will inspire you with new hope and you will say, "I can return to the faith of my parents." You will know the way back. It is a familiar road. You grew up in the Church. You know its teachings and its liturgies.

When you return, you will meet one stumbling block because you will not be fully reconciled. Some will say that this is not needed but you will know that something is missing. You cannot just overlook many years. You cannot remove your own sins. This violates all that you were taught.

March 18, 2011
## 19. Libya

## Mary

Why do they hesitate? Why do they look at one another waiting to see what each will do? The people are at the mercy of a dictator who wants to subjugate them. This is how the world acts. It seeks its own interests, and waits until it is too late, when nothing of real value can be accomplished.

Where is America? Have I not given it a special role in the world? It wastes its resources and cannot respond to the real needs. To those who would want my light, I say, "In Libya, rescue what can be rescued as quickly as possible, protecting what can be protected. Then wait for another day when America will have a different leader who will judge by truth."

If people pray to me, I will raise up this leader. Let this word go forth. America must pray for the right leadership. If they raise their hearts and hands to me, I will touch that leader's heart and he will accept the mantle of justice. Otherwise, he will just stay on the sidelines, because there is no divine anointing upon the political scene.

March 20, 2011
## 20. The Woman Who Conquers

## Mary

All is turmoil with the constant shifting of world events; all is turmoil. Human minds are helpless as new forces of evil and new forces of destruction emerge. The enemy has become legion, far too overwhelming and far too intelligent for mankind and its leaders. Destruction is everywhere, pouring out from its source, the human heart. There is no end in sight. Man cannot regain control.

Why does the world not turn to me? Am I not The Woman and must not the serpent await the crushing heel of my Son? Satan laughs and rejoices because I am set aside. He does not fear as long as man seeks no heavenly help. What must happen before man realizes, "We need the help of heaven"?

Must devastation continue? Continue it will because heaven is not asked to respond. Stubborn man keeps his back to heaven even when the road ahead grows darker. Hold your meetings! Call your conferences! Pile up your weapons! All to no avail. If you do not invoke me, I cannot save you. This is my message. This need not happen. This destruction could be avoided. It is late, but I will never say, "It is too late." There is always a moment when mankind can invoke me. However, the more it delays, the fewer people I can help.

### Comment

*Mary is the Woman (Genesis 3:15 and Revelation 12), the great enemy of Satan. She is saddened that the world does not invoke her, and tries to solve the problem by human means.*

March 21, 2011
# 21. Conversions through Signs and Wonders

## Mary

I speak to you whose hearts have no religious faith; to you who have never lifted your eyes to heaven, to you who have never sought a heavenly favor and to you who do not even believe that God exists. This is your hour, the hour when the stranger will become my son and the foreigner will become a citizen of heaven.

The old order is passing away. All is new. Those who have never listened to the message of faith will suddenly have ears of belief. I will take back those who have been stolen from me and I will bring back what has been carried away from me.

All are my children, the Muslims and the Buddhists and even those who claim no religion. In an instant, they will see what their culture has hidden from their eyes. I will no longer use ordinary means. In a moment, a nation will come to me. In a day, a whole tribe will turn to me. I will give signs in the heavens and will plant stirrings in their hearts. All from the least to the greatest will have a chance to believe.

What do these wonders mean? It is a moment of mercy flowing from my Immaculate Heart. A moment for the world. When all seems lost there will be an intervention of the Spirit of God, my spouse. Who can understand? Yet, in the moment of truth, all will be clear. All will have opportunity to become a child of God through the Immaculate Heart.

The stranger, the alien, and the person far from faith will be united through these signs. I will be saying to them, "You also are mine." Some will believe and be saved.

### Comment
*Mary will reach out to the whole world by signs and wonders. Everyone will have an opportunity to become a child of God.*

April 7, 2011
# 22. Explaining Divine Chastisements

# Mary

### Invitation
So many of my children are lost in the world's darkness. How will I find them? I will send forth my word in all directions. My children in distress will hear my word. It will claim their hearts and they will return.

### The Goal of Divine Justice
When mankind fails in the basic duties of justice, the heavenly Father must inflict Divine Justice to remove darkness and restore truth to the land. During this time, my children must remain in hope and light. When Divine Justice removes the architects of darkness, I will place the children of light on the lampstand. Until then, they must live in faith until the powers of darkness are toppled.

### Need For Words
To prepare for this cleansing of Divine Justice, I give my words to the little ones. My words, my words – I am always speaking about my words. Yet, this is the way I enlighten them. If they do not hear my words, they will not be prepared for my helps. I will provide many helps, but my words are needed to reveal these. If they do not listen, they will not have my helps and very few will survive the times of Divine Justice.

### Becoming Mary's Children
I speak these words to all, even those who are not my children. By reading these words and being touched by them, they will become my children. All can become my children!

### Revealing the Problems
To my children, I will reveal the enemy strongholds which Divine Justice must

destroy. If my children stay away from these strongholds, they will not be harmed by Divine Justice, which is like a surgeon's scalpel, cutting only what is infected.

So, to my children I say, "Stay away from sin. Do not go near it and do not tolerate sin in your midst. Be encircled by goodness. Then, the sources of sin will be evident to you so you can stay away from them. Each chastisement will be perfectly suited to cleanse an evil. Flee all evil. Have nothing to do with evil. God will expose the evil done in secret. This is his greatest glory."

## Protecting the Little Ones

How can I protect the little ones? Listen to my words. In the present, they must gather together in love for one another and in their desire to safeguard the family. I will open to them the doors of economic security to provide all that they need. Trying to act only at the moment of economic collapse will be too late.

Let them make decisions now. They must love one another. Be of one mind and one heart. Let the father be the head of the family, listening to the words of all the members.

As they agree on what to do, let them act in unity and in wisdom. If their hearts are correct, wisdom will be poured out. If each family seeks my wisdom about their finances, I will be in their midst, guiding their decisions.

*Comment*

*Mary's words are clear. God's Divine Justice will chastise evil. To prepare,*
*her children must withdraw from all evil.*

## The Coming Divine Justice

Everything is bubbling beneath the surface of world events, like water with a flame beneath it. As the heat is enkindled, the hot, destructive water overflows.

The fire is God's wrath and the water is the world events, the interactions of man. When the water boils over, the events become destructive. If the flame is increased, then the boiling over is inevitable.

Sins are enkindling God's wrath and the water will boil over where the sins are committed.

## Stay Away From Evil

To my children I say, "Stay away from sin. Do not go near sin and do not tolerate sin in your midst. Be encircled with goodness and the places of sin will be evident to you. The smell of sin and the vision of sin will be warnings to you. Stay away.

## Evil Movements

Many times people join their hearts together to bring about evil, for their own profit or to destroy their enemy. This is a great evil, but I will show you a greater one.

Some individuals have hearts that are seedbeds of evil (like Hitler). They enlist others to their cause. This becomes a gigantic evil, a movement which others join. They are drawn in because the movement appeals to their selfish instincts.

This evil takes on many faces and disguises so that even good people unknowingly contribute to this evil.

I must unmask these evil movements and reveal them for what they are. So, listen to my words. Do not judge new movements by what is on the surface, by the disguises it assumes. Look at the heart. Look at those who began the movement. Then you will discern the truth.

### Comment
*As society is threatened, some will take advantage of confusion. Jesus warned about "false messiahs." Mary does the same.*

Each chastisement will be perfectly suited to cleanse each evil. If the evil is violence, there will be death. If the evil is hatred and false denunciations, the evil will fall on those who spew these out. If the evil is dishonesty, they will be caught and exposed. For each evil, there will be a chastisement. Flee all evil. Have nothing to do with evil. Evil done in secret will be exposed. This is God's greatest glory. What is done in hiding will be exposed in the streets.

### Comment
*Clear away all evil, within you and around you. This is the best preparation.*

Divine Justice touches the problem like a surgeon's scalpel, cutting away only what is infected. To prepare for the time of Divine Justice, I give my words to the Little Ones. My words, my words, I am always speaking about my words. Yet this is the way I enlighten them. If they do not hear my words, they cannot prepare for the other helps I will offer. There will be many other helps, but my words will reveal them. I speak these words from the deepest love of my heart. If they do not listen, very few will survive the time of Divine Justice.

### Comment
*Mary promises many helps but only her words will reveal them.*

## Preparing for the Time of Divine Justice

I will reveal to my children the enemy stronghold which Divine Justice must destroy. By staying away from those areas, the little ones will not be harmed by Divine Justice. This is easy to understand. God restores justice by destroying places of injustice. He destroys greed by attacking those who control wealth. To avoid suffering seek only the necessities of life, which the heavenly Father will always provide.

### Comment
*Mary provides wisdom so the little ones are not touched by God's chastisements.*

April 9, 2011
## 23. Our Lady Speaks to the Nations

## Mary

### To the Church in the Middle East
How dark it is for my Church in the Middle East. Satan is uprooting the Church that has been planted for centuries, but I will place a new vineyard there.

The strife will continue and believers will be caught in the crossfire of constant turmoil. The Church will be severely damaged. I will weep and I will wait for my son, the Pope, to come and place a new vine in the old vineyard. Many will see it as small, but it will be young and vibrant, freed from the past divisions, a new Church, a free Church, an Israel Church, planted in the right soil.

### Comment
*The first part is already happening. The number of Christians in the Middle East decreases dramatically due to war. The second part is consoling.*
*A new Church will come forth.*

*The following locutions speak to countries and continents, revealing Our Lady's thoughts and desires, always giving directions that can be followed.*

The time is short. Soon the events will begin. At first, they will seem small and isolated, but then, like a match touched to a forest, the conflagration will spread. How can this happen? Are not the walls put up, the pacts signed and the treaties made? What is wrong? The sins of the past have not been removed by repentance.

### To Europe
#### Setting Aside the Church
You have set aside the Church that presided over your birth. The papacy is no longer heeded. You say, "We have no need for the Pope. We have created our own union." In

the Ages of Faith, I blessed Europe because the Vicar of my Son provided a oneness. Nations turned to him in the disputes and went to him in their crises. Even when the popes were unworthy, his office was accorded a role in peacekeeping. Now you say to the Pope, "Speak only to the Church. You have no voice and no role in modern Europe. We are secular now."

## Europe's Past Greatness

I still hold Europe in my heart. How many saints it has given me. How many missionaries it has sent forth, bringing the light of faith to Africa and to the Americas. All these came from the countries of Europe which were bathed in great faith. These missionaries went forth to save souls. How great were their sacrifices and their heroic deeds. They went in the name of my Son and of the Catholic Church, planting the cross on every soil. Theirs was a noble mission.

## A Secular Union

O Europe, now your churches are empty and you brazenly proclaim, "We are a secular union." Yes, a secular union which will be overwhelmed by the religious Muslims. They will devour you, not with their weapons, but with their faith, their beliefs and their religious practices.

Turn back to me or your European Union will collapse like the paper building that it is. Do not say, "Our economies are flourishing. Our way of life is succeeding." You have forgotten your Mother, the Church. Your union is like a little baby compared to my Church. How long have you existed? Not even a century. What is that compared with 2000 years?

Return to your mother. She awaits you. You need her wisdom. You need the spiritual life which flows from her womb and the nourishment that comes from her breasts. Your hearts are joined in money and in your economic system but not in the Catholic faith.

If you exalt my Pope, I will exalt you. If you listen to his wisdom, I will lead you along a path of survival. Otherwise, your destruction is near at hand because your union is a union of convenience, not of faith.

I ask you this. Would you die for one another? Would you shed your blood for your common faith, when you have no faith? Return now, while it is not too late. Fill the churches and I will drop down blessings from heaven and you will say, "The Age of Faith has begun again."

### Comment

*Mary points out the obvious. Europe's oneness came from their unity in the Catholic faith. The European Union rejects that source of unity and has adopted a secular model, making it vulnerable to the Muslim religion.*

My messages are not judgments or condemnations. They are warnings, spoken from love. People must understand what is weak and about to collapse because not built on solid ground. So much more to say. . . .

## To America

I hold America in my heart. It is so special and formally dedicated to my Immaculate Conception. It is built upon religious principles which are now covered over. What has happened to America? It is awash in material goods that it cannot afford, drowning in a debt that it cannot pay and killing its young before they are born.

What has happened to the light set upon the mountain? To the city set on the hill? America's foundations have been shaken. Slavery began the problem. Human beings were reduced to cattle. Then, blood was shed in the Civil War. A seed of evil was sown and not recognized – the seed of violence, brother killing brother.

## The Problems of America

A century later, a president was gunned down, the victim of a conspiracy that was covered over, and the seeds of lies were sown. America ceased to be the country of truth. Social institutions were bent to the will of the powerful. Truth was banished from the land and the institutions meant to uphold the truth were sold to the highest bidder.

Money. Money is your false god, America, and money will be your downfall. You will drown in the very money which you print so plentifully. It will not be worth what it says it is. It will become the laughing stock of the nations. The mighty dollar will be like a sick man who has no strength.

You are already sick. You must be carried by others, by the very people to whom you do not want to pay allegiance. They do not at all share your Christian faith. What have you done, America? You have sold yourself like a prostitute to whomever will buy your notes of credit, selling the heritage which the heavenly Father gave you, a heritage that stretches from sea to shining sea.

It is not too late. Turn back. In your years of prosperity, you helped those who were destitute. In your years of good fortune, you brought back to life those nations who were broken. Never will I forget your generosity. But if you do not repent, I cannot restore you. If I do not restore you, many will have nowhere else to turn.

### Comment
*Mary touches on America's special call, on its present problem of overspending.*
*America's future still lies in the balance, yet to be written.*

## To China

To a land that does not know me and to a people who have not heard my name. You are mine and soon I will take you to my heart, not just individually, not one by one, but as a nation, all at once. I will take you into my arms and you will ask, "Who is saving us? Who is setting us free? Who has suddenly loosened our bonds?"

Yes, you are in bondage to the darkness of your religious teachings. These bring you no light even though gods are invoked and prayers are said. These fall upon deaf ears, said to gods made by human hands.

I will give you a new God, a true Lord, my Son, Jesus. He is already walking among you in great signs and wonders. He is preached and adored in house churches. However, your government fears him and tries to control him. He will break out of their grasp. It is already happening. What is sown will break forth. New life is already in your midst, but you know it not.

A day will come when you will renounce your other gods and embrace Jesus. On that day, I will break your chains, the chains that have bound your hearts like you used to bind your children's feet. China will be free and the world's largest nation will proclaim my Son as its Lord.

### Comment
*For decades now, Jesus has brought forth great signs and wonders in China, resulting*
*in a multiplication of believers. These gather in house churches, which the*
*government strongly resists. Mary says that China will come*
*to Jesus, not just individually but as a nation.*

## To Russia

How gigantic you are, spread across two continents, encompassing various people and called a union of republics. A union you are not. You are splintered and fragmented, formerly held together by force and now united by political strategies. How I wish you were a people united in professing my Son. If his name were upon your lips, you would truly be one.

You beat down your people and tried to build an atheistic system on their backs. You took whatever was in your grasp, deceiving the West and making gains at the bargaining tables, destroying the rights of people who were not your own.

This is your twentieth century legacy to the world.

Where are you headed now? What new fields do you want to plunder? What new alliances are you forming? Why are you consorting with people who do not love my Son and who do not proclaim his as Lord? They exalt a different prophet unknown to you and foreign to your religious tradition.

Turn back. Your flirtation with the Middle East will not gain your goals. What are you seeking? A new role? A new identity? A return to greatness? If you had been truly great I would not have humbled you by breaking your system. I indeed have humbled you but you did not repent.

You just sought another road. "I will return to my former greatness," you say in your heart. "I will find new friends with whom to conspire. I will make new arrangements in the Muslim world. With these, I will rise to power again." You fool! They are plotting your destruction, just as they are plotting the destruction of the West.

You are not one of them. They laugh at you. They play your game but they will not let you rule with them unless you become one with them in their religious beliefs.

Will you sell them your religious traditions as you have sold them your uranium? Will you sell your people, the way you barter your secrets? They will not be satisfied with your wealth. They want your soul. Jesus, my Son, is the soul of the Russian people. Someday, they will be consecrated to me by my Pope. Then they will be mine and I will snatch them from your hands, from you who are so ready to sell them to a people who hate you.

*Comment*

*Our Lady loves the Russian people and their deep religious traditions. These words are directed to the Russian leaders who embraced an atheistic Communist system in the twentieth century and are now selling arms, uranium and technology to Muslim countries.*

## To Latin America

To you who are poor, who gather your little rations from your tiny fields while the world enjoys its banquets. I have not forgotten you and you have not forgotten me. I am sown into your hearts through the missionaries I sent to you.

Your religious traditions (placed in your hearts centuries ago) are fading and wilting as the modern world enters by its powerful media and messages. The new replaces the old. The young leave for the city or for other countries. Noise invades your quiet and restlessness spreads through the land. Change is everywhere. All is unsettled. How widespread is this march of progress, a progress which is rooted in the expediency of the moment. What can I do for you, a people close to my heart?

I see the old and the new, what was and what will be. How can I guide you from a past, so deeply rooted in the Catholic Church, to your future? How can I help you, so the values of the past are not surrendered to gain the blessings of the future?

I give you the rosary. The rosary will link you to one another and will chain you to me. Yes, chain you to me with chains of love which will never be broken.

You will need these chains. Only your mother can help you to survive the years ahead. The shaking will begin with the prosperous nations but will be felt most in the poorer countries, with a poverty you have never seen. Do not follow false leaders who preach a secular progress without religious values.

Who still calls on me? What people still seek me? These I will bless and sustain. Do not walk away from me as others have done. I am your mother.

Comment

*Mary confronts the problem that material progress can cause the loss of a religious tradition. She asks the people to say the rosary. They will be chained to her when they suffer new economic hardships.*

## To Muslims

To all who proclaim Allah as your god and Mohammed as his prophet. You have set aside my Son as the light of the world and have put another in his place. He has used clever words and strict rules. He has laid burdens on your backs and told you that you are a holy people. Yet, he himself cannot confer this holiness.

He tells you that you must work for holiness, that you must pile up good deeds that are greater than your evil deeds. What a bondage he places you in! What fears he plays upon. Is this religion – to pile up good deeds? Is there not a loving Father who has sent his only begotten Son to redeem and to make holy? Has not your prophet blocked the springs of living water that flow from my Son's side? Has he not turned you away from the gift of saving grace?

When will you learn? Salvation does not come from below, as you pile up goods, as if these could reach to the heavens. Salvation comes down from the Father of Grace. It descends upon mankind as a gift from above. It came through my womb which gave flesh and blood to the Eternal Son of God. All of this is yours, given as a gift and a grace offered to your freely.

Yet, you turn away from this gift to what you yourselves can earn by your good deeds. This is what your prophet has taught you. He has displaced the Son of God who pours out life freely and he tells you to work for your salvation. He removes the gift as if it had not been paid for and says, "You must pay again." Why pay again for what has already been bought by my Son's blood? Why bring the coins of your good deeds, when the Father will give you salvation paid for by His only Son?

This is the mystery which your prophet has set aside and is now hidden from your sight. Why has this been done? Why has the gift been set aside? Because you would not go to Jesus, my Son, instead of to Mohammed. By these words, I reveal what is waiting in my arms, your salvation. Come quickly and I will give it to you. You know me well. I am Miriam of Nazareth.

### Comment

*Mary points out the basic failure of Mohammed. He has removed grace, the divine life freely gained by Jesus' death and rising. He has reduced Jesus Christ to a prophet, lower than himself.*

### To Israel

Would I not speak to a people who gave me birth and nourished my faith – a people I have always loved. Yes, I will say it – people I have always loved. You are my people, not just the people of my heart but the people of my flesh and blood. You are my Son's people, of the same flesh and blood.

You are a wandering people. First, you wandered in the desert and now you have wandered for centuries. Dispersed and not gathered together. United only by the word, the Torah, the teachings and prophets. Yet, these have kept you together and given you an identity.

"I am a Jew," you say, a member of a proud race, begun by Abraham and gathered together by Moses, united in the glory of King David, sent into exile, gathered again in Jerusalem, dispersed by the Romans and now present in every land, waiting and waiting for the Messiah.

Have you ever asked, "Has he already come? Who is this Jesus, whom so many proclaim as Lord?" Have you ever asked, "Were we mistaken?" Did the forefathers kill the Son sent by the Father? Did they not kill the prophets before Him? Yet, today, you acclaim these prophets. Why do you not acclaim my Son?

No need to recall your history. Even more important, there is no need to allow these centuries to stand as an impregnable wall. Let us go back. Let us go back to the beginning. How did we get separated? How did we part our ways? How did those Jews who believed in Jesus get set aside?

Were their voices not heard? Were they not persecuted? Look at what Saul did before my Son appeared to him on the road to Damascus. Saul is my key witness. Study his life. Study his message. See him as one who persecuted the believers. Why did he change? Was he bribed? Was he forced to become a believer? Or, did he really see my Son? Did he encounter Jesus in the fullness of his resurrection? This is the question you must face.

You are a Jew. You will always be a Jew. I am a Jew. Paul is a Jew. Do not believe those who say that you cannot believe in my Son and remain a Jew. A believer remains a Jew, a Jew who has come to a fullness.

## Comment
*Mary's words strike at the heart of the question. Did Jesus rise from the dead? Did Paul see the Risen Jesus? Cannot a believer remain a Jew?*

## To Africa

Africa, beautiful Africa. You have been ravaged by the colonial powers. Your sons and daughters have been sent to faraway lands and placed in inhuman servitude. I love you. You are mine.

A fresh wind blows across your land. A new fire of faith has been planted in your hearts. In so many places, that faith is flourishing, due to the sufferings and toils of so many.

I have come to you and visited you at Kibeho. I am yours. I belong to you. I have embraced you and your many cultures.

The spirit of Kibeho will flow throughout your continent, not just the waters of Kibeho but its many seeds. They will be planted everywhere, North, South, East and West. There will be new Kibehos because I will continue to appear to those who call on me and obey me. So, listen to this word.

My Son will pour out the Holy Spirit with diverse tongues and powerful gifts. Do not be afraid of these new phenomena. They are part of my Church and were present from the very beginning. Do not be afraid of this New Pentecost. Do not close your doors to these new fires. These fires are sweeping your continent and I do not want these fires to be all around you while your doors remain closed. Do not lose these moments which are important.

Learn about the new fires. Study and prepare to receive. Let the priests be first, so the people are guided correctly. Then let all the people seek the fire. All must be done in order, but the fire must not be quenched.

You will dedicate this new fire of the Spirit to my motherly guidance. I will not let you lose your way. Then, when you send your abundant missionaries to every land, they will not just bring the solid Catholic teachings, they will also bring the Pentecostal fires, which they have personally experienced. This will be your gift to the nations. The youngest in the faith will lead his older brothers.

*Comment*

*Mary stresses two great sources of spiritual life, her personal appearances and the Pentecostal fires sweeping the continent. She wants the Church in Africa to be immersed in both of these streams.*

## To Ireland

To a land that I have separated from others so it can be totally mine. A land that I visited decades ago at Knock. A land which has walked with me for centuries.

I know the path that you have taken. You have followed another woman – Dame Prosperity. Now she has abandoned you and your house is in shambles. It is well that she has left you. You were drunk on her wine and corrupted by her lewdness.

"Where shall I go?" you ask. "Return to Knock." There you will find the answers that I gave you long ago and we will begin again.

It will not be easy. Much has been destroyed and you have not yet recovered from the shocks of your indebtedness. But we cannot wait.

I promise I will send someone to lead you and I will send others to help him. I will raise up a new priesthood. It will rise from the ashes, bold, vibrant and true, serving others not itself, close to the people and not claiming its own privileges.

If you follow me, I will raise up a new Ireland. If you do not, I must abandon you to those who will continue to rape you and destroy you. There are so many forces of division while time is wasting. I will be waiting for you and we will begin again.

*Comment*

*Mary speaks of the great religious centuries of Ireland, which has, in recent years, abandoned the Catholic Church and gone into deep indebtedness. She promises a new leader, a renewed priesthood and a new Ireland flowing from a religious stream of Knock.*

April 13, 2011
## 24. Mary Speaks to the Broken-Hearted

### To the Mother of An Aborted Child

Your child is with me, grown to full stature, just like every other child of God. It is you I am concerned about, and the burden you have carried for years.

36

First, let us go back to that moment of decision, when you said, "I will have an abortion." Recall the father of your child, and the role he had in your decision. Recall your fears, your qualms, the pressures you felt from so many sources. Recall the despair that filled your heart and the hopelessness of the situation.

Now recall the years of suffering since that decision – the sleepless nights, the endless questions, the despair, the darkness and especially that question which you always ask, "Why did I let it happen?" Recall all of this so I can respond.

You have suffered long enough. No need for greater pain or greater sorrow. No need for further accusations. There is need only for my saving word which will restore you. Listen carefully.

On earth, you will not be called the mother of this child because you did not give birth, but in heaven you will be called the child's mother because you gave life. In heaven you will hear the child call you "Mother," and its mother you will be. You will see your child in full maturity, grown to full stature. Your child will be waiting here to embrace you and I will be here.

There is only one difficulty. I must get you here. So, think about my words. Think of the child who so wants to have you in haven. Think about what awaits you. Set aside the past. Set aside the sufferings. You will be the mother you so much want to be. We both are waiting for you.

### Comment
*Certainly the child is in heaven and the child wants its mother to be there also.*
*The woman should not look back but forward.*

## To Women Who Have Never Conceived

I speak to women who want to conceive a child but have been denied this privilege because of circumstances. One has not found the right person to marry. Another has a husband who does not want children. With another, the mutual spousal love has never conceived. With another, conception has always ended in a miscarriage. Oh, the loneliness of a woman who so desires to bring forth new life! Each month there is the womanly flow which painfully reminds her that time is going by. I do not say "is being lost" for, in God, all time is holy.

Begin with hope. Always and everywhere, hope that God has a plan. Seek God's light. "What can I do? What steps can I take?" Often, there are surprising answers as you cast the light of hope upon disappointing circumstance. Finally, know that never to have given birth on earth is not God's rejection of you, nor does it condemn you to a fruitless existence. Look at those who have embraced virginity for the kingdom. Is their life fruitless? How many of these are saints that have blessed the world more than anyone else. I say this clearly. In your failure to give birth there is a seed of great life, a call to a fuller fruitfulness. Let me help you to search and we will find it together. As the psalm proclaims, "The woman who was barren becomes the mother of many children."

## To the Woman Who Experiences Unrequited Love

I speak now to the lonely wife, who gives loves but receives none. She would embrace her husband but he flees from her embraces. An unrequited love – going forth but returning empty.

The house has no love. Life is just an existence together. Two lives that pass in the night. Two streams that flow in separate river beds, never enjoying the fullness of a joining.

Can love be reawakened? Even your own love, because it has never been returned, has grown cold, even though still present. Let us try again. This time slowly and with great patience. Always await in hope. Always keep the door open. Treasure even the smallest coal of human warmth. When he needs you, be there for him. I will arrange the circumstances so that he sees that you have remained at his side, even though he has not always remained at your side. When the streams begin to join again, let his love flow freely. This will be a great sacrifice for you but there are too many years ahead for you to live mutually alone. The gift of reciprocal love does not return overnight, but it is a gift worth waiting for.

Do not seek the love of another man because his love would poison your heart. In loving your husband, you act like God who continually loves many who never return his love.

## To Parents Worried About Their Children

You see that your child is in deep trouble. Your child has spun out of control and walks away from you. You are helpless. All that you do is not enough. Learn much from my words.

I am with your child, walking with him, accompanying him in the darkness. I will be with him whether he is able to turn away from these destructive forces or whether he is unable to free himself.

So, I say to you, "Call upon me. Invoke my help. Use my name. Teach him to say, 'Mary help me.' Do not cease to cry out to me. I hear your every prayer and see your every desire."

Learn this lesson clearly. Everything is possible in my Immaculate Heart. This is a lesson which the whole world will soon learn but I reveal it to you much earlier because of your special need. "No one need be lost."

*Comment*
*Mary teaches total confidence in her Immaculate Heart. Parents will see true miracles in the change Mary will bring about.*

## To Parents Whose Son/Daughter Has Committed Suicide

The lonely hours and the constant questions, "What did I do wrong? Why was I not there to prevent this?" The memories still fill your heart, the memories of First Communion, the birthday parties and the graduations. These all flood your mind.

How much time has gone by! Yet the pain is still there, like an unquenchable thirst. It is a wound that seems never to heal, an unending agony.

Listen to my words. They will draw you to me. Then, read them again and they will touch you more deeply. As you continue to read them, these words will go to the center of your heart. A moment will come when my words will replace your words and you will be free. Let us begin.

Did he make a true decision, a real choice between good and evil? Was there not a narrowing, a closing of doors to other possible solutions?

Did you know his inner thoughts? How much inner light was present? What darkness had he stumbled into? Can anyone see the way when no light exists? These are the questions that I place before you.

Now, let us go on. Have you not prayed for him? Have you not asked God to have mercy on his soul? Do you not ask God to see your child as you see him? Where are those prayers? Did they get lost in eternity or are they gathered up in my heart?

Look at my heart. Your every prayer and sigh is there. Also, there are your tears, those tears which you have shed so abundantly. These, also, I have gathered up. They are not useless.

Now, come deeper into my heart so you can grasp the thoughts of the heavenly Father. The Father created him, brought him to life and charted his ways, recording every step he took. This path was not a sudden decision. The seeds of this decision were quietly slipped into his heart while he was asleep, like the parable of the enemy who sowed weeds at night. These weeds were numerous and they appeared everywhere, too numerous to root out, destroying all the wheat. This was the heart of your son/daughter. Your child could only see the hopelessness.

I was with your child in those hopeless hours, because you had called upon me. (I remember your prayers.) You had asked me to save him, because he no longer seemed to be yours. He walked a road that you did not understand.

So, I walked with him. I did not abandon his side, even for a moment, and especially, not in his final moment. I was there, within him, I whispered my name. I told him to call upon me. I could not save his earthly life because those weeds of death had grown too numerous. So, I offered him a chance for eternal life. In the little corner of his will, where freedom still had sway, I asked him, "Do you want me to save you?" "What was his answer?" you ask. I say, "Come to heaven. Seek always God's kingdom for yourself. All is not lost."

*Comment*

*Mary pierces the darkness of a suicide, and speaks of what we cannot know. The parents must seek to gain heaven for themselves, trusting that their child will be waiting for them.*

## To Those Who Have Lost A Loved One in the War

The memories are so sharp and clear. You remember the moment he told you of his decision. Suddenly, he was off to war, to an unknown land and to a people whom you did not know. These are the ways of war, the gathering of an army and the sending forth, while those who stay behind are filled with a thousand anxieties.

So it was, as it has always been, with the constant prayers for a safe return, so that your lives could begin again.

But this was not to be. Others returned, but not the one whom you loved so much. The place at table was empty now, never to be filled. The clothing he had stored away never to be used, at least by him.

What shall I say to you whose heart was broken by the cruelty of a war waged in a far off land? How can I console you, when he will never return? When you will never see him again? When you will never hear his voice or listen to his words? Let me speak because my words will bring you consolation and direction.

Some are meant to be here only a little while, to fulfill their task and to pass on, leaving behind a gift, the memory of their heroic deeds and of their great sacrifices. These memories live on. Do not drown them out. They are the seeds of new life. Remember what he stood for and what he tried to achieve. Remember his sacrifices. Tell them to your children. He gave his life for others. And when these memories overwhelm you and when the loss seems too great, call on me. I, too, lost a Son to violence. I will come to you and we will pray for peace so others do not share our sorrows.

## To the Young Person With a Broken Relationship

Your friend, your companion, the one who was always at your side is no longer there.

The friendship is broken and you have gone your separate ways. A loneliness sets in. Before you plunge into another relationship, let me, your mother, speak to you.

You have much to learn. Examine yourself. What blame must you shoulder? How will you be better in the future? Will your friend take you back, if you change?

There are other questions. Who can help you? Who will speak the truth to you? Who will speak a bold word? Who will be a good friend? Who will lift you up and ask you to live by higher ideals? Learn from a true friend before you begin another relationship. You will be different next time.

### Comment
*Many experience the heartbreak of a broken relationship. Mary asks the person to be truthful and to seek out someone who will lift them up to higher ideal.*

## To A Young Person Experiencing Guilt

Guilt covers your soul like a darkness, with the pain of a sharp wound, always present and never going away. You ask, "Why do I feel guilty? Can I find forgiveness? Can anyone remove my guilt?" Let me answer your questions.

You feel guilty because you are a person, conscious of self and of how you should have acted. Your guilt is telling you that you did not act as a person. To be freed from guilt, you must do some things that only a person can do. Be honest about where you have failed. If you hurt anyone, seek their forgiveness.

Then, come before God who created you as a person. Seek his forgiveness. If you are a Catholic, seek out a priest. He will absolve you and tell you what else to do. Take these steps and you will be restored. I am your mother.

### Comment
*Mary offers some simple steps to allow every human person to be freed from guilt feelings.*

## To the Young Person Experiencing a Call

What is that feeling which washes over you, calling you to serve others? What rewards and sacrifices does it hold in store? What will happen if you listen and follow? And if you don't? Let your mother explain what is happening.

My Son stirs within you, revealing the mission he offers to you. You see only the beginning steps. The rest of the road is hidden, so you must trust.

Listen to your heart. Follow your inner dream. Trust what Jesus has placed within you. Do not measure the sacrifices or allow others to discourage you. All is prepared. The next time you experience the stirring, say "Yes, Lord, I will follow you." You will see what to do.

41

## To the Young Person Who Cannot Find A Spouse

You have prepared yourself and made yourself ready, always looking, always hoping that you would find the right partner. The years slip by, but the desire perdures. In moments of great hope, you say, "It will surely happen." Then come moments of despair. You ask, "Where can I even look and hope to find someone?"

Questions are everywhere. "Should I take this opportunity?" Yet the other person is so far from what you had hoped for. Is not time running out? But what is the alternative? Many look for sexual favors. Few seek a relationship and even fewer share your dreams of marriage and family. What do I say to you who are caught between your desires and the reality which frustrates your hopes? Let us begin.

Listen to my voice within. Say often, "My mother will provide." Then, walk where I would walk. Seek relationships that only I would have. Stay free from those who do not share the desires of your heart. They will only absorb your time and leave you empty.

Go where I send you. Search and seek. Do not be afraid to knock on some doors. Seek new groups, always with the noblest of purposes. I have placed within you a desire for parenthood, to bring forth a family with a spouse who shares your faith and your values. What is wrong with that? Is this not a noble ideal? Then believe that I will help you to achieve it.

Trust that I have placed in you those qualities which will both attract the other and help the other. See what you can bring to the relationship. If you do this, you will be more sure of yourself and your relationship will be based on mutual support. The relationship can then grow. True love can spring up and a moment will happen when you see that you are meant for each other. That is the important moment.

## To the Young Person Who is Not Ready for Marriage

There are others to whom I must speak. You seek to marry but you are not ready. You have not prepared. Your values are too superficial and your choice of a partner would be the wrong one.

Deepen your life. Seek true values. Return to Mass. Grow in your faith. Stay away from debaucheries. Form your own lifestyle. Choose friends wisely. Do not be led astray. Marriage is a serious enterprise and few are adequately prepared.

When you have done all of this, when you have matured, then you can seek a partner because you will choose much better. You will reject that person whom before you would have selected and you will be drawn to the person whom you formerly would have shunned. The right person was there all along but you were not yet the right person for the other. Lift up your lifestyle and you will choose a partner at a higher level.

### Comment

*A person tends to choose according to their level. If the person is lifted up by a better lifestyle, they will meet and choose a better partner.*

May 1, 2011
## 25. To Those Who Never Heard the Gospel

# Mary

I speak to you who have never heard the Gospel because you have been deprived of a great light. Everyone on earth has a right to hear the Gospel of my Son, but sometimes missionaries did not reach you. Governments have refused them entrance or even ejected them from your land. No more. Governments can no longer banish a word that goes forth electronically.

I speak first to you because others have had their chance to hear the Gospel. It is a new day. I will preach and you will hear. No one will stop the gift.

### The Conception of Jesus

I begin with a mystery which was hidden in my womb and first revealed in a Jewish culture, 2000 years ago. God became man. He took flesh and blood. He came among us and was seen and heard by those who lived in Israel.

Why Israel? Because God had prepared them for centuries. They knew there was only one God. He had spoken to them through the prophets. As a young girl, I was instructed in these sacred books. I was a daughter of God and a daughter of Israel, prepared by my sacred culture to be the mother of God. Yes, I am the mother of God and I want to be your mother.

### Life of Jesus

My Son's name is Jesus. He performed miracles, signs and wonders. He proclaimed that the Kingdom of God was breaking through and that his life would begin this great event. The leaders of Israel were jealous. They were angry because my Son denounced many of their practices. They feared him because large crowds followed and believed. So, they killed him, nailing him to a cross. I was there. I saw my Son die and his heart pierced by a sword. We buried him in a new tomb and I sorrowed, more than any other mother. He was my only Son and I was a widow.

However, all of this was only a preparation. He entered the tomb to deprive it of its power. That is the great message that I bring you. My Son won the victory. He destroyed the power of death. On the third day, he rose from the dead. His body is now in glory – unable to die or to suffer. This same glory is for you. That is my message. You do not need to fear death if you believe in my Son. This is my first message. It is basic but even now you can see how deprived you have been by not hearing these words. I promise I will make it up to you.

*Comment*

*The good news of Jesus Christ will go forth electronically, preached by God's greatest messenger – Mary, God's mother.*

*May 3, 2011*
## 26. Gaining Holiness in Mary's Heart

Everything that is holy is in my heart. You are free to enter because my heart will be open until the end of time. Then it will be sealed for all eternity.

What is not in my heart is not holy, not of God's kingdom, worthy only to be cast out on the final day. All that is in my heart is the Father's will. When you enter my heart, you will receive a desire to do the Father's will. As you remain in my heart, that desire will become pervasive and deepen, extending to every thought, word and deed. This is not the work of just one day or one year, but it is the sure and easy way to goodness because you will experience a vehement desire to do God's will. I will show the easiest way to accomplish what the Father wants.

*Comment*

*In these few locutions, Mary has invited the soul to a conversion from sin, to fidelity to God's will and to holiness – all accomplished easily if the soul enters Mary's heart.*

*May 4, 2011*
## 27. Receiving the Holy Spirit

# Mary

Peter, the leader of the disciples told the crowd about the events which I have told you. He explained the purpose of my Son's death – to take away every person's sins and to send the Holy Spirit into their hearts.

The people experienced great sorrow for having killed my Son and asked what they had to do. Peter said that they had to repent of their sins and be baptized in the name of my Son. In this simple and easy way, they would receive my Son's Holy Spirit. Peter baptized 3000 persons that day.

This little story raises many questions which I will answer. Who is this Holy Spirit? He is the Spirit of the Father and the Son. The Father is God and my Son is God. Also, the Holy Spirit is God. When you receive the Holy Spirit, you become a child of God. God lives in you and, on the last day, He will raise you from the dead, just as He raised my Son from the dead.

I told you that my Son conquered the tomb and you do not need to fear death. By the Holy Spirit, you will live forever. Death is not the final state. My Son gained eternal glory for himself and He gained it also for all who believe the story. I will explain more the next time.

*Comment*

*Mary gets quickly to the great gift of Jesus – the Holy Spirit who bestows eternal life.*

## What You Have to Believe

Many books form the Christian Bible, but you need not read all of them before being baptized and receiving Jesus' Spirit. In these little talks I will give you all that you need to know. Let us begin with God.

There is only one God. We call him the "heavenly Father" because Jesus taught us this title. Centuries ago, he created the whole world – the earth, sun, moon and stars. He created all that lives – the fish and the animals. When earth was ready, he created the first man and woman, from whom comes every man and woman on earth. They are our common parents.

You have a body and a spirit. Your body came from your parents. Your spirit was created by your heavenly Father. But this was not enough. Your human spirit can receive God's Holy Spirit. As your body lives because of your human spirit, so your human spirit lives because of the Holy Spirit. Without the Holy Spirit, your human spirit has no life. My Son died on the cross so He could give you his own Holy Spirit and you could live forever with his heavenly Father. I will talk about that the next time.

*Comment*

*Mary is so clear about the human person. The human person has a material body taken*

45

*from human parents and an immortal spirit created directly by God. This human spirit can live forever by receiving God's Spirit. What great mysteries explained so clearly!*

May 5, 2011
## 28. Mary Ascends the Electronic Pulpit (the Internet)

## Mary

So many of my children who used to be in my heart are missing. They were baptized and taught the truths but they are not here. I am their sorrowful mother and I must look for them. I will ascend the pulpit of the world. I will call out to them in the clearest of words. No matter where they are, my words will reach them.

Since their world no longer includes the Church, I will enter their world through the Internet. I will find new pulpits and give the clearest, most inviting teachings. At the same time, I will touch their hearts. They will know that it is a mother's voice which invites them.

### Translated into All Languages

I ascend the pulpit of the world to speak to all people in their native language. The words will go forth on the Internet and will be translated into all languages by the little ones whom I hold in my heart. You will accompany me into the pulpit and record the words as they go forth.

### Explaining All the Truths

The God who created the world wanted to reveal the mysteries of heaven. To do this, he chose a people to be his very own – the Israelites, also called the Jews. These are my people. He formed them by his word, which they collected into books.

He revealed many things but the most important was that there was only one true God. This truth separated the Israelites from the other nations. Although they knew that God was one, they did not know God's inner life. Only Jesus, my Son, who is God, could reveal and explain God's inner life. This is what Jesus explained.

God is a Father who brings forth his Son. The infinite love which they have for each other brings forth the Holy Spirit. The Father so loved the world that He sent his Son, Jesus, to save the world, (All of this I will explain later.) and to give to the world the same life which the Father and Son enjoy together. This life was given when the Father and the Son sent the Holy Spirit who begins to live within you when you believe in Jesus and are baptized in the name of the Father and of the Son and of the Holy Spirit.

*Mary gives a clear summary of Divine Revelation. God is one and in this oneness are three divine Persons. By the Holy Spirit, all can share in God's inner life.*

## Disobedience and Obedience

Having spoken of what God did, I must now speak of what man did. Inside of you are powers not shared by the animals. You have a mind that can know God and a will that can obey him or disobey him. You can say "yes" or you can say "no" to God.

The history of man is filled with "no." This is called "sin." This tendency to sin (to disobey God) is now planted in every heart. It is a selfishness which destroys all that God would do.

Because I was going to be the Mother of God, God did not allow this power of sin to be planted in my heart. No power of disobedience ever touched me. I always said "yes" to God. Jesus, also, always said "yes" to his heavenly Father.

Because he was obedient to the Father, the leaders of Israel crucified Jesus. All the way to his death on the cross, Jesus said "yes." I, also, said "yes" as I stood at the cross of my Son.

The heavenly Father heard this perfect "yes." So, the Father and the Son poured out the Holy Spirit (their mutual "yes" to each other). This Holy Spirit empowers people to say their "yes" to the Father. Therefore, the Father can glorify us, just as he glorified Jesus. I want to explain exactly what will happen.

*Comment*
*Jesus saves us from our "no" which separates us from God. He gives us the power to say "yes" which joins us to God and allows him to glorify us with Jesus.*

## The Glory of God

My Son, Jesus, always enjoyed life with his Father. This life we call "God's glory." By disobedience to God, man had lost God's glory.

Jesus lowered himself and became a man. He even accepted death on a cross. His Father exalted him, raised him into glory and made his name above every other name. All who call on this name can be saved.

You are "saved" when your human spirit receives God's Holy Spirit. This is God's glory. This Holy Spirit raised the human nature of Jesus from the dead. This Holy Spirit will do the same for you as he did for my Son, Jesus. The important proof of this truth is that He already did this for Jesus. Let me tell you what happened. In this way you can believe that Jesus rose from the dead.

*Comment*
*By becoming man and dying on the cross, Jesus made God's glory available to us.*

## The Appearances

When Jesus was 30 years of age, he left our home and began to preach that the kingdom of God was at hand, the special moment that all of Israel had awaited for many centuries.

Jesus told everyone that God had sent him and that he was God's Son. To prove this, he healed sick people, drove out evil spirits and even raised people from the dead. Many Jews believed and placed faith in Jesus. Some became his disciples, and from these he chose apostles, who were called the twelve.

Jesus predicted to these disciples that he would die on a cross and that he would rise from the dead. The disciples did not believe that he would be killed and they did not understand what "to rise from the dead" meant. Yet, both took place. After Jesus rose from the dead, he appeared to these disciples for 40 days, proving to them that he had risen and instructing them about their future tasks.

These disciples were the important people in God's plan. They told this story to the whole world. They had no fears. Many were killed because they preached this new way of life.

These disciples believed because they had seen the risen Jesus. Those to whom they preached believed because of the disciples' words. Also, the disciples healed people and drove out demons. This little group was not educated, yet they preached to the whole world. This is what I am doing now. By their preaching, many received the opportunity to gain eternal life. Those who heard believed, were baptized and received the Holy Spirit.

This is why I am preaching now – preaching to the whole world by the Internet – so all receive the same opportunity for eternal life.

*Comment*
*Just as the disciples went to the whole world, so Mary's words go forth, telling what Jesus gained for us and giving all an opportunity for these riches.*

## A New Way of Living (Jesus is Lord)

Jesus proved to these disciples that he was God, the Lord of all creation. He was God's only Son and, with the Father, the source of the Holy Spirit. These disciples went forth telling the whole world to put aside their many false lords and to accept the true Lord, Jesus, into their hearts. This meant adopting a new way of life. The disciple has to live like the Master and the servant like his Lord.

Jesus lived in obedience to the Father and to his commandments. He lived in truth, in service to the Father and to others. He lived in chastity and purity of life. All of this I will explain now.

Your human nature is selfish, controlled by your passions. You are a slave to sin. Baptism frees you from your slavery to sin and makes you a servant of goodness. You are a new creation, called out of your selfish darkness into Jesus' light. This is how Jesus is different from your pagan gods. You offer them sacrifices but you go on leading your selfish lives. With Jesus you are lifted up, made a child of the light, guided and helped by God's Holy Spirit. I will take this up again.

### Comment
*Many reject Jesus as Lord because this requires a new way of life.*
*Choosing the true Lord demands a change.*


## The Christian Community

When the believers were baptized and received the Holy Spirit, they could not return to their former way of life. So, they supported one another. They joined together for prayers and the teachings of the apostles and the sharing in the Eucharist.

This same method was used by the missionaries. Baptism demanded that the new believers leave behind their sinful way of life. To accomplish this, the believers formed new Christian communities. They came under Jesus who had promised to stay in their midst until the end of the world.

This is true even now. The baptized must remain with the community. Jesus has already given himself as the food for the community. That is my next teaching.

### Comment
*Mary stresses the communal aspect of Baptism and the believer's duty to gather.*


## The Eucharist

The Holy Spirit forms the Christian community. He lives within each member and unites them. His goal is that every member proclaim Jesus as Lord. To gain this, he recalls all that Jesus did and taught.

Even more, he overshadows bread and wine so that Jesus himself lives in their midst and is food for their divine life. I will tell you how this gift was given.

One day, thousands of people gathered to hear Jesus preach. This was in a deserted place and the hour was late. Jesus took some bread and fish into his hands and blessed them. He gave them to his disciples, who distributed them. All 5000 were fed. This multiplication of food was a sign to everyone of Jesus' special powers.

The next time that they gathered, Jesus used this miracle to promise a greater gift. He would provide bread come down from heaven, his own body and blood, to give them eternal life. He promised that if they ate his flesh and drank his blood, he would raise them up on the last day.

At this time, many did not understand the promise. First, Jesus had not yet died and been raised to glory. Second, they did not understand how he could give his flesh to eat and his blood to drink. I will explain this the next time.

*Comment*

*Mary leads into her teaching on the Eucharist by describing the preparatory events – the multiplication of food and the promise of the Eucharist (John, Chapter 6).*

The Last Supper

On the night before he died, Jesus was at supper with the twelve apostles. He took bread, blessed it and gave it to them to eat, saying, 'This is my body that is for you. Do this in remembrance of me." Then he took a chalice of wine and said, "This cup is the new covenant in my blood. Do this, as often as you drink it, in memory of me."

Now the twelve apostles understood the promise. The bread and wine had become the Real Presence of Jesus. When they would say the same words in his name, Jesus would always become present. As they ate and drank, he would enter their souls with the divine life he had from the Father, uniting them to God through his body and blood. Celebrating the Eucharist is the central act of Christian worship.

*Comment*

*Mary explains clearly the daily Catholic practice of Holy Communion.*

The Apostles Creed

I have taught you long enough, explaining all the basic beliefs. Now, I want to gather you. Your world is filled with darkness and Jesus is the light. If my words have stirred you, then read them again and again. I have instructed you as simply as I could.

Our names are important. I am Mary, the mother of God. Jesus is my Son. He was born to give you life, to save you from darkness and from the evil spirit. Do not wait. If you believe, seek Baptism from Christians in your land. If there are no Christians, then believe and baptize each other. First, learn this prayer:

I believe in God, the Father almighty, creator of heaven and earth. I believe in Jesus Christ, his only Son, our Lord, who was conceived by the Holy Spirit, born of the Virgin Mary, suffered under Pontius Pilate, was crucified died, and was buried. He descended into hell. On the third day, he rose from the dead. He ascended into heaven and sits at the right hand of God, the Father almighty. From there, he shall come again to judge the living and the dead. I believe in the Holy Spirit, the holy Catholic Church, the Communion of Saints, the forgiveness of sins, the resurrection of the body and life everlasting. Amen.

*Comment*
*Mary prepares all for Baptism through the Apostles Creed written explicitly to prepare believers for Baptism.*

Explaining the Creed

I have explained these truths in the course of my teaching but let me review them in a systematic way.

God created the world. Jesus is God's son. Pontius Pilate, the Roman governor, sentenced him to death in Jerusalem. I was there when he was buried in a new tomb, not used by anyone else, made out of stone with a large rock across the opening.

On the third day he rose from that tomb and began appearing to the disciples for 40 days. Then they saw him taken up to heaven to prepare a place for all who believe in him.

On the final day, he will come down from heaven and will judge everyone. Some he will take to heaven. Others he will send away because they did not believe in him and did not receive his Spirit.

The Holy Spirit forms the community of believers called the Catholic Church. This Spirit forgives sins through Baptism and other sacraments. The Spirit will bring about your resurrection into eternal life. Jesus promised his disciples, "I go and prepare a place for you. I will come back for you, so that where I am you also may be."

"Amen" means "I believe," "I say it is so." If you believe all these truths and want Jesus to be your Lord, then you are ready for Baptism. Just begin. The one who is baptizing you should plunge you into the water three times saying, "I baptize you in the name of the Father, and of the Son and of the Holy Spirit. You answer "Amen." These names Father, Son and Holy Spirit, are familiar to you.

*Comment*
*Ideally, only a baptized person should baptize another.*
*However, these words might reach people who are not baptized.*
*A non-baptized person can baptize as long*
*as they do three things:*

1. *Plunge the person into water three times, or pour water on their head three times.*

2. *Say the words, I baptize you in the name of the Father, and of the Son, and of the Holy Spirit.*

3. *Do all the above with the intention of accomplishing what the Church and Mary want accomplished, namely, to make the baptized person a child of God.*

May 6, 2011

## 29. Preparing for the Chastisement

## Mary

### A Chastisement of Mercy

A time of great trial will come upon the world, a great distress of the nations. Many will die. Others will not know what to do. However, those who know me and know my words will have enough light to get through this period of darkness.

The world will be purged by this extraordinary divine intervention. This is the purpose of the trial because the Father would not do this if he had any other choice. He cannot allow the world to go on as it is. If he did not intervene, as drastic as this is, life on earth would be even worse. Man would inflict on man unheard of sufferings as the weapons of mass destruction are released by those who are under the control of the Evil One. So, what looks like divine chastisements are really acts of his mercy. God will purge the world before man destroys it.

*Comment*

*Mary says that God must act to cleanse the world and also to avoid greater suffering inflicted by man himself through nuclear arms.*

### God's Care for the Living and the Dead

Those who live in light and believe my words will know this is true. Even in the worst moments, they will see God's purposes and know what to do. Some will die but they will accept their deaths in a spirit of faith, knowing that they have used their lives to love and serve God. They will have no regrets and the Spirit will console their inner being.

Others will be preserved from death by the Spirit so they can form the new Church that will arise, the light of the new mankind that will be fashioned by the Father. This will include people from all over the world. They will be people of faith, even if they did not believe before. They will have come to faith in the middle of the trials because of the signs in the heavens and the wonders upon earth. They will know that God has saved them and they will tell the story to their children and their children's children.

*Comment*
*Both good and bad will die. God's rain falls on the just and the unjust, but the Spirit will be able to console the good. He will also care for those who survive and have come to faith.*

## A New Creation

It will be like a new creation. Man will once more realize that he owes his existence to God's choice. He will no longer say, "The earth is mine to do what I want." Instead, he will say, "The earth belongs to God and I am the caretaker of his creation."

Man will once more stand in God's presence and will rejoice in the title "Children of God." Faith will be everywhere. Man will see clearly that all life comes from God. A new world will begin, "as it was in the beginning."

Man will still be free, still able to choose good and evil, but man will be so filled with light that good will be easily chosen and evil will be easily rejected. All of this can only take place after the world is purged.

*Comment*
*Seeing the final result of the purging gives hope and purpose.*

## New Lights for People of Faith

I say all this to prepare you for these events. Prepare, you must. Whoever is not prepared will perish from hopelessness and despair, devoid of all light and understanding. Satan will put out all the lights of the world, all that men hoped would save them.

However, I will shine my light, new lights, extraordinary lights, seen only by people of faith, words heard only by those whom I have trained to listen. Let me explain.

The heavenly Father wants to communicate with his children by the powers of the Holy Spirit. This Age of the Spirit has already begun but too few are aware, even in the Church. I have appeared to some and have made certain places sources of divine messages. These are a sign to all, but my plan goes much further. The Father will pour out the Spirit on all mankind and I am his messenger.

*Comment*
*The Father speaks to his children by the Holy Spirit. We must learn how the Spirit speaks and guides us.*

## True Light – Extraordinary Yet Essential

Two things must happen. All must be open to this new inner light and all must be aware of false lights. There will be extraordinary true lights and extraordinary false lights.

I will raise up leaders in my Church who will know the true light by their own deep personal experiences and by their solid theology. They will point out the true light and will reject the false light. Follow them. Plunge into this true light for it will be the only light that you have in the darkness. Get used to the light and learn how it guides you.

All of this is extraordinary but the darkness will be extraordinary. The deep personal light of the Holy Spirit guiding individuals and families will become essential.

### Comment
*God's light will be new and, before the darkness, we must become familiar with it.*

## Gathering in the Light

You cannot be like the foolish virgins who believed that they could get oil for their lamps at the last minute. You cannot gain this new light when the darkness comes upon you. You must become a child of the light now. I say "now" because the Spirit's light is available and he will train you in the light. You will learn to act in his light. You will also gather others, because many must walk in this light.

You must gather. Gather in praise, exalting my Son, Jesus. This is the Spirit's method to give light. Gather daily. Lift your hands in praise and the Spirit will descend upon you. Otherwise you will never learn his gifts or receive the light that I intend.

Do not ask me to tell you when these trials will begin or to give you signs. Doing that is useless. Even with the clearest signs, people will not listen. My words are enough and they are clear. Why talk about some future sign when I have already told you to begin now. If you do not believe and if you do not start now, will you start in the future? Will some sign jolt you into belief? You will be jolted but not by my signs.

My words are signs and I tell you clearly that this is the Age of the Holy Spirit. If you invoke him, he will give you personal signs, especially a unity with others.

### Comment
*Mary tells us to invoke the Holy Spirit. Gather with others. Praise God in unison.*
*Learn the charisms, how the Spirit reveals his words. Special signs are useless.*
*Her instructions are enough.*

## The Scattered Children Must Gather

I sorrow over my children because they are scattered. Their little light cannot overcome the darkness and they cannot survive even now, before the great darkness comes. What will they be like when Satan puts out all the lights?

When people invoke the Holy Spirit, he joins them together. They find a common voice of praise. They lift their hands to the Father. While they pour out their praise, the Spirit joins their hearts. They are no longer alone. They have others on their side.

I will be with all of these little groups. They will be called Marian Gatherings of the Holy Spirit. Even if just three or four gather, this will be enough. I will teach them and they will learn together. This advice is very easy but this is how you will prepare for the darkness. Gather with others in a Marian Gathering of the Holy Spirit. Do not put this off. If you go and search, I promise that you will find others. Then you will discover my plan for you. You will rejoice and say, "Mary has provided me with others. Together we will prepare for the darkness. May I find you together when I come."

### Comment

*Mary's advice is easy. Her children are too scattered. They must come together in a Marian Gathering of the Holy Spirit. They will be blessed as long as they stay together.*

## A Clear Plan of Action

What will you do when you gather? You will read my words. They will teach you. More important, you will give me your hearts as slaves of the Immaculate Heart as taught by St. Louis de Montfort.

This is only the beginning. Let each one use their gift of the Spirit. Let each heart, touched by the Spirit, bring forth a word, a hymn, a revelation. Serve one another with the spiritual gifts. Do not wander into other concerns. The Spirit must do his work in you and you must learn his ways. Enough for now. I have given you a clear plan. Begin to act.

### Comment

*You are told what to do in these gatherings. Read Mary's words. Consecrate yourself to Mary in True Devotion. Use the Spirit's gifts.*
*Learn the Spirit's ways. Do this right now.*

## Family Preparations

Different structures must be built. Tiny structures which can multiply and be present everywhere. These structures will survive. They can be built right now. Whose authority do you need to gather in your home? Whose blessing must you seek for family prayer? I give you my authority and my blessing. Begin now, before it is too late. Gather your children into the Marian Gatherings of the Holy Spirit. Since this is where everything must begin, I will speak to the parents.

*Comment*

*Mary wants these groups to start immediately. The easiest place is in the home.*

## Anxieties of Parents

How anxious you are. You have brought your children into the world, but now you see, only dimly, the great questions about the future of the human race. What will be the future of your children who have so many years ahead (years when you will not be with them)? Even now, fear covers you. You can see all the problems on the horizon. When you hold them in your arms, do you not ask, "What is in store for them? How will I keep them safe?" These questions must lead you into action. Follow the safe path which I offer to you.

*Comment*

*The future problems can be seen on the horizon. Loving parents inevitably suffer from anxiety. Mary will provide a plan of action.*

## Four Pieces of Advice

First, you must believe that I will keep you and your family safe, but only in my Immaculate Heart. That is why the heavenly Father wants to establish devotion to my Immaculate Heart. Do not follow any other path. This is the sure, the easy and the short road. You will never arrive by any other means.

Second, you must give me your heart so I can purify it of all its sinful desires.

Third, you must bring to me all the members of your family so I can purify their hearts. There is no salvation without purification.

Fourth, you must gather together in my heart. This is not optional. I can only bless those who gather. I can seek the scattered sheep but only so that I can gather them with the others. A scattered sheep is a lost sheep until it learns to stay with the flock.

*Comment*

*These four pieces of advice are basic. They must be fulfilled for Mary to give greater help.*

## More Advice

Now I must go deeper. My words are true treasures that come from my heart.

First, read God's word. Take it to heart. Love that word. Let it be a light for your path. Let the word live in your family. Live by the word. Study it. Memorize it. Too many Catholics are ignorant of the word. I pondered the word that I was taught at the synagogue. You, too, must ponder it.

Second, purify your home. Remove whatever I would not want to be there. Make it a Marian home. Clean out the secret recesses. Let nothing unclean enter your home. I will bless a purified home. I cannot bless a home which tolerates sin.

Now, let us go still deeper. I want love among the family members and peace in their relationships. I want truth to reign, together with honesty and purity. I want family meals and time for the children. I will make all of this possible if only you have faith in me and allow me to act. I ask only good will and a willingness to begin again when you have failed.

Any home which does this, I will bless and I will make it a light for others. When the darkness comes, these lights that you and I have set in place will not go out.

*Comment*
*These are perfect guidelines. Each parent will be touched by different sentences. Each command also carries some promise of Mary's help to implement it.*


May 10, 2011
## 30. Mary and World Events


## Mary
### The Darkness of the Mideast Uprisings

Some nations are already in darkness. Others are in twilight, retaining some light. However, nothing is secure. Everything can change and much will change. Many nations are now in tumult, faced with the uprisings of their people. The West looks on, unable to comprehend what is happening, unable to see what will be the final result.

These uprisings are the beginning of the darkness, the first stirrings, the early signs. Yet, no one sees them for what they are. Many in the West think they are the first stirrings of freedom and democracy. You fools. These are not stirrings of light. They are stirrings of darkness. These nations are in twilight and these uprisings will put them into complete darkness.

I want these people to be free, but years have passed and who has preached the Gospel of my Son to these nations? The West has never understood. Only the Spirit of my Son can set free. Whomever the Son sets free is free, indeed.

These are not religious revolutions, where people of light throw off the darkness of a dictator or the darkness of a system. These are secular revolutions and these nations will go from one darkness to another. What is secular is dark. What has no roots in God's word cannot bring about life and freedom.

The West has forgotten this. It has pulled up its own religious roots. You have only a light which is left over from centuries of abiding in God's word. This word you have rejected. Soon, your light will go out, also.

*Comment*
*Mary sees all the uprisings in the Middle East quite differently than Western leaders.*
*These nations have killed Christians and the missionaries. How can they now*
*have a true light or true freedom?*

## A Son Whom I Will Call to Jerusalem

I will call a son from the West and he will go to the Middle East. He will bring no armaments of war, no secular powers, no large bureaucracy. He will come because I have given him my word. He already knows to come. To come and to lay down his life and to plant afresh the seed of God's word. He will be my Pope. With him will come others, not to conquer any land or to claim any kingdom. They will come only because I said to them, "Go to where I lived. Go to where my Son preached." All of them will go in faith and when they come, they will do only what I tell them to do. There will be only a short time, just as my Son preached only a short time. They will find disciples and they will carry on the word.

"What can be accomplished by a Pope?" you ask. He will plant a light, a light at the top of the mountain, a light that will never go out, a light that all the nations and all the Churches and even all of Israel will walk by. It will be the Lord's mountain and all will say, "Let us climb the mountain of the Lord."

When nations climb the Lord's mountain, then their weapons will be beaten into plowshares and peace will come to the nations. This is the true light and I will bring it about, but only after a long darkness that convinces the world that it possesses no light at all. It will be a seed, planted in faith, which will become a gigantic tree that all the nations can rest in. Jerusalem will be the city of world peace as all the nations realize that my Son's blood was shed there, the blood which still cries out to the heavenly Father for peace to men of good will.

*Comment*
*Jesus' blood, shed in Jerusalem, still has power to sanctify the city so that*
*Jerusalem will be the light of the world. However, many events must*
*happen before that takes place.*

## America's Shriveled Roots

America, you have killed your enemy, Bin Laden, but you have not solved your problems. Your difficulties lie in your roots. The roots of your life have shriveled and the roots of your desires have grown. These roots are planted in a lava waste and drain away your life. You are dying from within, unable to reverse the tide that has been unleashed by your turning to the secular.

Your roots were religious, based upon the strength of the Churches and the high morality of your people, in the sanctity of life and the holiness of marriage. You guarded your young against pornography. All was in order. You flourished in the discipline of your life and in the discipline of your spending. This was the high level, the truly American life, where human life was human life meant (always) to be protected.

You can see what has happened. The roots of life have shriveled and the life that you enjoy now is a remnant from the past, given to you by your religious roots which brought forth America, one nation under God. I ask you, "Who is under God now?"

I want to draw you back to where you belong and where you will thrive again. I would draw you to a nation under God, but you will not come. You want your freedoms, even those which violate God's will. You do not want to be a nation under God. You cry out, "Do not speak to us, O God. We do not want to know your will. We do not want to ask, 'What is God's will?'" When voices are raised about God's will, you say, "We have separation of Church and State."

Shall we go our separate ways? Do you want to form your secular state? Is this what you want? Are you asking for a divorce? A divorce from the woman who gave birth to a nation?

Think it over again. Ask yourself, "What course am I choosing? Do I really want to follow the road of Europe? Or, should I go back to the Churches? Should I ask them to teach me again? Should I say to the Churches, "Teach my children for they no longer know right from wrong. I have taught them what works. I have given them skills. But, they have never learned who created them or the way of true life. Here, take my children and teach them the ways of the Lord."

It is not too late, America, but our separation must be ended. You have listened to the wrong voices and have cast out the mother of your children.

Can it happen? Can religious life be restored to its proper place? Just open your doors. Do not listen to those who want to kill your religious spirit. The roots are shriveled but they are not dead. Restore your roots and they will give life.

## Comment

*The disease of the removal of religious thought from public life is pervasive, resulting in the least religious young adult generation in America (shown by all the statistical polls).*

*Religious life and thought must be invited back in America's public marketplace.*

The Need for Peacemakers

Slowly, ever so slowly, I reveal my plan, a plan of love where every heart is turned away from hatred and revenge. From the evil in men's hearts come wars and exploitations, now seen on a scale never imagined before. Only love, forgiveness, repentance, reconciliation, a putting aside of the past is the road to walk. But who walks this road?

Where are the peacemakers? They have vanished from public life. I must raise up a new army and once more stir the consciences of the world. These peacemakers will be gunned down, as were the others who preached non-violence. The blood of these martyrs calls out. They ask, "Has our message been forgotten? Has the soldier become the hero? Have the weapons of war become the new idol of America? Where is the stream of peace that used to flow so strongly in the hearts of the young? Where are the peace movements? Where are the prophets who would shed no blood but would allow their own to be shed?"

Do we no longer raise the question about a just war? About appropriate means? About the costs of armaments? Or is it the blank check which we provide to the military complex, saying, "Produce the best technology at any cost?"

You have wandered down the wrong road, America, taking to yourself prerogatives that you do not have. Return to the heart of the republic. Let the voices of peace be raised. They have not been heard from in a long time.

*Comment*

*Mary recalls an earlier era when political leaders had to pay attention to peace groups that protested the Vietnam War. Since there is no more draft, these voices have not been heard from recently.*

May 11, 2011
## 31. Mary's Role – Statesperson to the World

# Mary

Mankind must be lifted up. It needs the words of statesmen and poets to form a conscience, to call political leaders to higher ideals. Since these voices are missing in America, I will become the statesman and the poet. People will hear a new voice, because others have forsaken this task.

I will touch the heart of the country which I love so much and which I have made so powerful. Its greatest moments and its most important tasks lie ahead. First, its heart must be lifted up, or else it will falter. Even worse, it will turn aside to a goal that is unworthy. This is the real temptation for America.

Listen to me, America. I have not raised you up to conquer the world. I have not raised you up to invent new weapons. I have not raised you up so you can sell your weapons to whomever will pay your price and support your economy.

America, I have raised you up to feed the world. Look at the farms I have given you, a fullness of natural resources. I have raised you up so you could export your medicines, not your weapons. I have raised you up to eradicate disease and to bless the poor. Instead, you send forth your soldiers; not your doctors, your weapons not your food.

You must see all that you can accomplish with your discoveries and your methods. Fund governments that will welcome your help. Use your farmlands that deliberately lie fallow. These unused lands are an abomination to me. Open up new rivers of aid, let your riches flow in new ways. Then you will have friends among the nations.

Do not listen to your bankers. Listen to the cries of the poor and the hungry in other nations. If you care for them, I will care for you. If you let them grow hungry, I will let your children also taste the evil of famine. I have given you a destiny but you have turned away from it, ignoring the prophets of peace.

### Comment
*Caring for the world demands a heart that loves the world.*

May 12, 2011
# 32. A Commentary on the Modern World

## Mary

### Revealing Her Secrets
All the doors will open – the doors to nations, the doors to leaders, the doors to the hearts of the people, the doors to my secrets, and the door to my heart. Nothing will be hidden. All will be revealed to know and to see and to believe. The words will reveal the truths behind the reality. Just let the words flow like a stream. Let us begin.

### Comment
*All will be touched by the words that follow revealing the realities beneath the surface.*

### The Streams of Heaven's Blessings
When men harden their hearts, the stream of heaven's blessings cannot flow into that place. God did not place every blessing in creation. He reserved some powers to himself. He held back the power to create the human person, reserving that to himself.

This is only the first "holding back" because the Father also holds back every spiritual blessing. He "held them back" in the sense that they are not in the power of

61

man. God did not give to man the power to create the spiritual. Man cannot create peace or goodness or forgiveness. He also cannot overcome spiritual evils – hatred, envy, lust. Overcoming these is beyond his power.

Yet, look at mankind. Does it not believe that everything is within it powers? Then, when society is pulled apart, when violence erupts between nations, mankind is surprised and asks, "Why does this happen?" Man does not understand the heavenly stream that flows from the throne of God. This stream contains every blessing that mankind so desperately needs. The Father has provided everything but mankind does not look to the Father. Mankind operates with the false notion that he contains in his hands all that is needed to form human life and world peace.

Mankind wants creation for himself. He wants to take it and say, "This is mine." O foolish man. Creation is not yours. Creation belongs to God. You do not have everything in your hands. The Father knew you would take everything to yourself. He knew you would appropriate what is his. Creation is not owned by man but by God. Let your wars, your killings, you revolutions, your intrigues – let them all speak to you. You will not listen to the churches so listen to your worldly news. Just listen to what is broadcast each night on your televisions.

Tell me, O conceited man, do you have peace? Look at the stirrings on every side. You do not have enough bombs, enough drones, enough technology to bring about peace.

War, war, war. There is war everywhere and the seeds of greater wars are already planted and waiting to be harvested.

You have forsaken the heavenly stream that flows from the throne of God. Come, turn back. If you begin again to drink from this stream, you will not need your guns and your bombs. Whoever drinks from this stream tastes peace and when anyone tastes peace they say, "Never again. Never again the war." That is when you have true peace. I am your mother, sorrowing over her children as they kill one another.

### Comment

*Mary pinpoints the problem. Mankind does not have all power. Many needed blessings come only from God but mankind does not look to the Father.*

## The Collapse of False Hopes

Can you dream only of material goals? Are your hearts limited to the sensual? Is this the way the Father made you? Did he not place a different dream in your heart? You ignore this. You are a stranger to your own heart. So many truths are planted there. Read them all. I will be your teacher. Let us begin.

It is spring. The flowers are fresh. The winter is over. All is hope. Nothing has come forth yet but all is beginning. Who placed hope in your heart? What is its purpose? Hope is often mangled, twisted to false goals. When this happens, hope becomes ambition, greed, a climb to power. False goals abound. When they are gained, they bring disillusion. You ask, "What is life all about? Why did I seek this? Why did I believe the false promises?"

You have misread the hope which the heavenly Father placed in your heart. You have misused the promise of your life's springtime. Go back. Find true hope, a hope that deals with heaven and with a life that you cannot see.

It is not too late, even if your earthly career has crashed. Do you not see? It is your false hopes that have collapsed. Now that they are scattered to the winds, you can search again for the true hopes. These are planted in your heart by the heavenly Father. You are made for God. Nothing else will satisfy you. You are made for heaven. Earth passes away.

Do not say, "I am without hope." Look again in your heart. An unopened gift still remains there. It reads, "If you wish, you can be a child of God and a citizen of heaven."

*Comment*

*This is a beautiful teaching on hope. Directing hope to earthly goals mangles it.*
*Destroyed earthly hopes recalls that a true hope is still an*
*unopened gift planted in your heart.*

## Mary Sorrows Over Lost Souls

I want to share my sorrows. There are some who died today who will never live with me and some who will die tomorrow and not be with me. Many do not hear the Gospel because they live in cultures of darkness. So my words must reach the darkest places of the world.

At first, my words will not be accompanied by signs but the time will come when my words are challenged. Then, I will give signs, not for those who challenge, but for the little ones, that they would continue to believe. Therefore, be open to the greatest of divine favors, even revelations of events that will take place. I will speak of the future actions of God and man. I will speak of diabolical actions and reveal them ahead of time. I do all this because of my great sorrow for souls. The greatest divine favor is to love souls as I love them and to share in my sorrow over lost souls.

*Comment*

*Mary's heart is broken over souls who will not enter heaven.*

May 15, 2011

# 33. Understanding Worldwide Evil

# Mary

## The Trojan Horse

Good and evil are not separated. They are intertwined in every event and in every moment. Evil inserts itself into all that is good and good is present even when evil seems to be triumphant. This is the mystery I will explain. Except in those actions which are totally divine, all of human history is a mixture of good and evil.

Not understanding that human events are a mixing of good and evil, man often proclaims as good what is only partially good. He, then, opens his heart to it, not knowing that evil enters with the good. If the evil is not impeded, it takes over the good and destroys it. There remains only the selfishness of man, not the goodness of God which initially inspired the action.

Look at human history. So many events and movements have begun with the good but have ended with evil. See the French Revolution that began with high ideals but soon became the tool of evil, causing social disruption, overturning the divine and making reason the new god of mankind. So much evil goes back to that revolution because man was not aware that evil attached itself to good, like the Trojan horse, to enter unnoticed into the city.

### Comment

*Mary points out what man often overlooks, the evil mixed with the good that enters history unnoticed until the effects are seen.*

## Explaining Why Man is Confused

Now, let me explain good and evil. Each has its own fruits and its own source. Good comes from God alone and is given freely to all creation. God saw that everything was good as it came from his hands. Man and woman were created in God's own image. They were rooted in divine goodness, more than any other material creation. Man was meant to be the bearer of divine life and the purpose of material creation. Yet, man became the door to evil, the only door that Satan could have used, the only creature with free will. What was good (the free will of man) was used for evil and became the door to chaos.

The world is now filled with a goodness that comes from God and an evil that enters by man's free will. Man does not understand this. It is like light and darkness. As if man forgot that all light comes from the sun. So, he walks away from the sun and is plunged in darkness and he does not know why. Man forgets God. He turns away from God and wonders why the world is plunged into evil. Then, he blames God for the evil that does not come from God.

## Progress That is Not Progress

O Man, you must turn back to the source of all goodness. Purify your works of evil. Otherwise, you are blind. Your solutions will be no solutions until you understand that everything which man brings forth is a mixture of good and evil. Without God, the good will always carry evil with it. Without God, the good that was originally intended will soon surrender to the evil that accompanied it. It is a purified mankind that I seek, when creation will once again be creation, "as it was in the beginning."

Without God, progress is not progress. To each new invention, evil is attached. I do not say, "Halt all progress." I say, "Let your progress be done in God and it will be true progress. Progress without God carries only greater potential for destruction."

O Man without God, look at the world you have brought about. Is it progress that your bombs are atomic bombs? Is it progress that your technology destroys the very earth that you live on? Look at all your technology. Look at the powerful Internet that causes so many problems. Look at everything. Everything you produce for good is taken over by evil. This is the mystery that I put before you. You are building a world without God. You are building a destructive creation. God must purify creation before creation destroys itself.

### Comment
*Mary answers a confusing question, "Why is the world less safe when we have had so much progress?"*


## Approaching a Disastrous Moment

The world is approaching that moment when the power of Satan will have two aspects. First, he will have linked his evil into what is truly a worldwide system. Second, this system will contain the power to destroy most of the world.

I say this. The heavenly Father will not allow this but he has only two alternatives. Either he purifies creation by divine chastisements that totally disrupt what Satan is putting in place so that all of creation is not destroyed. Or, the world comes into my Immaculate Heart and I reveal a much easier salvation, by which hearts are touched and the evil attached to progress and inventions is purified. In this way, the power is used for good and not evil.

The choice is a solemn one, filled with a thousand ramification which touch the hearts of people and the fibers of society. I say this again and again – the secrets of God lie in my Immaculate Heart. That is where the Father has placed them.

### Comment
*What Mary says is almost self-evident. Man is approaching a moment when he not only*

*can destroy himself but the forces of evil are present that are willingly and even hope to destroy large segments of humanity. What she reveals is even more important. The only way to avoid world-wide disaster is to listen to her wisdom.*

May 27, 2011
## 34. Jerusalem – The World's Center Stage

## Jesus

### Killing the Pope

For years, I ministered with my disciples in Galilee. I placed in their hearts, the treasures of my words and the memories of my deeds. However, the culmination of my life was in Jerusalem. I went there in the heavenly Father's time. It was Passover, with great expectancy in the air. The Jewish leaders wanted to kill me. Pilate, the Roman governor, was in Jerusalem for the feast. All was according to the Father's plan.

Jerusalem is the world's center stage, where two dramas are played out. The first was 2000 years ago. The second will be in modern times. Jerusalem is the world stage where the kingdoms of good and evil clash.

There will be efforts to gain peace for Israel but these will fail. These efforts are good but the world leaders do not see the depth of the problem, or the deeper clash that only faith reveals.

I preached for some days in Jerusalem so all would know that I was present. Then the drama began. Violence was the force used against me and death was the result. However, the victory was won. The great treasures were placed in the hearts of the disciples who preached my word to the world.

There will also be a modern drama. At just the right moment in the Father's plan, the Pope will go to Jerusalem. Again, there will be anger and hatred. He will go as a man of peace. The enemies will use violence, as they have so often used terrorism. Their hatred against Israel will spill over. Their weapons will kill the Pope. Yet, he will be the victor. By his death, the weapons of violence will be seen for what they are – weapons that would strike down my Vicar, the great man of peace, who came to Jerusalem in my name. His death will usher in the gift of peace for the whole world, especially for Jerusalem.

*Comment*
*Jesus again highlights the importance of the death of the Pope*
*that will take place in that city.*

## Mary

Jerusalem held two dramas for me. When Jesus was a boy, I found him in the temple. He said, "Did you not know that I must be about my Father's business?" I realized that he was no longer a child who belonged to me. He was a Son, who belonged to the heavenly Father.

Years later, when I went to Jerusalem for the Passover, I knew this drama would be repeated, but in a greater degree. I again would lose him to the will of the heavenly Father.

There will be another drama. I will go with another son, my Pope. He will enter the city like Jesus, a messenger of God's peace. But, I will no longer be just a daughter of Israel. I will be the Woman, clothed in the sun. I could not control the events of the crucifixion or the cruelty of the Roman soldiers, but I will be able to control these events. There will be the Pope's death, but I will temper the sufferings and remove the unnecessary torments. Death will come suddenly and quickly.

### Comment

*Although world leaders give no special notice to Jerusalem, except for its political importance, both God and Satan see the city as the place of their first clash. This resulted in Satan's defeat, but he is confident that he can conquer, using the same force, hatred and violence, that he used previously.*

June 3, 2011
## 35. Reactions to Scarcities

## Mary

When some darkness enters human life, Satan stirs people to react selfishly so that a much greater darkness results.

This first round of evil will begin with scarcity, but the greater evil will result from the selfish response to scarcity. When nations and groups see themselves as threatened, they will begin to horde for the future, setting aside much greater resources than they really need. This creates even greater scarcities because they do not think of others and they overestimate the problems. The unity that has been forged in what is called "the global economy" will be tested, stretched out, and, in some cases, broken.

### Leadership in America

Even in the greatest of all unities, the United States, the scarcities will begin to affect life. America was built upon abundance and, with abundance, the belief that all should share. Scarcity will be a new experience for modern Americans. I say that it is not too late for America but people must pray for new leadership.

I say this strongly. America must come out of its darkness, led by new political leaders. Now these leaders sit on the sidelines. I do not say to them, "Get off the sidelines." Rather, I say to America, "If you pray, God will change your political climate, so that those who can lead you will be stirred to step forward and assume the responsibilities. If you pray and repent, changing your goals, then I will send people to lead you. America, it is not too late but you must act quickly."

Comment

Mary again addresses the need for constant prayer to create<br>a political climate of change.

June 6, 2011

# 36. The Middle East Disruptions

## Jesus

Human life is a drama. The heavenly Father does not write all the parts because everyone has free will. The Father does not control the timetable (although he knows what will happen) nor all the events. Much is left to man's free will.

The Father's original drama was destroyed by sin. Then I came and preached that the kingdom was at hand. This new drama began with my death and rising. Yet man remains free. He can accept the kingdom and become part of the Father's drama. If not, he remains outside of the drama and his life is useless.

World events involve the clash of the kingdom of God with the kingdom of Darkness. In all of this there is man's free will. This determines the timetable and even the specific events.

A person who loves the kingdom and always seeks the kingdom moves up the timetable of completion. A person immersed in evil slows the timetable and tries to place obstacles to the kingdom. From these obstacles come the events of darkness which are now happening. An important event is the widespread disruptions in the Muslim countries. Many do not see the great evil contained in them. I will explain what is happening.

In the Muslim world, there are people of light. These accept those parts of the Koran which are shared with the Jewish-Christian beliefs. They live these values in a Muslim culture. Other Muslims are neutral, so to speak, they are not children of light but they are not given over to radical darkness. Then, there are Muslims who accept and follow the darker teachings of the Koran which are totally at odds with my teachings on love and peace.

In these Mideast disruptions, the radical darkness of the Muslim world is hidden but when the current leaders are toppled, they will use this opportunity to diminish the number of the other Muslims, to increase their own converts and to assume leadership in these countries.

These deceptions will not bring about an Arab spring but an Arab winter of desolation and destruction. They will not bring about the kingdom of God. They will only enhance the powers of darkness which oppose the kingdom.

*Comment*
*These disruptions, although toppling dictators, will lead to a greater darkness –*
*the rise to power of radical Muslims.*

June 8, 2011
## 37. The Center of the Darkness

## Jesus

The wisdom and power of man are as nothing. They have no force and are totally ineffective in the face of evil.

Does not the heavenly Father have a plan and does he not have power? All of the darkness of evil has a center. From this center, the darkness emanates and receives its life. This center will be overcome by the light of truth.

All of the events of the Passion had one purpose, to lead me into the center of darkness where I could overcome the Evil One. I was captured, led to Pilate and then to Calvary. All of this took me into the center of darkness.

Previously, my life had been threatened but the Father preserved my life because I was not at the center. The center of darkness was in Jerusalem.

*Comment*
*The worldwide darkness that we are all experiencing has a center. Trying to*
*overcome the darkness is impossible. God will get to the center and*
*remove its power and life.*

## The Wounded Side

## Mary

Why was Jesus' heart pierced when the redemption of the world had already been accomplished? Jesus had no more free will. His soul had left his body. He had already entered into his glory.

This piercing took place for me and for all who would gather with me. The wound guaranteed that the Precious Blood would pour out constantly. The wound is also a place where all can enter. The wound was for me and for my accomplishing my task.

*Comment*
*Mary explains the two-fold importance of the wounding – so Jesus' blood can pour out and so we can enter.*

June 12, 2011
## 38. Raising Up A New Church

### Jesus

Throughout America, the enemies of the Church are united. They share their secrets and their methods hoping to ruin the Church entirely and reduce it to silence. The Church is my bride but she has fallen into the hands of her worst enemies, who want to tear her to pieces. How I weep. What will I do?

I will raise up a new Church, a Church that worships in Spirit and in truth. While my enemies are destroying the institutional structures, I will raise up those individuals whom they cannot destroy. Suddenly, it will happen. A new Church, built upon the Spirit, so that those who attack the structures will be helpless.

On this Pentecost Sunday (when the Church was born) I begin right now to give birth to a new Church. Within a year, you will see before your eyes what I have done, whom I have raised up, whom I have touched, and the methods I have given.

Later, I will deal with those enemies who have wounded my bride so seriously.

*Comment*
*Jesus loves his bride and he will respond by strengthening the Church Spiritually and, later, dealing with her enemies.*

### Mary

On the first Pentecost, I saw the Spirit guide Peter from beginning to end. He knew what to preach, what to say when questioned and how to complete the gift by baptizing the new believers.

I left Jerusalem for Ephesus with the Beloved Disciple and there emerged a new Church. John's Church was held together by love and not by structure. So, there were two churches, the Church of structure and the Church of love. Often, the latter is set aside.

Now is the time to focus again on the Church of the Spirit because the Church of structure is under attack. There are two Churches, united in one. When one is attacked, the other must respond. That is what is needed today.

### Comment
*As the official, structured Church is under attack, the Church of the Spirit must grow powerfully so it can support the structured Church.*

## The Lights Going Out
The lights of the structured Church will go out. This seems hard to believe because these lights are all over the world, but much is possible for Satan, especially with the new means of communication.

Once the light of the Church was strong in North Africa, but it is no longer. Once it was very strong in the Middle East, but it is no longer. So, do not be secure. What exists can be destroyed and what you have can be taken away.

### Comment
*Jesus is not trying to scare us. He is warning that in this great darkness, Satan, by using the modern means of communication, can totally discredit the Church. We see this happening already in America.*

June 25, 2011
# 39. Truth – the Source of All Blessings

# Mary
Truth must not be concealed. This is the work of the Evil One who constantly hides the truth from man. If man were to see the truth, he would be free, for God is truth. Instead, the truth is covered over, clever words are used and devious reasonings lead men away from what is obvious. In these messages, I have come to reveal the truth, to pull away the demonic covers and to place the truth as a light on the mountain, for all to see. Today, I begin with the heart of man that is so twisted.

When truth is presented to modern man, he does not accept it. Instead, he judges it. Truth is from God and is never meant to be judged. Truth is the judge. To bring about its blessings (and all blessings come from the truth), truth needs to enter the heart in a complete and total form, untarnished by lies and not mixed with opinions.

This is not what happens today. Man makes himself the judge of truth. Man thinks that what is true is what man accepts and what is not true is what man does not accept. But truth stands outside of man. Truth exists first in the will of God. Man cannot change God's will. And God, in his love for man, reveals his will. The revealed will of God is truth and is the source of all blessings, but only if man receives truth into his heart. This is so clear. Truth begins in God's heart and is meant to be placed in man's heart, so that God's blessings can flow. If man rejects truth, then he absolutely cannot receive God's blessings. He has rejected the source of blessings, my Son, who is the truth.

*Comment*

*Rejecting the truth does not just put man into darkness, it makes him incapable of receiving God's blessings.*

## The Power of Words

A word – how powerful is a word. A true word opens the heart to goodness. An evil word turns the heart to darkness. How many words spew forth from the mouth of men. Today, I would speak about the evil of deceitful words.

Evil words were first spoken by Satan to Eve. Satan knew that these words were not true. They were meant to accomplish his purposes, which were totally opposed to the blessings which God had in store for all mankind.

Deceitful words led the human race away from the path of God and led mankind down a road of frightful suffering and destruction.

The same is true today. Satan uses the same tactics. He raises up people and he places deceitful words in their minds. He promises them great powers if they just speak these words. When they do, then Satan's power is extended. He brings about exactly what he accomplished in the very beginning. He leads men down the road of deceit, a terrible road which leads only to confusion and despair.

That is why my Son said, "I am the Way, the Truth and the Life." The true word leads mankind along a road that brings life.

Satan's people will always speak words of deceit. They will always try to lead people away from truth. Their voices now are legion, and the powers they have to communicate their deceits are more powerful and more extensive than ever (and will continue to expand).

What can I do? I can gather my children to listen to my words. Those who listen will walk a path of life and all the deceitful words, no matter how powerful or how multiplied, will have no power over them.

*Comment*

*Deceitful words are satanic yet said and multiplied every day, deeply affecting mankind. Mary's children need to constantly listen to her words – the antidote to satanic deceit. Please read on.*

June 28, 2011
## 40. Romantic Relationships – True and False

### Mary

I want to lead my children into truth but in the world they hear deceiving words. These deceitful words have great power. They are said cleverly, spoken by those who claim an expertise. These words are multiplied by the media and people feel that they are arriving at some new understanding. The world has followed a path of deceit and it has led to nowhere. Now, I must invite them to turn back, to return to the truth. I will do this by teaching what should be obvious.

The love of a man for a woman is sacred, and inviolate. This is the way it should be from the beginning. The woman must be respected and lifted up in the heart of the man who loves her. She must be special to him, holy and sacred, in a sense untouchable.

If he acts this way toward her, she will be ennobled and his love for her will increase and grow, until a moment comes when he will say, "She is the one chosen by God to be my partner for life. She will be the mother of my children."

What a glorious moment, when the divine mystery, the eternal plan of God is revealed to a man and a woman through the circumstances of their meeting, their mutual attraction, their willingness to share special moments, and especially because they walked in truth.

Contrast this with those who have been deceived by the world which teaches that these attractions should serve selfish interests. Lust grows and strangles the budding romance. It never flowers and is soon discarded, wilted and never reaching its full beauty. Then, when the man is lonely and the woman is rejected, they experience a resentment in their hearts. Really, they have been deceived. They have choked off the possibilities that existed in the gift of each other.

To the young, I say, "Cast off the deceits of the world. You are wasting these vital years of your youth. Live in truth in your romantic relationships. They contain a great promise, but if you squeeze these flowers by seeking your self-interests you will never discover what could have been."

### Comment
*Obviously, Mary is speaking about purity and mutual respect in a man/woman relationship, claiming that the great promise contained in these attractions are ruined by selfish love.*

June 29, 2011
## 41. The Protection Around Israel

### Jesus

I speak to you about the Middle East and the growing darkness. The blocks of protection that surround Israel are being chipped away. Israel is totally aware that its safety and its existence are more at risk.

### Comment
*From the uprisings, Israel's protecting buffers are much weaker.*

July 1, 2011
## 42. The Fires of Destruction

### Mary

Why is the world so troubled, so agitated and filled with such turmoil? Look around. All is in disarray. Armies line up, trying to preserve peace and there is no peace.

All turmoil comes from the heart of man and it goes forth from there. Yet, no one speaks about man's heart and no one claims power to quiet the heart of man.

They have rejected my Son. His heart was gentle and he was able to make the hearts of his disciples gentle. Having rejected him, the world has no power to quell the inner fires of destruction. Only Jesus' gentle heart is able to say, "Father, forgive them." Only his gentle heart can say, "Love your enemies. Do good to those who hate you."

Even those who profess his name do not possess his gentle heart and do not live according to his words. That is the state of the world.

Fire after fire breaks out but these are the fires of destruction, not the fires of love. Love is found in only one place – the Sacred Heart of my Son. When will mankind learn to seek this new fire. Instead, it holds on to the human fires. It launches its destroying fire, claiming that this is how peace comes about.

O foolish man, your hearts bring forth every possible evil and yet you believe that you can restore creation to its original goodness. Can fools bring forth wisdom? Can what destroys bring about restoration?

You need a new heart. Yes, that is what mankind needs – a new heart – a heart transplant. That is what I offer you. Come into my heart and I will give you the heart of my Son. Otherwise, your intellects will create greater weapons and your hearts will try to solve your problems by destroying the earth. This does not have to happen, but it will, if you do not enter my Immaculate Heart.

*Comment*
*Can the human heart be changed? Can the destruction cease? It looks impossible. The two hearts of Jesus and Mary are the only door of escape from worldwide devastation.*

July 2, 2011
## 43. Self-Love Destroys a True Relationship

## Mary

Because love is a fire which consumes, my children must be concerned about what they love. Too often their hearts go in the wrong direction and the fire of desires burns them.

That is why I invite every human heart to enter into my Immaculate Heart where I place a true divine and human love. Without divine love, human love is weak, fickle, unable to be sustained and subject to the scourge of self-love. When self-love is present, a hundred becomes fifty and fifty becomes twenty. Self-love steals and robs, taking for itself what was meant for the other. It is like a tax, selfishly draining off true love. As self-love grows, true love grows less. A relationship which began with great generosity soon becomes a test of wills.

The relationship which began with great promise finds itself burdened with self-love. The relationship limps along, a caricature of what could have been. Sometimes, the relationship is broken and the couple separates.

None of this need happen, if only the couple would realize that self-love destroys true love. Their love must always be purified and they cannot do this by themselves. How many couples have asked, "What can we do to regain our original love?"

On this feast, I speak to husbands and wives, to young people who are in a serious relationship, even to all the world. Every day, place your heart in my heart and I will place you in the divine fire. Your love will be purified and your relationship will be free of the burdens of self-love.

July 3, 2011
## 44. Bringing Mankind to Its Knees

## Mary

Everything spins around with little direction, subject to the whims and desires of the human heart, yet, beyond the control of mankind, which is caught up in forces that he does not understand, and cannot control. Yet, man thinks that events are in his control and that he can turn everything to his advantage.

As a result, nations struggle against other nations, trying to be superior in the world markets and in political affairs. Meanwhile the average person is overlooked. The poor are set aside. A new class is always emerging. The "rising class" they are called, but they leave the world no better and even far worse than before they emerged.

Will it never end? The Spirit of God has been replaced by the spirit of man. Man has been set loose, unrestrained by God's word, following his own inner light (which is no light at all).

When will this era of "reason and enlightenment" come to a halt? It will come to a screeching halt. Two world wars and two atomic bombs could not bring man to ask, "Where have we gone wrong?" What will it take to have an age of faith replace this age of reason?

I see what it will take. Too horrible to describe. Yet, that is where mankind is headed. People ask, "Why does God not prevent this?" I answer simply, "How can God prevent this when mankind does not listen to God"?

So, I come as God's messenger, heralding a new age of faith, when mankind again will call upon God and live according to God's word. The new age of faith will come – but how it comes depends on mankind itself. This is why I am sent and this is why I am speaking so clearly.

This new age of faith will certainly come. It will come either by way of destruction, a destruction never before witnessed by mankind which will bring the world to its knees. Or, it will come by my word. My word also will lead mankind to its knees. Mankind will end up on its knees before a living Father and the age of faith will begin. There are two paths – of destruction or of my word. That is why I speak. Man must choose.

### Comment
*Mary describes the present – a world out of control because man has followed reason not faith.*

July 5, 2011
# 45. A Purified Earth

## Mary

Divine love is like a single drop in the gigantic ocean of man's sins. Yet this single drop has the power to cleanse the entire ocean.

Now the ocean is dirty, polluted by man's selfishness. People drink from it because that is all they know. This water enters into every heart and from it comes all the ills of society.

Who can cleanse these waters? When will the Age of Faith be restored? The task looks hopeless. The little ones scurry to form their little groups to resist the onslaught. Many see the problem clearly and try to respond so faith is not lost. I bless all these efforts and want them multiplied so that, in this time of cultural darkness, there are little places of light. But this is not what I am talking about now.

I am talking about a new Age of Faith, when the air is purified and the water is cleansed, when faith is the air that everyone breathes and peace is the water that everyone drinks. Who can even imagine these moments. Yet, this is my goal, brought about by a special action of the heavenly Father and which I will announce ahead of time.

When this divine action begins, I do not want the little ones to despair. The Father does not want the destruction of the earth or the end of the human race. He wants a purified earth and a new mankind to come forth.

These are the great mysteries hidden in my Immaculate Heart – great mysteries, mysteries which hold the future of all mankind in their light. But who seeks this light? Those who come into my Immaculate Heart. All are invited and I will reveal these mysteries to all who seek with a pure intention, that is, with a desire to live according to God's commandments. Come, let us begin. All of good faith are welcome.

*July 5, 2011*
## 46. The Powerless Age of Reason

## Mary

All the world is in an upheaval, far beyond the powers of man to quell. Forces are released that overflow all the protective walls established by God to safeguard the human race.

This ocean was released centuries ago. It began as a tiny stream, a few voices of dissent which clothed their message in terms of human freedoms. In truth, it was a hidden revolt against God, for these voices wanted to throw off what they saw as the divine restraints upon their human freedoms.

Quickly, they convinced others. "The earth belongs to man," they said. "Man, not God, should rule human life. We are people of reason. We can order our lives by the gift of reason." So, reason was exalted and faith was put aside. When faith was put aside, God was put aside. Man wanted a world of man, a world free from divine constraints.

O man, now you have your world. You have had it now for a few centuries. Look at your world. Look at what you have done to it. Look at the rivers of destruction that have been unleashed. You never foresaw all of this. You are powerless. You cannot restrain the rivers of destruction. When will you learn? How high must these waters get before you finally say, "Let us turn back to God because we have taken the wrong path?" When will leaders arise who will preach this new faith? They must begin now. Their voices will be few and weak, but others will hear and these younger hearts will re-echo the message.

My heart turns to the young. You are the hope. Do not listen to your elders who have destroyed the world. Their message is discredited. Go back to the earlier eras. Go back and find the voices of faith, the saints of the past. Listen to them and become a new voice.

### Comment
*Mary wants action now. She wants voices of faith to prepare for the future Age of Faith.*

July 6, 2011
# 47. The Spreading World-Wide Problems

## Mary

No one knows the future events which will shape the world, nor do they know how to prepare for them. However, those who listen to my words will be made ready. Although the forces of destruction will be great, they will not destroy my little ones. So, listen carefully.

It will seem as if everything will be swept away – all the structures of society and all the safeguards to human life. There will be breakdowns because many will be selfishly stirred, thinking that they can better their lot by toppling those in power. Really, Satan just uses these uprisings to serve his own goals and to inflict even graver hardships upon the people. This has already begun and the end is not yet in sight. The turmoil increases. The wars drag on. Both sides dig in their heels. This is what delights Satan – constant, daily, ongoing death and suffering.

The problems will spread. They will not be of the same nature because circumstances vary but they will have the same essential qualities. When some conditions are not right, Satan will stir up protests. He will raise up those who will cleverly lead the people down Satan's path. Many will follow, duped by the clever rhetoric but also hoping that their condition can be improved. This will always be his bait – the hopes of people to improve their condition.

I would gladly improve the economic condition of my peoples. I would show them how to call upon me, how to join together in ways that would truly benefit them. But they do not call upon me or learn from me. Instead, they listen to other voices that lead them down destructive paths, which center upon overthrowing what they see as evil. There are other means and other ways. I would gladly point these out. People can build a new world, not one based upon destruction. Do you build by destroying? Do you gain peace by stirring up unrest? What power to stir unrest exists in today's world! A click of the Internet, a careful use of the electronic media, and thousands are stirred to unrest. The modern world is not prepared for these new stirrings.   Man thought he had all the answers!

### *Comment*

*Mary comments on the new phenomena of the Internet fostering revolution.*

# LOCUTIONS TO THE WORLD
## PART 2

## JULY 7, 2011 – SEPTEMBER 7, 2011

# TABLE OF CONTENTS
## PART 2

July 7, 2011
## 48. God's Final Preacher

## Mary

Why does God wait? Why does he not intervene? Do you not see? He is always trying to lead man away from self-destruction. He sends his preachers. He sends his teachers. But these are snuffed out. Their words are not listened to and their invitations are rejected.

So, finally, he has sent me. I am his final teacher, his final prophet. I am his last opportunity to change the course of history. There is no one behind me, no other message, no other signs than the ones that I will give.

When I tell the world that it must listen to me, I am not speaking from a selfish and arrogant spirit. I am speaking as one who sees the destruction, the hopelessness of mankind if my words are not heeded.

What are my words? They are clear. They are the same as my Son's. My message is the Gospel message. Repent. Believe that the kingdom of God is at hand. Do penance and you shall find eternal life. This is a message of hope.

You see the demands of the Gospel. I will help you with these demands. I will be at your side. I will lessen the difficulties. I am a Mother, not a taskmaster. I will take much of the burden on myself. It will be much easier than you think.

The Father has said to me, "Go, and help them to live the Gospel, and I will be able to turn away from my wrath." That is why I am here, why I have come. Will you accept my invitation? Right now, ask me to come. I will help you and we will begin.

*Comment*
*What a message of hope! Yet, also a message of warning.*
*Mary is God's final preacher.*

July 8, 2011
## 49. Where Mankind Is Headed

## Mary

All of history is before me – all that is past and all that is to come until the final days of the human race when my Son will come in glory, escorted by all his angels. What will happen from now until then is known to me but it is not yet decided by me. It all depends on the free will of man.

My Son came to Jerusalem on a donkey, an animal of peace. He was not a military

84

Savior but a Man of Peace. He preached peace and accepted the violence done to his own body in peace and forgiveness. He would lead the world into the ways of peace, but the world does not listen to him. Therefore, the Father has sent me. I see where mankind is headed and I come with an urgent message. Do not look for my message only in these words. More important words are spoken in your own heart. Listen to them. The Spirit is speaking to you. They are words of life. Follow them and you will live.

July 10, 2011
## 50. <u>A World Receiving Divine Glory</u>

## <u>Mary</u>

The whole world can receive the divine glory. This is what I am preparing for, a gift come down from heaven that will touch every heart, a divine illumination, in the interior part of every human being.

But that event must be prepared for. The Church must be aware. The people must be told. But who will tell them? What preacher is adequate for this task? That is why it has become my task to prepare the world through these teachings.

I will be very specific, even though I speak of future events. I will give exact teachings, even though I am speaking of experiences that are familiar to few. Let us begin.

First, there will be a period of signs and wonders. This should alert people to the coming manifestation. Unfortunately, the world will remain in darkness. However, because of worldwide communications, individuals will have access, both to my words and to the news about these manifestations (which have already begun, especially at Medjugorje). At least, part of the world will be prepared. Even some secular media will note these events, not from a religious purpose but merely because they are newsworthy. This, too, will further my purposes.

Now, I will describe some of the forthcoming phenomena. I will appear to many of my little ones. People will hear these reports and wonder how this could be true. Each of these will be a little spring of devotion, some larger and more known than others. This, too, has already begun to happen.

I will also begin to touch the hearts of secular people. These will be good people but not known for their religious faith. Their stories will be told. People will learn of their religious conversion and of the sincere, Christian lifestyle which they have adopted. This, too, will be a special witness of the events to come.

Finally, the graces will be even more widespread. There will be religious stirrings in

85

the hearts of many who have set aside their faith. They will be led back to devotions.

I say all this for two reasons. First, the Church must be prepared to respond. Second, as each of these graces is given, all must be ready to believe.

July 11, 2011
## 51. Leaders for a New America

## Mary

All of this comes about because of my special care for the world. Only because the world is buried deeply within my heart does the human race exist in its present form. I say present form, meaning that there are so many people spread out all over the world. I am the one who led Christopher Columbus and my name was on his ship. I am the one who sent the missionaries and people of good will to these new lands, bringing the faith and the civilization of Europe. I am the one who has kept at bay the atomic power unleashed for the first time so many years ago, but never used since. I am the one who has limited natural disasters. I am the one standing between the Father and the divine chastisements.

I have worked through others but now I must intervene directly, openly taking the initiatives which I foretell with these words.

First, I must raise up new leaders, leaders of faith whom I form in my Immaculate Heart. These leaders will have lives of integrity. I will bond them together because if they stand alone they will be ineffective and vulnerable to the world's darkness. Let these leaders arise.

I am calling them forth. Let them be aware. Your mother is calling you. Be stouthearted. You, who are reading these words, you know I am right now calling you to lead my people.

You must gather with others, who could help you in this leadership. Servants of Mary you will call yourselves. Deeply religious in your hearts but totally competent in the secular world, for that is where I need you.

Come close to me. Bond with others. Prepare your skills. Go forth into your culture. I will guide your steps. I am talking now to thousands, leaders of every kind. I need you to be in place, to be accepted by others as just and fair, as a preserver of peace and a force for justice. The gifts come down from heaven but they must be used on earth. Only with holy leaders, consecrated to me, can I fashion a new nation of America.

July 12, 2011
## 52. I Will Walk with God

## Mary

There is a certain road that the world must walk. By these messages, I will lead. All must follow. Do not swerve to the left or the right, because the road is narrow. I am speaking about the road of life – found by few and walked by even fewer. Now, all can find the road because I will reveal it. All can walk this road because I will walk with you as your mother.

Many will say, "This is impossible. Mankind is too selfish." But, I say, "Come, let us believe. Let us trust that mankind can change, that men will respond to the light."

Why will they respond now, when they have not responded before? Because my light is new. It is different. It is not a blinding light that causes men to fear. It is an attractive light that invites them, like a mother inviting her child to take his first steps. Are not a child's first steps followed by a lifetime of walking? If only I can get mankind to take these first steps, soon they will delight in this new power that they have. "I can walk with God," they will say. "Why did I reject him? Why did I set God aside?"

These will be the feelings inside the human person. Who does not want to walk with God? This is the greatest call of the human heart. "I will walk with God" is the greatest decision of mankind. This is my goal. Do you see how gigantic it is? I want all of mankind to proclaim, "I will walk with God." I want every heart to make that decision, "I will walk with God." My voice goes out to the whole world. I am your heavenly mother. Your earthly mother invited you to walk. I will invite you to walk with God. Let my voice reach your ears. You are walking away. You are walking to your destruction, but it need not be so. My voice will grow louder. My words will be more appealing. If you continue to listen, you will come to a moment when you will say. "I can walk with God. I will talk with God." Do you not hear my voice right now? Why not say those words, "I will walk with God." Walk with God and soon you will be accompanied by others – your friends, your family. They, too, will walk with God.

### Comment
*Mary has gigantic hopes. She believes there can be a total conversion of all mankind.*

July 13, 2011
## 53. A Release of the Heart

## Mary

I will make these messages so attractive that many will come to believe. I shape the truths of the Gospel, putting them in a form that all will say, "I now see Jesus' teaching in a new light." I do this because this is the final preaching, the Father's final attempt to have the world accept His Son. So, let us begin.

The heart of man must be released. All is now pent up. He holds so many things in his heart. These he must let go. He has his sins (infections which poison his whole life). He has his memories of failures, of selfishness, even of cruelty and hatred. There have been moments when he was not himself, when temptation caught him unaware, conceived sin and gave birth to evil.

The person did what they thought they would never do. My Son preached repentance. What does this mean? I will use a mother's words. Repentance means "to release your heart."

Yes, repentance is a release. You no longer need to hold it in. You can allow it to flow out. You can confess your guilt. Like a dam that has burst. Where will it go? Into my Immaculate Heart where the fires of divine mercy will consume it forever.

You will have a free heart, a heart that can begin again. That is what I offer to mankind. That is what I offer to you who read these words. My Immaculate Heart offers you a freedom that you have not experienced for years. It is not too late. Let everything pour out. Let the tears come. There is so much to pour out.

Afterwards comes the freedom and with the freedom comes new responsibilities, but only after you are free. I have come to set mankind free. How can I build a new world unless man is free again?

### Comment
*As sin multiplies we forget the effects on the human heart.*
*Mary knows exactly where to begin.*

July 14, 2011
## 54. A Gift for the Secular Person

## Mary

The heavens will burst open and it will be a time of unprecedented grace, available to all – to the religious spirit and to the secular man. Those who know me will be more sensitive. Those who do not know me will be puzzled at first, not understanding what I will call "the first stirrings of faith." It is to the secular man, the person who has no religious faith, that I speak today. Let us begin.

This modern age has stolen from you the greatest power and privilege of man – to be a child of God. The world has given you every possible convenience and pleasure, hoping that you are content with its earthly gifts and will call yourself a "child of this world." In this way, the world can number you among its members and be sure that you would oppose any intrusion of my Son into the world.

My Son came into the world. I brought him into human life, but the world did not want him. The same story that happened in Israel, happens every day. My Son, risen from the dead, wants to come into each culture, but the world will not allow it. The world makes sure that its members resist the intrusion. This is called the secular spirit, the spirit which now controls you to whom I speak.

The world can only hope that you are satisfied with what it can offer you, that you never examine the treasures put in your heart by my Son. If you do examine your heart, you will discover a special gift that you have not opened as yet. (This is what the world fears.) You are made new when your eyes are opened and you say, "I am meant for God."

O secular man, I love you. My Son died for you. I do not come to give you a gift. The gift is already within you. You are born with a desire for God. Do not be afraid to open the gift. The only danger is if you never open it, and go through all your life without understanding that you were made for God.

What will happen when you do open it? I will be there with you. I will show you how to open it without destroying anything in your life that is of God.

A voice speaks now in your heart. It is my voice saying, "Do not be afraid. Do not put aside the religious stirrings that I have planted within you. Open the gift. Open the gift. I can do nothing for you until you open the gift. But after that, I can flood you with life."

### Comment
*Mary invites the secular person to become a child of God.*

July 16, 2011
## 55. A Love Waiting for You

## Mary

My heart overflows with love for all mankind. No human heart is excluded from my love. This is why I ascend this pulpit of the world. So I can reach out to all men. Today I reach out to the neglected, to those persons who have received so little love in their life. You do not believe in a God of love because you have experienced so little love. To you I speak. Let us begin.

How different you were from the other children. You experienced a life of constant emptiness. You did not realize this until you were old enough to understand. Your home was different, empty of human affection, sometimes filled with gigantic disorders (which I will not list). Then came false love, the love you sought from those of your own age. You always met with constant failures. Then, you chose a marriage partner and found yourself inadequate. How could you respond in love, when you had never experienced love? And so it has been. Love, love, love. It has never been there and you have never been able to receive love or to give love, even though you tried so hard to do so.

Now the years go by and your life narrows. You foresee a future in which true love is impossible. The world has cast you aside. You are no longer young (at least as the world defines young). What do I say to you?

First, my heart goes out to you. You have truly been deprived of life's greatest gift – love. You have searched – oh, how you have searched for love – but so many times in the wrong places. Now, I will turn your heart with these words. "It is not too late because my Son has planted a river of love within you called the Holy Spirit, a veritable fire of every kind of love. You will be able to experience his love as so many others have. His is a redeeming love. His first task is to wash away all your sins, quickly and immediately, so that you experience a freedom. The past will have no control over you. Then, this Holy Spirit will release the heavenly Father's love for you, and you will know you are his child. Jesus will take you into his arms, for you are truly a straying sheep. Then I will grasp you and offer you the warm love of a mother." All I can do is to tell you that this love is waiting for you. Take my hand and I will lead you there.

*Comment*

*Many are deprived of human love. No one needs to be deprived of Mary's love.*

July 16, 2011
## 56. Sin Destroys the Marital Relationship

## Mary

People are pulling in all different directions and the oneness of mankind is being shattered. Who can unite mankind? All is divided and the forces of division multiply each day. This is not the Father's plan. He dreamed of a united human family but this sin destroyed this unity.

Dividing man from woman made them almost enemies in their own relationship. Yet, they had a continual urge for each other and man had a loneliness for a companion in his trials. This is the problem I will address because all other problems flow from this sexual war, the inability of man and woman to fully enjoy a loving relationship. If man and woman were at peace, then there would be peace in the world. But, there is no peace. So, let us begin.

Every man and woman is selfish but they do not understand this. They enter into marriage believing that they can be a good husband and a good wife. Soon, however, the realities of their relationship become apparent. The sinfulness of the husband encounters the sinfulness of the wife and problems emerge. They try to resolve these problems, even in a sincere way, but they are not totally successful. Then, they distance themselves. Their sexual contact becomes less frequent. They even question their original attractions. They function together but the full intimacy is missing, not just of body but even of friendship. Something important is missing in the family. This is transmitted to the children. The fullness of God is not present.

I must reveal the problem and offer the true solution. The problem is the universal presence of sin which lies hidden and unseen in every human heart. The solution is to see this selfishness and by repentance to remove it. This, however, is beyond the power of the husband and wife. Forgiving and removing sin belongs to God. So, every marriage without God is doomed to some level of failure because of sin in the human heart.

Let every husband and wife explore my words. Use them to open your eyes. You will see your sins, but also you will see a God who will free you. Mutually accept your need for my Son and a new road will open before you.

July 17, 2011
## 57. The Effects of a Home without Love

## Mary

So many parts of human life are bent and twisted that the human person finds it very difficult to turn to God and to seek Him. That is why I am his messenger. Like John the Baptist, I am called to "make straight his paths." Where will I begin? As always in the human heart.

When the person grows up in an atmosphere of loving parents and a home that is in order, free from strife and turmoil, he can easily perceive the goodness of God because he sees life, love and happiness all around. However, when the original plan of the Father for the family becomes far removed from the original model, then a darkness covers the mind and a heaviness comes upon the feelings. The person is not free to

91

choose the light or to respond to love. Everything is bottled up within, the result of years of an unsatisfying home.

What can be done when this is so widespread? The normal, loving home has become the exception, not the rule. Especially, I address you who are reading my words right now. Your lack of faith is not rooted in the lack of goodness in my Son. It has its roots in your family where so many disorders entered and where faith was dim. I have not come to blame anyone but to offer you a very special gift.

I will be your mother. For many reasons, your own mother was not able to provide and nourish you, could not pour out the warmth and protection that you needed. I will wash away those memories that still hurt within you. I will help you to see everything in a different light. I will open up those feelings that have been closed for so long. Believe me. Everything can be changed. Let us begin right away. Know that I am your mother, loving, powerful, always with my eyes upon you. Always saying to you, "Come and feel my warm love. Come and listen to different words. Come, there is another world that you have never experienced. Come, because everything can change. It is a warm, motherly love that you need and a warm love is what I have for you. Come and you will receive."

*Comment*

*Mary says the cause of little faith in the world is due to disordered family life and a lack of love which she will supply.*

July 18, 2011
## 58. Declaring Endless Wars

## Mary

There are disorders everywhere – in the family, in society, in governments and in international relationships. Nowhere is there peace. Cannot men discern that this universal unrest comes from the Evil One who stirs everywhere? Wherever there is turmoil, he is there, exploiting it to his own purposes.

I am here on the scene to actively engage in battle. I am the Woman. The Evil One and I are foes, eternal foes. The battle will be fought to the end. Let no one doubt that I will win and that he will be vanquished. Let no one doubt that peace will be restored, that human life will again gain a tranquility of order. Yet, let no one doubt that until that special moment brought about by my Son's blood happens, there will be endless wars.

I will fight him everywhere. I will raise up my army, with new skills and greater powers of the Holy Spirit. I will give new signs and wonders to encourage them. I will hold them close to my heart so that they will never be deceived. I will give them the greatest of comforts for the trials they must go through. I will prepare them, send them forth, give them a definite task and bring their work to a completion, even if this sometimes means their own death.

First, I must call them into my Immaculate Heart. Many times they are deceived. They do not see the newness of this situation. They go forth as they usually do but encounter only failure, sometimes falling into the very evils which they are trying to overcome.

Let these words go forth. This is a new and more dangerous situation. Destructive powers have long been at work that have changed the very landscape, not just the individual heart. There is no longer peace. War has broken out and so many of my children are unaware. Many have fallen in battle, not even knowing that a battle is raging.

That is why I say that before going forth, they must come into my Immaculate Heart. I must train them in the new ways of warfare. Otherwise, the enemy will easily destroy them.

### Comment
*Devotion to Mary does not mean withdrawal. Her army will attack*
*but first they need to be trained.*

July 19, 2011
## 59. The Flow of Blessings

## Mary

I come only to bring blessings, blessings of every kind. When man withdraws from God, he withdraws from the source of all blessings. First, one blessing is gone and then another. Man grows jealous. He sees his neighbor with blessings of which he is deprived and then he steals his blessings. Strife and discord begin and from these come open conflicts that escalate. The evil in one man's heart spreads to a nation. One nation sees what it can steal from another. The darkness grows. What can be done? Let us begin.

I must take mankind back to the source of all its problems. To exist, mankind needs God's blessings, the blessings of food, of land, of water – all the material things which God has given plentifully to the earth. Mankind also needs God's blessings upon his heart – the blessings of peace and especially the blessings of mutual love and respect. With these spiritual blessings, mankind can regulate correctly the flow of earthly goods, making sure that even the poorest nation is supplied with enough. When man receives the blessings of God, especially the blessings on his heart, then man wants to bless others. By their very nature, blessings flow out. They are never contained and they are never selfishly hoarded. If they are, they cease to be blessings.

So it is with the blessings of wealth. These are meant to flow out to others. God will replenish them. When they are selfishly stored up in barns, they burn the heart and destroy the rich. Blessings are like a river. They are meant to flow, always enriching the places which they pass through.

The problems begin when God gives these blessings but man forgets their source. They think that they have generated the blessings and that the blessings belong to them. "This is mine," they say. O fool, the blessings are given to you to pass them on. Then, you will have greater blessings.

All evils come from this one source. Man does not acknowledge God as the source of all blessings and does not see the great privilege of being a source of blessing to others. Yes, I will say this clearly, "Man can be like God. He can share in God's powers and be a source of God's blessing to all."

July 20, 2011
## 60. The Power of the Evil One

## Mary

Where do I begin when everything is in disarray? I must stay with the essentials. What is the heart of these problems? What is behind the scenes? What is causing this universal disorder, a disorder that extends to every aspect of human life? I must speak about the Evil One and his minions, what is called the kingdom of darkness. His kingdom is vast and his resources are gigantic.

He entraps people. Some seek him out and make pacts with him. He gives them whatever they desire. He blesses them. Protects them. Leads them to high places. He waits for that day when he will need them. He knows that he owns them.

There are others over whom he also has power. These have made no pacts with him. They might not even know or believe that he exists. However, they, too, are in his power. These people have cravings, desires, ambitions that totally absorb them. They would do anything to gain their goal. This suits the Evil One very well. He just shows them what to do to gain their ambition or to satisfy their craving. He enlightens their intellects in the ways of evil. So, even if they do not believe he exists, they are one of his minions. They build selfish systems, destroy everyone who stands in their way and they release a gigantic stream of evil. Look at Hugh Hefner.

Finally, there is everyone in the world. All, at some time and in some way, can be an instrument of the Evil One. In a moment of weakness or a moment of passion or in a moment of ambition, the person acts not according to their usual manner. They are just caught up in that single moment. This can be repented and, with my help, the damage can be reversed. I just say this so everyone is aware that they can be one of his helpers in a given moment.

### Comment
*Mary wants us all to realize how Satan uses people as his workers.*


July 21, 2011
## 60a. The Power of the Evil One


## Mary
"Wait. Wait. Wait." That is what the Evil One is always saying to those who love me. "Wait, there is time. Wait, there is no hurry. Wait, it can always be done tomorrow." His voice lulls them to sleep. So, I speak to awaken them. Let us begin. The time is short. Oh, you have heard this before. Preachers have used these words. Popes have used these words, but you never listened. Now, your mother will use these words, but with a new power and a different message. I will speak with full knowledge. I know what is ahead and I know the time for each event. I say "each event" meaning what will happen if nothing is done, because the forces have been put in place and they will erupt if nothing is done.

I do not want these events to occur. They are destructive events that will tear down what I have put up and destroy what I have built. Let me repeat, "I do not want these destructive events to occur." Some would see the need for these events, so that people will repent and see the error of their ways. This will not happen. The destructive events, for many, will be the removal of their last hope. No. It is far better if these events are avoided by prayer and sacrifice.


July 22, 2011
## Mary
The power of evil and the forces of good are drawing up the battle lines, but this is not seen by many. A war is about to break out, but so many do not see the obvious signs. So, I must teach my children. Let us begin.

In the beginning, the forces of good were in control, and the Evil One could do little. A morality governed the world, a sense of right and wrong. The powers of evil were restrained. These bonds were broken by the two world wars, especially with the creation and use of the atomic bomb.

After it was dropped, the Arms Race began, together with the Cold War, the partitioning of Europe, and the forming of the Iron Curtain. For decades now, vast sums have been given to developing and maintaining vast supplies of arms. Meanwhile conditions declined. Hunger grew. Problems that could have been solved were allowed to fester. Drugs increased, as did every other type of immorality that degraded the human person. All of this was a fertile field for the growth of the powers of evil.

Now the sins of the past, unrepented and even unknown, have destroyed the human spirit. No one believes that the world of the future will be brighter. All are waiting for the next outbreak of terror, or the next economic collapse. There is defeatism everywhere. In this atmosphere, the powers of evil thrive because no one hopes. The Evil One has stolen hope from the heart of man. No one proclaims a better and brighter world. No one except myself.

This is what I preach. These are the words that must go forth now, while the darkness grows and midnight approaches. I preach light. I preach hope. If no one else's words stir the human heart, my words will. So, listen carefully.

The greatest light that has ever shone upon mankind will come to it as a gift of the heavenly Father. This moment must be prepared for by hope. Yes, you must hope when there seems to be no reason to hope for the future. Hope, that is what I preach. I will explain later. For now, let all my children begin to hope. Your mother sees what you cannot see.

July 23, 2011
# 61. Scattering the Powers of Darkness

## Mary

As time goes on, the powers of darkness grow and increase. Greater powers of destruction are created every day. Those who do the works of darkness have greater powers to bring about their designs. All of this is cleverly intertwined. These forces are linked together by an intelligence given over to the works of darkness. I am eternally opposed to these intelligent creatures, but I am a mother to those who are entrapped in these powers of darkness. I must free them, even though it is difficult for those who are deeply initiated into the darkness to respond to my light, but let us begin.

My first task is to separate those who are in the forces of darkness so they do not encourage one another. I must turn them against each other. I must divide Satan's household, setting father against son and daughter against mother. I must sow discord among those who are under his powers. I will sow these seeds of discord in the Taliban, in Al-Qaeda and in all the terrorist groups. Let my people pray for this. Let them lift up their voices, asking me. This is the simple prayer they are to say, "O Blessed Virgin, Mother of the Savior, scatter the forces of evil so they are not engrossed in darkness but can come to light."

Notice the prayer. I do not want these people's destruction, but their scattering. If they are scattered, then I can surround them in light and they can believe and turn to me.

There are legitimate efforts to destroy their influence, but this only unites them in their darkness and consolidates the hold of the Evil One over them. I will take a different approach, scattering them and making them vulnerable to the light. Yes, I say "vulnerable to the light" because their hearts are made for the light, just as is every human heart.

What is important is that millions of my children begin to pray that I scatter the forces of darkness. Say the prayer right now.

### Comment
*Mary outlines a non-violent way of destroying Satan's power.*


July 24, 2011
## 62. The Way to the Way


## Mary

The world no longer believes. Without belief, it cannot call upon God and cannot use the heavenly stream that is always flowing from God's throne. The stream must bypass those whose hearts are closed. My task is to bring the world to a beginning faith. So let us begin.

Why would the world turn away from God? What are the basic teachings? He is a Father who loves all his children. Seeing the helplessness of man, and even the cruelty of man against man, he sent Jesus to save the world and to bring about a new opportunity for man to live at peace. My Son did not preach violence or hatred. He preached forgiveness. He preached works of charity. He took up no sword and told his followers to accept persecution and to pray for those who persecuted them. What is offensive about those teachings?

He sent the Holy Spirit, who is the Consoler, the Friend, the Advocate for everyone who receives Him. Are not all of these truths attractive? Why are they rejected? This is my point. All of these truths show a God who gives, who pours out himself, who

97

blesses, who understands the sorrows of man and wants to be of help. Why does man not believe and seek God? This is the contradiction.

Man is lost. He is wandering. This is why I come. Even though my Son has come to earth, man does not know the way. Jesus alone is the Way to the Father, but man does not know the way to the Way. This is why I come. I am the way to the Way. In Jesus, the Father will embrace you and give you eternal life, but the modern world has hidden Jesus. He is set aside. He can no longer be found. His voice is lost in the many strange voices that are now claiming men's attention.

You who read these words, take my hand and I will lead you to Jesus. Once you find him, your heart will open wide and the stream of heaven can enter you forever.

July 25, 2011
## 63. A Surprising River of Heaven

## Mary

When I open up the treasures of my heart, I want everyone to be prepared. Otherwise the treasures will pour out uselessly and fall to the ground, not into people's hearts. How can I prepare them? I can only speak of what is to come so their eyes are opened. I am not speaking of future trials but spiritual and even earthly gifts. The heavens will open, slowly at first. A continuous stream of blessings will descend. Then, as the whole world is gradually awakened and as many hearts begin to receive, the heavens will open even more, and a gigantic river of blessings will descend. This will be a continuous river, flowing into every heart that is open. The Church will never have seen such a river since the early days of Pentecost with its signs and wonders.

Theologians will wonder what is taking place. They will examine it and be unable to discredit it. They will be forced to say that these are valid blessings, extraordinary in nature but seemingly ordinary, that is, abundant to all. In this way, they will put their seal upon these phenomena.

The Church will be reluctant to speak at first, but it must not hold back, as if silence is the most prudent course. For too long it has tried to take this road but the modern world moves too quickly. The Church is left behind, arriving with its blessing after everyone else has already passed judgment. No, the Church must be bold and speak out early, so the faithful will not be filled with doubts. Otherwise, many will hesitate and the waters of grace will fall uselessly to the earth.

What are the rivers? Every type of blessings, beginning with repentance and sorrow for sin, but leading quickly to a personal relationship with my Son through my intercession.

That is enough for now. There is too much to explain. I will teach this later.

July 25, 2011
## 64. The Surprising Door to Economic Recovery

### Mary

Everyone is in confusion. All are running around to find a solution, but the seeds have been sown for too long. These are seeds of waste and extravagance, an America which has been out of control for decades. O America, how could this have happened to you whom I have blessed from the beginning? You took my title away from your largest river. (The Mississippi was originally called the River of the Immaculate Conception.)

Now, you further strip yourself of your religious clothing. Well, continue. Continue your secular course and I will have you stand naked before the nations, an economic laughing stock. You have put aside your traditions. You have set aside the accounting procedures that made you a model for the world. You are no longer a model. You are a scandal and you are about to take the whole world down with you in your economic collapse.

You will not listen to those who would strengthen you. You are sick and you refuse to take your medicine. You refuse to see how deep is your illness.

You talk of recovery, an economic turnaround. There will be no recovery because you lie to yourself. A true recovery is based on truth. You hide the reality and your people want to be lied to. Leaders and people, you are tied together by unhealthy bonds, the profligacy of your lifestyles, the unchecked spending and the lack of any discipline. You have had it all for so many decades. Now you will surrender nothing.

No need to surrender. It will all be taken away from you by your creditors. They will close your doors and shut down your excesses. Must it come to this? Is there no solution? I can offer you solutions, but you will not listen. I can point out a road, but you will not follow. Still, I must try. I cannot give up on America, the nation I have taken as my own.

I give you another chance because you have been generous in the past. This is also your future hope. To save your economy, turn your eyes abroad. See the starving of the world and feed them as you have never fed them before. As your food enters the stomachs of the world's hungry, then my economic blessings will flow into your financial systems. That is my promise. The hungry of the world are the doors to your economic recovery.

July 26, 2011
## 65. The Causes of World Problems

## Mary

### Debt Limit Crisis

As everything continues to swirl and events happen with no one (not even those with the greatest powers) able to set a direction, I want to explain what is behind the confusion. The leaders believe that they can use human reasoning to find a common ground and set a direction. However, these forces have a mind of their own. They go off in any direction, heedless of the consequences and unable to be brought into control. This is not one force, but multiple forces. It is not a question of bringing one force into line. None of the forces are aligned. There is no line. It is always shifting. But this is what inevitably occurs when economic selfishness has been fed for so long. Even reasonable restraints are seen as draconian. Everything is amiss and this is a stage of affairs which America has brought upon itself.

For so long they have not listened to me. They have gone their own way, throwing off the restraints upon their selfishness which is demanded by my Son in his Gospel teaching.

The great divide began with abortion. That issue set up the walls. Go back. Look at the political process before the legalization of abortion. Was there not a bipartisan approach, a trying to work things out? Abortion changed all that. Those who followed God's law suddenly saw an issue where there could be no compromise. Many had to withdraw. Others compromised their beliefs. Abortion is the great divide and abortion will always be the great divide. I will not compromise. I will not forsake the unborn, even if America has forsaken these smallest of her citizens.

I will divide you and divide you and divide you. I will let your economy collapse. I will tear your congress apart. I will rip up your constitution. As long as America says that every woman has a constitutional right to kill the child in her womb, I will hold your constitution as unconstitutional. It is no longer a valid document. America, you only think you have a constitution. The Debt Crisis just reveals what I have been doing to you since your Supreme Court made its 1973 decision. Now, I will strip you naked in the streets, for all to see.

You cannot solve your crises because you cannot solve your divisions. Will I allow a house to stand which kills its unborn, millions and millions of these, and all done legally? Legally? By whose law – yours or my Son's? America, your debt crisis is rooted in your divisions and your divisions are rooted in your Supreme Court abortion decision. Find a middle ground! Find a middle ground! This is your cry: Yes, I want you to find a middle ground but your middle ground is not my middle ground. My middle

100

ground is life. Your middle ground is death. A country can only be united to preserve life. How can you be unified when you protect those who cause death?

### Comment

*Look at the history of America since 1973. Have we ever been truly united since Roe vs. Wade? Look at the large number of states which are automatically in the blue or the red column. This is a new phenomenon in America.*

## The Cause of the Explosions

There are explosions everywhere. Money markets are shaking. Wars break out. Revolutions take place on the streets. Dictators kill their own people and America is shaking (in the breakdown of unity). Should not mankind ponder the deeper causes? What causes these explosions? Are they linked together? Why are so many explosions happening at the same time? Should not mankind ask these questions?

I will ask them. I will put these questions before the nations. They must answer these questions before it is too late. I speak of too late. It is already late and my words are a final effort to bring light. Let us begin.

Look beneath the explosions. Study the qualities and you will see a pattern. Man is meant to help his fellow man because some are strong and some are weak. Some have more resources than others. Some have more political powers. Some nations are better trained and organized politically. The strong are meant to help the weak. But what has happened? The strong always think of consolidating, of firming up their position, of gaining more of the marketplace. The poor are excluded from the table. They are taken for granted. Their needs are never factored in.

They are seen as how they can be exploited and how they can feed the stronger nations. Is this not all backward? When will the rich nations think of the poor? When will they shift their policies so the poor are blessed and fed at the table?

All of these explosions have resulted because mankind does not see others as their brothers and sisters. What happens within a family? Is there exploitation? Do they charge one another interest? Do they keep accounts of favors? Or, do they seek the good of all? Are not the family relationships quite different? That is the reason for all those explosions. Mankind does not live as a family.

Only my Son can bring you together. He has restored the family of mankind. Reject him and your family is destroyed. Then you have explosions.

### Comment

*If God is our Father, then we are a family. All are brothers and sisters. To reject God is to destroy the idea of a family and to make mankind into strangers to each other.*

July 27, 2011
## The Economic Disasters

## Jesus

Your eyes see only what happens now. I see what will happen two to three months from now. You see the shaking of the American economic system and the default crisis. There will be no default. At the last minute an extraordinary emergency measure will rescue America from this problem. However, the economic system will be weakened, especially in the eyes of the world.

This will send forth waves of uncertainty. Money supplies will tighten, as will credit advances. The effects of this will be felt in all the nations. There will be greater pressures and higher expectancies. The result will be felt most in those countries that are already weak and already have trouble in keeping up with the others. It is like a man with a weak heart. If the pace is slow enough, he can keep up, but with a struggle. However, if the pace picks up, then he cannot keep pace. He falls behind and eventually drops out of the race. He sees the writing on the wall and loses hope. This will happen to some countries who are on the fringe of the world economy, who already have problems and cannot respond. In these countries there will be major economic disasters.

### Comment
*Even though there will be no default, the political problems will*
*send shock waves through the world economy.*

July 28, 2011
## 66. When God Withdraws

## Mary

No one understands. No one grasps the destructive forces that will soon be unleashed. They will be unleashed by men themselves. No one should blame God. Yet, when these forces are released, many will ask, "Why did God let this happen?" So, I must explain the deeper truths, the greater realities.

Although man lives on earth, he does not understand earth and he refuses to listen to my Son, who would teach him about these destructive forces. The power of sin is rampant. It infiltrates every aspect of human life because it resides in the heart of man. Wherever man is, there is a power to do evil and, at times, to do enormous evil. Only God keeps these forces in check. He does this by his protecting hand, quelling

102

the evil in men's hearts and preventing the enormous evils that these hearts can bring about.

When men blaspheme God and when they reject God (and who would dare to say that this is not the case in America), then God must show his power. He cannot be silent in the face of this rejection. He cannot continue to act as if no rejection is taking place. What do you do when you are rejected? You withdraw. You leave the place. You shake the dust from your feet. This happened at Nazareth and my Son withdrew. This happened to the apostles in some villages, and they withdrew.

Now, all is clear. What is happening in the world? The world rejects God and he withdraws. When he withdraws, there is no force/power present to restrain the destructive forces that men carry in their own hearts. There are destructive forces everywhere and the divine presence has withdrawn.

What are you to do? Invite God back. Ask him to return. He will come. He listens to his children. Invite him into every part of your lives, your homes and your communities. Restore the statues that remind people of God. Let hearts join in public prayer. Especially, invite him into your own heart. You will see the forces of evil withdraw, because a greater power confronts them.

When these destructive forces break out, make the right conclusion. Do not ask, "Why did God allow this?" Say rather, "This happened because we have rejected God's presence and protection."

### Comment

*Man does not realize that destructive powers are present in every heart.*
*Without God, these powers will always break out.*

July 29, 2011
## 67. Rich Nations Must Repent

## Mary

When the nations gather, they do so in their own interests, mapping out their strategies and plotting their ways. They come to agreements that satisfy themselves. They shift the agenda, speaking always of what they want accomplished. Never, never do they ask, "What does God want to accomplish? What does the heavenly Father want done? Why has he given us the goods of the earth?"

Everything is shifted to the powerful nations. Each nation moves off in its own direction, speaking of its "national interests." I must address this problem.

The heavenly Father loves mankind. He has foreseen all that is needed. He has placed on the earth unimaginable blessings. These blessings are stored in elements of the earth that man has not yet explored. The earth is rich, able to sustain human life. There are blessings that have not yet been discovered and remain untapped.

Yet, what will man do when they are discovered? He will do the same thing. Each nation will act selfishly. The powerful will shift everything. The places where the riches are discovered will be exploited. There will be no fairness because men do not ask the central question, "How would God want us to use these blessings? After all, He is the one who has provided."

You have built a world that is out of balance. It is tilted, shaken off its axis. All the blessings flow in one direction. How far down this road you have traveled! And you wonder why God will release his chastisements? What will get the nations to repent? How many forces hold them prisoners to their own foolishness? "This is the way it has always been," they say. "It is too difficult to change."

Is repentance possible? Let us begin. I will help you. Do not delay because you have a long way to go. Take the first step and the bonds that hold you will quickly unravel.

### Comment
*Mary condemns the exploitation of earth's blessings by the powerful nations.*

July 30, 2011
## 68. America's Great Sins

## Mary

Why are the chastisements delayed? Because the little ones stand before God with their arms upraised in intercession. Their prayers rise as sweet incense and the heavenly Father's justice is blinded to the sins of men. How long can this continue? How long can the intercession of the few cover over the sins of the many? This is why I speak. The world is enjoying a time of reprieve, yet it does not understand this. The world feels that it has many years of future blessings. The world believes that God will not act. Oh, he will always act as a Father, always tempering his justice, always seeking another way to correct the situation. But a time comes when the children have decided the issue.

That is my teaching. The children of this world decide the issue. They are the ones whose hearts are free. They refuse to turn back. They continue to move ahead. They lead the world astray. When some children lead others astray, can the Father do nothing? Must he not act for those who are being led astray? This is how you must see the issues. For the good of those who can be saved, the Father must act.

104

Before that moment (Oh, that terrible moment when I see what must happen if men do not repent), the Father has sent me. He has told me, "You will be my final preacher. If they do not listen to you, then I have no one else to send. If I send my Son, Jesus, it will be the end."

In the midst of all man's sins, what will I preach? If I condemn all that needs to be condemned, the list will be too long. Men will be confused and lose hope. So, as a good preacher, I will pick out one sin, the most heinous of sins, the one that most arouses the anger of God. I will preach against that sin. My message will be easily understood and this is my promise. "If the world repents of this one sin, I will hold back the chastisements of God and there will be a springtime without a winter. Otherwise, the deadliest of winters will settle upon the earth."

The sin that stirs the anger of the Father is the killing of the unborn. Repent of this sin and turn back to life. I will protect you, if you protect these little ones. Do not say this is impossible and that the political forces are too great. Let us begin. I will bless your efforts, stirring the hearts of others to join you.

### Comment

*Mankind has many sins, too numerous and too confusing to even list. Mary picks out the great sin of abortion and promises that the Father's anger will abate if mankind repents of this.*

July 31, 2011
# 69. Cutting Samson's Hair

## Mary

Slowly, ever so slowly things grind to a halt. Where is the former power of America? Where is the former greatness, the ability to accomplish and to do great things? First, one power is gone and then another. America is becoming like a Samson whose hair is being cut. Let me explain what is happening.

Your greatness came from your religious roots. From these flowed your vitality. You, however, misjudged yourself. You thought the power was your own and you said, "What need have I of these religious roots? They are from another century. They hold back our progress. They offend the sensibilities of some of our members. We will cut them out. We will limit their growth. We will impede their influence."

Yes, America, that is what you have done. You are becoming like Europe. You are removing the title religious and substituting secular. Like Samson, you have fallen into the hands of Delilah and she is taking away your strength. Wake up before she cuts off all your hair and delivers you over to your most hated enemies. That is exactly what will happen. Your enemies look on. They watch and wait. It is not yet the moment. You still have some strength but soon, yes, very soon, you will be their prey.

Wake up. Wake up. The word religious is fading. When it is totally erased, you will fall. This does not have to happen.

*Comment*
*Mary clearly explains the waning power of America.*

August 1, 2011
## 70. A Prophecy of Future Events

## Jesus
Pakistan will be a source of great problems. The support of the United States and its ties to Pakistan have been weakened by the killing of Bin Laden. The present government, weak as it is, is the only fence standing between the rebels and the nuclear arms. When the government is toppled, America will try to secure the arms, but its military might will not be enough. The rebels are too large and too firmly implanted – too extensive among the people.

Even if the people do not belong to the rebels, they feel no enmity to the group. That is why the government is so weak in its fight against the terrorist group. It does not want to offend a large segment of its people and must make some political responses against the United States.

The Suez Canal is no longer protected by Mubarak and can no longer be seen as under the influence of the United States. Understandings with Egypt about the use of the canal are now meaningless.

Russia will continue to press its relationships with the key countries of the Middle East. These countries see Russia as a force which can help them gain their quest.

In all of this, America is no force for Israel or for true Middle East peace. The president sits on the sidelines and allows the forces in the Middle East to go unchecked.

Many see these problems as Middle East problems, far distant and not important to the West, but all of this will affect America because of its need for oil.

All of these events will tilt the power to the Muslim world and many Muslims will rejoice to see that they are gaining the upper hand much more quickly than they thought possible.

The most important issue has been overlooked. Up to now, the Muslim world has been divided because of the various dictators. Now, these have been or will be soon toppled. There is a new possibility of Muslim unity brought about by radical Muslims.

This sudden possibility of some union of Muslim nations under a religious leader will lead many to believe that they can be that leader. Important people will begin to move toward Muslim unity along religious lines. These men will not succeed but they will move the process along.

Then, one will arise who will take advantage of all of these forces and will somewhat unite the Muslim world for his purposes.

### Comment
*Jesus allows us to see beneath the surface of world events.*

August 4, 2011
## 71. How to Survive

## Mary

When the time comes, it will be too late to prepare. Those who have called on my name will know what to do to survive. Their hearts will tell them and I will guide them. Those who are selfish will act selfishly. They will condemn themselves because they will see all their past efforts destroyed in one moment. They will have nothing to live for. They will make efforts to control the situation, but their efforts will be in vain and they have never learned how to live in faith.

This is my teaching, how to live in faith. People with few resources will survive because of a deep-rooted faith. People with more resources will not, because they cannot find any faith in their hearts. This is why I grieve. A time is coming when men will need great faith to survive, yet faith has grown cold. Let me explain.

When there is prosperity, many set aside their faith. They do not need God's help. Their own power secures their needs. Their eyes turn away from heaven because they see all the goods of earth. Two things result from prosperity. The person no longer looks to God and the person gives their heart to earthly goods. Faith is lost.

Then, however, comes the divine chastisement. This is the only option which mankind leaves to God. They have rejected every other path. (That is why I am speaking so clearly, so that mankind accepts this last opportunity offered by the merciful Father.)

In the chastisement, the earthly kingdoms fall. Terrible jolts come upon society. In the beginning, no one notices. However, as the jolts continue, all begin to see that their society, which provided all these goods, is collapsing. For a person without faith, this is all they have. They have nothing and do not know how to turn to God for their security. They are lost and each day is worse than the last one. They stumble in an insurmountable darkness. For them, everything is destroyed. They cannot go on. Indeed, many choose not to go on. They destroy themselves.

I speak to you, secular man. Look into your heart. You will find no faith. You have no relationship to God that will sustain you in the difficulties that lie ahead. I will teach you a prayer. Say it often and I will come to you and you will see a flower of faith growing in your heart. This is the prayer, "O Mary, when I am alone, I realize I am empty. I believe this feeling is my search for faith. O Mary, plant the seed of faith in my heart and I will let it grow."

### Comment
*Mary wants the secular person to receive faith so they can survive the darkness.*

August 1, 2011
# 72. Electing a President

## Mary

The holes are opening up in the American economy, gigantic gaps that no amount of money can fill in. American life is spiraling downward and out of control. No one can see how fast all of this will transpire. There is still an aura of unreality, as if this could never happen in America.

O America, you will tumble and tumble, wondering when this downturn will bottom out. "When will we turn around?" you will ask.

Who are your leaders? Whom have you elected? Did you not vote your wallets? Is it not always the economy that determines your choice? You have gotten the leadership that you deserve. These are the ones you have chosen, because you always vote by the wrong standards.

You must hold your elected officials to higher standards. They must be good people, who protect the unborn and protect marriage. To you, these issues seem unimportant, as if they are on the sidelines. Yes, for you they do not matter. If Satan could fix your economy, you would elect him your president.

This is my promise. If you place first what I place first and elect officials who hold my values, then your economy will turn around. However, if you continue to elect those who are unworthy but promise you economic blessings, your economy will continue to tumble.

Look at the next elections in light of what I have just told you. Those who do not protect the unborn and who do not protect marriage cannot protect your money.

### Comment
*This aptly describes the American voter who chooses those who promise prosperity.*

August 7, 2011
## 73. Recapturing American Generosity

## Mary

Just as people leave their valuable possessions behind, not realizing that they have lost them, so America has left its most valued possession behind, the gift that made it a great nation.

It has forsaken the well of living water. Its cisterns have been broken. Its culture no longer values truth. Everything has been thrown away that preserved the ancient heritage. The old has been rejected. The new has been embraced.

Motherhood is now set aside for the career. Family is now sacrificed for the gaining of goods. Children are devalued. Large families, where children enjoy many brothers and sisters, have been replaced by what is convenient to the parents.

The children learn these values. Selfish parents bring about selfish children. Parents who severely limit their children bring about children who will abort their children.

Selfishness is a stream which many hearts quickly accept because it serves their own interests. Generosity is a river that finds few hearts open to its blessings because it demands sacrifices.

America used to be a generous country. It would make many sacrifices to gain what was true and good for others. Now, it is a selfish country, where everyone looks to their own interests. How can I save you, America, a country so close to my heart? There is only one path. Return to the generosity and sacrifice that made you great. Return to the truth that guided you.

Begin now. You, who are reading these words, do not wait for others. Begin today to recapture a generous heart. I will help you.

### Comment
*America must realize that its most valuable possession is its generosity.*

August 8, 2011
## 74. Leaving the Father's House

## Mary

Forsaking the Father's Wisdom

Why are the nations in tumult? Why this stirring on the earth? All is anxiety and turmoil. The pot boils over. The sins of the past come to the surface. What was planted in secret now brings its harvest – a harvest full of weeds not wheat. This economic turmoil was not a harvest sown overnight. For decades, the nations have hidden their debts, buried them, saying, "Let a later generation pay the bill." Now, the bill has come due. The collector is at the door and he wants the whole house. He owns it. His accounting is correct. He has added up his figures and now he presses his case. Oh, poor mankind, burdened with so many years of folly, like a man awakening to reality. Yes, the harsh reality of an economic system that cannot pay for your lifestyle. What can I say in the face of this worldwide problem? Let us begin.

Years ago, you left your Father's house, where all was in order. You said, "Give me the inheritance that is due to me." You were of age. You could claim what was yours. You took your Father's money but you did not take his wisdom. "It is different now," you said. "The truths of economics that my Father used are no longer the guide." So, you made up new rules, the modern way that borrows now and pays later. "This is the way of growth. This is how we expand," you claimed.

But you overlooked one truth – the selfishness of man and the constant postponement of responsibility. Look back. See the wisdom of your heavenly Father, a wisdom you have rejected. Return to your Father's house before it is too late! Regain the ancient truths upon which your society was built. You have forsaken the religious spirit. You have become secular. Fine. Taste the secular wine. Eat the secular food. It will make you throw up. Hopefully, in your agony, you will return to your Father's house.

*Comment*
*As the worldwide economic markets are shaking, Mary teaches the causes and the solution – a regaining of the religious spirit.*


The Prodigal Son

I speak with you as a mother to her child and I reveal to you the longings of my heart, the heart of a mother. Yes, I am a mother who sees all too clearly the state of my children. They have left the Father's house where they could daily experience my love. Now they have chosen to scatter, not even recognizing their brothers and sisters. They are divided and clashing, and want to gain superiority. They leave behind the relationships within the family and adopt the relationships of the street. They have chosen this, wanting their freedom, and being discontent to remain in the Father's house where they were loved and fed, where they were accepted and had a place.

Why, O why, did they leave? I watched them go forth. I felt the sorrow in the heavenly Father's heart. I knew what lay before them. They saw only the false promises. They would own and prosper. They would have their own house. They were a human race "come of age." These were all their false hopes. They forgot that the Father held them together.

In the Father's house, they cooperated. The Father kept everything in order. The human race is now a world without a Father. They are like the Prodigal Son. They have spent their inheritance. They have no identity. They are not recognized for what they are – children of a loving Father and children of a heavenly inheritance. Can all the ills be solved? Yes, the answer is yes. That is why I speak to the world. One decision is needed. "I will arise and I will return to my Father's house."

O world, you do not even know how to return. That is why the Father has sent me. The journey is a long one because you have strayed so far. Take my hand. Let us begin the return journey.

*Comment*
*Mary makes clear the source of all the world's problems. Led by false hopes and*
*without realizing the full consequences of their decision,*
*the world has left the Father's house where there was a family relationship.*

## To the Generation Born in Darkness

I want all my children to return home. I will call them. I will place new stirrings in their hearts. They will remember the way it used to be. But what about those who never knew the Father's House? Those who have no memories? It has been so long now. Children have been born outside of the Father's House to parents who left and abandoned the Father. What will I do about them? They are children born without any religious memories. Oh, what time has done! A generation which has never tasted the springs of religious faith. They thirst and have no idea of where to find true water. They are even more difficult to draw back than their parents, but I must reach out. Let us begin.

To you who have no religious memories, who were born and raised in a secular culture. For you, religion is only an item in the news, usually associated with political controversies. To you, I speak these words. You have no idea of the gift of a religious spirit and of the consolations offered by faith.

You have no idea of the peace that comes from a relationship with my Son, Jesus. You do not know all that He will do for you.

Instead, you wander in darkness, not knowing the true longings of your heart. I cry for you. I weep for you. This was not your decision. Your parents left the Father's house. They never taught you the truths that they had learned. In rejecting their religious life, they lost it for you also.

111

I do not see you as a generation which has rejected my Son. Your parents rejected him. You were fed a secular milk. This is how I see you – a deprived generation, an offspring that has never existed before in America. Know that you are welcome in my heart. I await you.

*Comment*

*The young adult generation is the least religious generation in America's history. Mary does not scold them. She sees that they have been deprived. She waits for them.*

## Is There a God?

Why does the world not return to the Father's house, especially in the West where the faith was so strong? The memories have faded. They have forgotten the peace that settles into a person's heart when it is right with the Father. They have forgotten the order that comes to a society when all its members accept the Father's commandments. They have forgotten all the blessings that come from an Age of Faith. So, I come to lead them back. They cannot return because they do not know the way back. That is why I speak. Listen carefully.

The way back to the Father is not a far-away distant path. It is near. It is in your heart. The path back begins within you. Even now it has begun with the stirrings caused by my words. Others are praying for you. All the saints and angels intercede for you.

Faith surrounds your heart. Faith is like the air all around you. You need only to breathe to take it in and be blessed by its presence.

Let your mind and heart rise above what you see and experience. For just one moment be willing to ask, "Am I made for God? Are the ancient teachings true? Will I live forever? Did God create me? Is Jesus his only-begotten Son?"

In the ages of faith, people knew these questions and lived by their light. Begin with the first one. "Is there a God?" Keep asking yourself that question until the light dawns. Everything begins with that question.

Do not shut the question from your mind. Do not put it away. To ask this is the first breath of faith.

*Comment*

*Modern society has forsaken God for so long now, that the average person does not know how to return to him. Mary shows the road's beginnings –*
*to ask the simple question – Is there a God?*

## The Loneliness of the Secular Person

When the darkness begins it will be too late. The return to the Father's house must

112

begin now, so you can be joined with others in faith. I want to explain this gift. Let us begin.

When a person leaves the Father's house, they also leave behind all the relationships and friendships they enjoyed. They not only break their relationship with the Father but also with the others. This is the high price that man pays for what he sees as his freedom.

He goes out into a world which does not know the Father. The relationships which are formed are not relationships of faith. People unite in pragmatic ways, in ways that serve their interests. They form relationships according to their own will and fancy. How fragile are these relationships. How many times they break off, unable to withstand the forces that come against them.

Some forces are internal, the passions and the selfishness of those involved. Some forces are external, the trials and difficulties encountered in the world. As relationships are broken, innocence is lost and isolation sets in. The person is vulnerable, unable to respond or even to hope, because they stand alone. They never foresaw all of this as they left the Father's house. What must be done quickly because so much has been destroyed?

Begin like the Prodigal Son. Say, "I will return to my Father's house." Seek out a Church and seek out people of faith. Give yourself to these relationships. Be formed with others into the Body of Christ.

Find others! Find others! This is the secret. Find others who believe. Form relationships of faith. Together, profess my Son as your Lord.

### Comment
*In the Ages of Faith people were joined together by the heavenly Father whom all acknowledged. As that faith was lost, the relationships with others were lost and society suffered its greatest disease – individualism.*

August 12, 2011
## 75. The Egyptian Uprising

## Jesus
### The First Scene of Satan's Drama (and the point of no return)

With the Egyptian uprising (January 2011), the events of darkness have passed the point of no return. The great confrontation between the devil and the Woman has begun. People do not grasp that events have entered a new stage. They think these are just a new level of the old problems. January 2011 was the point of no return because Satan decided to begin his drama.

The Egyptian uprising has meant that Israel has lost some layers of protection. Israel knows that it is endangered more than before. So, the drama has begun. Satan has sent out the first actors in front of the curtain to begin the show. Soon the curtain will pull back and everything will begin in its fullness.

No director begins the first scene unless he intends to follow it with all of the other scenes. No director begins a show unless the script has been written and well rehearsed. No director begins a show unless all the actors are on hand, especially the most important ones. Yes, they are all on hand and after this opening scene of the disruptions in the Middle East, the curtain will rise and Satan will introduce his important actors.

These will move the script along and lead up to the main actor. All the important action will wait for his arrival on the scene. When he comes, I will point him out to you, even giving you signs ahead of time.

You will identify all these actors and note how they are reading the script and bringing about the story. All will be clear through the revelation of the Holy Spirit. One after another they will come upon the scene, but only when the most important actor arrives will the full power of darkness be seen and manifest.

### Comment

*The confrontation between God and Satan has begun. The Egyptian uprising was the first scene.*

August 13, 2011
## 76. Ability to Destroy Israel

## Mary

The events spill out of control and man loses his power to shape the history of the world because Satan has stepped onto the scene, using people whom he has prepared for years, many of them since their birth.

These events have their roots in the past, in a culture of darkness. However, they are different. They have taken on a new power, a new sharpness, and a new level of destruction.

These powers of darkness have now surpassed the powers of the West to contain them. Right now, the West is absorbed with its own economic problems and in attempts to find solutions. This, too, is Satan's plan. Since their own houses are not in order, they cannot give attention to the Middle East and to the drama that is taking place there. These are the shifts in the Muslim world.

114

The dark side is coalescing, coming together, increasing its arms and getting its leadership in place. Certainly there are internal struggles and sometimes they go backwards, but the movement is forward. They go to greater military strength, to more coordinated functioning, to a harder resolve and, especially, to a belief that their day will soon come. Confidence in their ability to finally destroy Israel grows daily.

All of this comes from religious fervor which the West does not understand because it has lost its own. Fervor must be fought with fervor. Religious fervor with religious fervor. This is my promise. I will rekindle religious fervor. I will open the eyes of all who want to see. I will touch hearts, even of those who have no religious background. When you see the fires of this new religious fervor you will know that I am keeping my promise. Do not despise the day of small beginnings. A little fire can enkindle a mighty blaze.

### Comment
*Satan uses people with a false religious fervor which drives them to extraordinary sacrifices. The West lacks this fervor. Mary will rekindle new fires. They will be small but extremely important. When needed, they will become a mighty blaze.*

August 14, 2011
# 77. A Place Prepared in the Desert

# Mary

So quickly, as if by a gigantic surprise, Satan will suddenly move his people into place. They will remain hidden, ready to come forth when he calls them. But, I will not allow him to complete the fullness of his plan. This would be too much. There would be desolation everywhere with no hope of any escape. This is the type of plan which he hopes to execute, but I will do two things.

First, I will not allow him to deploy all of his forces. I will not allow him to put them all in place. Some, which he puts in place, I will not allow to function as he would like. They will be in place but I will render them helpless. Their voices will be discredited ahead of time.

Secondly, I will open up gatherings of faith and my children will be aware of them. They will not know why I have led them to these gatherings. They will just know that I am leading them in this way. Only when Satan's attacks begin will they see that these are saving gifts – the windows and doors that I have opened so they can escape. Yes, I say "escape" because to remain is to be lost. To foolishly cling to homes or material goods is to be swallowed up. Just as a place was prepared for me in the desert (12:6) where I was kept safe, so I will prepare places for all those who hear and receive my

115

words. People must learn to go out into the desert, those places of solitude where I can gather my children. Did I not go into the desert? Would I not go to prepare a place for my children? This is how I will save them in the times of great trials that lie ahead.

### Comment

*Mary speaks in images. These are easy to understand, although what they refer to in the concrete is not yet clear. I am sure that she will explain this later.*

August 16, 2011
## 78. The False Light of Television

## Mary

What light does man walk by? This determines the path he takes. Everyone should examine that light because often that light is darkness, but the world calls it wisdom.

There used to be the light of faith. It was so strong in the Ages of Faith. Some men rejected this light and walked their own path, but they were seen as rebels against the truth, and they did not endanger those who remained in the light, who were solidly supported by others in their beliefs.

Now, all of this has changed. The great light of faith that guided the nations has been shattered into many small lights. In the lack of unity of the Churches another light has emerged, able to be used by whoever has the power to raise money, to collect an organization, and to rise to power among the mass media.

The light of faith has been replaced by the light of the television from which pours forth every darkness. It creates a culture, a way of thinking, a standard of morals. It forms its disciples, preaches its Gospel, and enforces its laws by shoving aside the people of faith. It is godless and has led society far astray. Its powers grow. Its channels increase. Its views harden and claim greater power, destroying one law of God after another. It is not rooted in faith and would like to destroy faith so that it would be the only voice.

I must speak about this power which has only come on the scene in these final decades. Yes, I say final decades because if the power of television is not transformed then these will be the final decades, where faith is extinguished. But, I will not let that happen.

### Comment

*Mary speaks first of the great light that united the West – the Catholic Church.*
*She mentions the breaking up of the Church as the great light became many little lights.*
*In this division of the Churches, television could emerge as a new light,*
*a secular light that destroys faith.*

116

August 17, 2011
# 79. The Consecration of Russia and the Jerusalem Papacy

## Jesus

When all is put in place and all the events are about to occur, I will raise up a son to be the Pope. He will be well instructed in my ways and he will not fail me. I will have instructed him for years and then, through the most extraordinary of events, I will lift him to where no one thought he would ever attain.

He will be a man of faith and will walk only in my ways and in my light. All will be clear to him because I will have revealed everything ahead of time. There will be no doubt and no hesitancy.

## The Two Goals of a Short Papacy

Because of the confusion of the world, he will set aside many of the usual tasks, and will focus on the tasks that I had revealed to him ahead of time – the consecration of Russia to the Immaculate Heart and the moving of the papacy from Rome to Jerusalem. These are the two important goals of his short papacy.

My Church will be positioned again, just as I positioned the Church when I placed Peter and Paul in Rome and led them to their martyrdom. This planted my Church in Rome, where it has been for all these centuries. Now it is time to root it again in the soil of Israel and in the Middle East. It is in Jerusalem that all will find peace. No longer will my death and resurrection be set aside. All will see that Jerusalem is the holy city. Because of that holiness, peace will come to the world.

All will tell the story, the fathers to their children. They will tell the story of what I accomplished in Jerusalem and why Jerusalem is the center of the world. Yes, I say, the center of the world. Other cities will exist and have their own importance, but it is to Jerusalem that they will look for their wisdom. Presidents and kings, men and women with political power, will submit to the wisdom of Jerusalem and all the nations will walk again by my light. See all the events in this light. It will not be accomplished in one step or two steps.

How can I shake the present order? How much that now exists must be set aside? I will use many to accomplish my plan, even the strategies and the powers of the Evil One will unwittingly bring it about. Step by step. All will proceed until all the nations see what I have done to exalt the mountain of Zion.

### Comment
*Jesus is the Lord of history. He wants all the world to remember what he*

*accomplished in Jerusalem. To do this, he must exalt Jerusalem and make it the center of the world. Only when people see Jerusalem exalted will they remember the events which happened there.*

August 18, 2011
## 80. Sunday Shopping, Sports and Entertainment

## Mary

When the good are confused and when the stouthearted begin to waiver, I must bring about a new light and a new firmness. Otherwise, all will perish. I speak words of life which counteract the corruption of life. These words can be painful in removing what needs to be put away. Many will not want to hear these words and will set them aside as too foolish. They are the foolish ones, not seeing the great danger in which they live.

I must cut away, detaching my people from what has become so ingrained. I must cut away your Sunday shopping. I must cut away your addictions to Sunday sports and entertainment. I must shake you out of the web that the world has woven around you. It has stolen the day from my Son. Oh, it has happened little by little, a gradual pouring out of a sea over the sacred island called the Lord's Day.

Step back and look at the day. What has happened to it? A part has been chipped away for national news. A part has been given to endless sports. And, if that is not enough, even the nighttime hours are consumed. Entertainment. Entertainment. That is all you give yourselves to. Then, you expect my Son to lead you and guide you. I must cut away your Sunday shopping and your Sunday entertainment.

Move away from it. Gather the family. Learn the ways that used to be. If you do, I will teach you the ways of the Lord. If you do not sanctify the Lord's Day, if you do not offer the day as a pleasing sacrifice to the Most High, then I cannot lead you on any saving path.

### Comment
*All admit that American life is in a mess but few remember Sunday as it used to be and really should be. Making the Lord's Day holy is a clear obligation. Mary says much more. It is the first step to restoring life to America.*

August 19, 2011
## 81. The Coming Worldwide Darkness

## Mary

Can you not see the path where mankind is heading? Look back and see the light which used to bathe the world. Look now and see the twilight. The lights are more dim and many have been extinguished. Now, look forward and see that this path must lead to darkness. Yes, all will enter the darkness. When the lights go out in a room, it is dark for all, the good and the bad, the selfish and the unselfish.

I invite my little ones, through these words, to leave this path, to withdraw from the paths which the world trods.

How can this happen? Are not all caught up in the forces of culture? Can a person detach themselves from their society? Let us begin. Yes, let us begin now. The call is urgent. Time is short and the powers coming against my children are great. Let us begin.

### The New Gift – A Covenant in the Spirit

Everything begins within by a fresh stirring of the Holy Spirit. Natural wisdom is not enough. Even spiritual wisdom does not hold the answers (although it offers sound guidance). My children must be aware of the method I will use. I will outline this so all can understand.

First, everyone must pay attention to the fresh stirrings of the Holy Spirit. Yes, I say fresh stirrings because these will come suddenly. All must pay attention because the Spirit will be enlightening everyone. If they do not pay attention, they will either not notice the light, or they will not give the light much importance.

Many in the same area, in the same group, in the same parish will receive this light. These lights must come together. One light will not survive and one light does not contain everything.

The parish that receives this light must cherish it, live by it, and allow the light to call people together into a covenant of love. This will be a mystical joining of hearts. In this joining, the people will discover a new life. They will call it "Our life in the covenant." They will know that the covenant is a special gift which they must cherish. In the covenant will be contained all that they need. The Holy Spirit will be in their midst as never before.

*Comment*
*Mary explains God's plan and gift. How else can God lead except by a stirring of the Spirit? This stirring must draw people together or else it will die out.*

August 20, 2011
# 82. The Coming Elections

# Jesus

The confusion in America will continue because the safeguards have been weakened. The figures belie the true picture. The years of high unemployment have taken away the hopes of the people. This is the most important point. The confidence of the American people that their country will be strong again has been shaken. There is no end in sight.

The solutions that will be put forward to solve the economic crisis will not be the right ones because everyone is looking at the elections. The suggestions will be political and the American people will be even more disheartened. Time is slipping away. Opportunities are lost and nothing is being accomplished.

America will then go to the election and make a choice, a choice between light and darkness. Their issue will be the economy but the economy is not my issue. My issue is life and the protection of the unborn. My issue is truth and the protection of marriage. My issue is holiness and the keeping of the commandments. If America votes for my issues, then I will care for its economy. However, if America votes in a selfish way, electing those who will not protect life, who will not protect marriage and who will not protect my commandments, then I cannot and will not save America.

It will enter into a total darkness, without any hope. People will wring their hands and ask, "What can be done?" It is too late. They have made their choice and they scorned my issues.

Let the word go forth and let all see clearly before it is too late.

## Comment

*Americans focus on the economy. God focuses on other questions. Voting is extremely important and people must judge every candidate according to God's priorities. It is already late in the game.*

# Mary

## The Modern Day American Judas

Too many problems for modern man to handle. They crash in upon him – wars and deficits, uprisings and defaults. Problems arise on every side. Mankind never understood the world that he was building, or rather, the world that he thought he was building. Really, the world was being constructed by the Evil One who used the selfishness of man for his own purposes. He said to one, "Do this and you will be blessed." To another, "Build this and you shall profit." Meanwhile, he remained in the background, allowing man to do his work.

When this stage was finished, he felt bold enough to step up his efforts and to bring

120

to the forefront those hearts whom he had owned for a long time – the hearts of Osama bin Laden and those who followed him. For the first time, he confronted the world with his demonic power in the burning of the Twin Towers. How did the nations react? They still did not repent. They did not turn to heavenly help.

Now, he is preparing a third offensive, which will take a new form, not easy to detect. I want to reveal this before it happens but only to show the validity of these words. In this way, many will listen to my words that will reveal so much. Let us begin.

The problems for the West will come from the West. Your eyes are looking to foreign borders, to cultures not your own. However, the Evil One has, for a long time, gained the hearts of your own – your own leaders, your own statesmen, your own bankers. They are like Judases, ready to sell you out, ready to betray you for their own interests. They placed their trust in you when they saw you as strong. Now, they realize that you are weak. "America is not the place to invest. Let us take our money elsewhere." This is what will happen. Your own sons will abandon you. They will not stand by you in the time of trial. Your weaknesses will be magnified by their departure. O America, when will you turn to me?

### Comment
*America is certainly in crisis. Mary predicts a betrayal which will multiply the difficulties.*

August 21, 2011
## 83. The Sunday Dollar

## Mary

America is like a field that has been neglected for so many years. Formerly, it was a fertile field, bringing forth the fruits of goodness. It had the houses of worship, families which prayed, and marriages that lasted. Now, all its fruits have spoiled because an enemy has sown his fruits. What will I do with this field that was mine and is no longer mine, with a nation that was consecrated but now renounces its consecration? Are you ready to declare like the European nations, "We are secular"? The words are already on your lips. Do not say them. Do not let me hear those words. This would be the final break. Your ties to God are already tenuous, yet there is some life. Can the religious spirit regain its fervor? Let us see. Let us examine the situation. I will point out the problems.

You have filled the Lord's Day with your concerns. "Why close the stores?" you say. "Why deprive ourselves of this day, when so much can be sold?" Yes, much is sold – it is your soul that you are selling for the almighty dollar, but your dollar is no longer almighty. Store up your dollars. Soon they will be of much less value. Sell your goods. Soon your people will be in debt. Open your stores. They are filled with goods made in other nations. Is this want you want, America? Is this the American dream?

Well, I have a different dream and if you do not accept my dream, then yours will soon be a nightmare, and that day is not far away.

This is my dream for you, America. I want a Lord's Day when your Churches are full and your stores are closed. Do not the two go together? Can a family be at both? Are not your open stores a challenge to the Churches? Do they not appeal to the selfishness of man? Will he not always think of what he needs? He thinks of what he can obtain, even when he is already in debt.

Many will not listen to me. But those who hear my words can act. Keep holy the Lord's Day, and I will keep you safe in the coming trials.

### Comment

*To keep alive the religious spirit demands a setting aside of secular pursuits. When secular activity goes on as usual, many forget their religious duties.*

August 22, 2011
# 84. Purged from Selfishness

## Mary

I am Queen of heaven and earth. Everything is drawn into my heart. All is present there. An earthly queen reigns over the good and the bad, over those who serve her loyally and over those who stray from her commands. Many do not know that my Son is Lord, and many do not know that I am the Queen of heaven and earth. If this were understood, then order would come upon the earth and peace would reign.

Men have rejected God, and when he sent His only begotten Son, they rejected him. Now the Father sends me, the final chance for the salvation of the world. "Who is she?" they say. "She is only a creature." This is true, I am a creature, coming forth from the hands of the Father, just like everyone else. However, I am different in one respect. All that the Father gives to me returns to the Father. I keep nothing for myself.

This is what I must teach to mankind. All blessings come from the Father, but mankind says, "These are mine." He takes them to himself, never acknowledging that all these gifts come from heaven above. They never return to the Father and are never purified, like dishes that are never washed, filled with stains and unworthy to be used at the banquet.

Learn from me. Everything I receive I give back to the Father and he gives me greater gifts, pure gifts, untainted by selfishness.

Selfishness is the cause of man's problems. "How can we be purged of selfishness?" This should be the question in man's heart. This gift comes down from the Father, like all his other gifts. Seek this gift and you shall live.

*Comment*

*Mary is different from us in one way. At no moment in her life was she selfish.*
*She will lead us to the same gift if we proclaim her as our Queen.*

August 24, 2011
## 85. Strangling the Breath of Faith

## Mary

Holes will open up; even some gigantic holes will appear in society. Some have already appeared. People felt that the walls of protection were strong and that the fibers of society were tightly woven together, but so much is frayed, so much worn away, so much left unattended for so long. The human spirit has not been nourished. What holds together a society?

People will say "the great institutions, the Constitution, the laws, the political offices." They will point to all those things outside of themselves. Yet, what brought them into existence? What breathed life into this nation? How was it born? What kept it vital? It was the human spirit, fed and nourished by faith. This nation was built upon faith in God. Faith was the breath that breathed life into America. Now, that breath is gasping for life. It is being deliberately choked to death by those who would remove religion from American life. And the death of faith is being witnessed by those who cannot grasp the role of faith in breathing life into the institutions.

### Life of Faith

The life of America is the life of faith. It is your churches that breathe life into you. The churches give you citizens who are ready to serve. The churches give you families committed to goodness. Why are you killing the Churches? Why? Why are they falsely portrayed? Why are they slandered? You have taken up another agenda. You have taken up the rights of women to kill their unborn. You have taken up the rights of those who want to change the nature of marriage. You have taken up the rights of so many and you have set aside the rights of God. When the churches raise their voices to challenge your agenda, when the churches speak about right and wrong, you say, "Let us kill the

123

churches. Let us silence their voices. Let us call them radical. Let us diminish the churches."

Need I say more? And your young stay away. They see the churches as you depict them. You are strangling the faith that breathes life into your institutions.

### Comment
*As America marginalizes the Churches, the important gifts of the Churches to America are destroyed.*

August 25, 2011
## 86. The Door of Repentance

## Mary

Why does the heavenly Father wait so long? Have not the sins been piling up? Could he not have acted long ago? Yet, he waits and waits with great patience, always giving time to repent. Repentance is needed now but people do not know what the word means. It has been stricken from their vocabulary and is now an unknown topic.

Formerly preachers would say "repent" and people would understand what to do. Now, they do not even know what is needed. So, I will give a simple and clear teaching. Repentance is the only way to avoid the wrath to come. The Father has delayed and delayed, hoping to see some signs of repentance. I will explain what everyone can do to repent.

Repentance means to acknowledge your sins, to realize where you have failed, and what obligations you have not fulfilled. You cannot see all of these at once. Some become visible only as you go higher. So, begin with the most obvious. This is how.

### What Would Change

Ask yourself the question. If I were to come before God right now, if I were to die today and face his judgment, what would I have wanted to change? Just answer that question. Do not ask other questions. Just that one. Keep asking it until it is as clear as the noonday sun. If I were to die right now, what would I repent of most? Keep asking this until the answer comes.

When it comes, then begin. Make a resolution. Hold yourself to it. Ask what helps you need. Whom can you talk to? Even tell another, someone who will affirm your repentance. Repentance is a gigantic door. I wait on the other side, holding in my hands all the gifts you need. Open the door of repentance. You have entered God's house.

*Comment*
*The Bible always says that God delays his punishments so we have time to repent.*

August 26, 2011
## 87. Destroying the False Lights

## Mary

People are attracted to light. They gather around this light and congratulate each other that they have found this light. They recount the profit of this light and speak about this light to others, rubbing their hands together as a sign of their good fortune. Yet, they do not see that they have been drawn together by a false light, a light that will go out and leave them in total darkness. They have been deceived. This need not happen. If only they had examined the light. So, I will speak now of all the false lights. I must put out these lights, so my people can be freed from their power. Once freed, they can follow a different light, a softer, more gentle light that will never go out. This light is my Son, Jesus. He does not promise you pleasures or power or human luxury, but he alone is the light of the world. Let us begin by destroying the false lights of the world, because these hold so many in their power.

First, there is the light of what others think. This is powerful. It draws many along, like a powerful stream. This light creates its own values and establishes its own goals. How difficult to be freed from this light! Difficult to reject the voices heard every day!

You, O soul, must hear a different voice. You must hear my voice. You must read my words every day. There will be a special moment when my word suddenly sets you free. When my word says, "Come in this direction. This is the way of life. Then, you will walk away from the false lights. You will take a different path. On that path, you will meet my Son, Jesus, and you will find the true light."

How difficult to explain before it happens. Say this prayer, "Mary, destroy the false lights that now capture my mind." Say it over and over and soon you will identify your false lights.

*Comment*
*The light of Christ is not seen because the world has now constructed*
*so many of its lights.*

August 27, 2011
## 88. Nuclear Proliferation

## Mary

Some will say that my words will have little effect. Others will say that they have little power. Still others will even question the method that I use. But all of these will be proved wrong. This word goes forth from my Immaculate Heart and this word will stand the test of time. People will come back to this word, especially as they see the events unfold.

Why would I speak unless there was some necessity? From where does this necessity arise? It comes from the total and complete danger in which the human race now finds itself. Yes, "finds itself," but it is totally unaware of these dangers. It misinterprets the events. Puts a spin on them, as if they will go away.

O mankind, you are hurtling toward the cliff of total annihilation, unconscious of the forces that soon will be released in your midst. What can be done? That is why I speak and teach and try to show the way. Let me begin.

### Read Your History

Open up your history books, just the recent history of the past century. You have had two major wars but these were limited, yes, "limited," because the great weapons of destruction were limited. Now, they have proliferated. It was dangerous when these weapons were only in the hands of America (a land that loved peace). The danger grew when these weapons were gained by Russia (a land so interested in expanding its interests and its borders). In October, 1962, the world held its breath as these two powers were in a confrontation.

What will happen now, fifty years later, when these atomic arms fall into the hands of those who would destroy you? Yes, that day is coming. No one can prevent it.

That is why I speak to you. What will you do in those days? Will you turn to the Father for help? Will he hear you when you have ignored my word? Begin now. Read my messages. Everything will be contained in them.

#### Comment

*The world has lived so many decades with nuclear proliferation, that many are lulled to sleep. Mary wants to wake us up and make us attentive to her helps.*

*August 28, 2011*
## 89. The Power of the Culture

## Mary

Why do all men walk along the same path? Does no one question the conventional wisdom? There is a mindset which I must break and set my children free. That is what my

126

words accomplish. My children must allow me to shatter the worldly chains that keep them bound. Like Peter set free by the angel, they will be able to walk out of their prison. Yes, they are in prison to the thinking of the world which is an enemy to the Gospel. Let me begin.

When you listen to others, do not immediately accept their values. Question them in light of the Gospels. Yes, make the Gospels your light and my Son's words a guide to your path because no other light exists.

## Culture of Light

Form little communities of the word. In this way, the darkness of the culture will be cast out and the little seed of God's word planted in your heart can grow.

You can see my plan. I must raise up cultures of light, where the darkness of the world is seen as darkness. But even more where the light can be sustained and people can live according to the light because they are encouraged by others

My greatest desire is to break that culture of the world which is an enemy to my Son's word and which draws so many into its darkness.

Its power grows every day by the propaganda put forth. Yes, the propaganda, the constant drum beating for what is evil and which violates God's commands. This is the problem. My children awaken each morning to the blare of a thousand trumpets proclaiming the freedom of man to create his own world, when really he is destroying his world. This is my dilemma, the great problem that I face.

*Comment*

*Every day, in a thousand ways, the message of the world reaches everyone's ears.*

August 29, 2011

# 90. The Pope's Death

# Mary

Although I do not reveal the exact time and dates (for this is not yet needed), I point to the signs of the times which all can read. When the exact moments come closer, I can be more specific because all can understand. Before the culminating events, other moments will happen which will lead up to it. It will not come as a surprise to anyone who listens to my words. This is why I speak, to prepare you so that when all the events occur you will be kept safe. Your house will be built upon rock and will not collapse.

I can see the forces of evil building up. Each of those under Satan's power are

127

storing up their own evil. They are each in their own houses, so the time is not yet at hand. No one has come on the scene to call them together, to bind them as one. I will delay his coming. I will put obstacles in his way. I will cause dissension among those whom he would want to gather.

In this way, the little ones will have more time to prepare.

## A Delay Not A Postponement

Yet, I do not want you to be disillusioned. Pushing back the time of these events is just a delay, not a postponement. The clash must come. This is the only way to dispel these forces of evil. They have claimed too many hearts and the message of repentance does not reach these hearts. They are intent on a holy war and on the destruction of Israel. They will not turn back. They believe that their cause is a holy one and that they will quickly dominate the world. This force has been building for centuries, consolidating its powers, suffering losses at some moments, but always moving forward, convinced that its cause is true and will inevitably conquer.

What can I do with such an evil force, which uses the sword to gain its goals? My Son told his followers to put away the sword and to lay down their lives for each other. This will be the turning point, when my son, the Pope, will lay down his life. Then, the Spirit of Jesus will be poured forth upon a world in shock, a world made ready to weep and repent. Before that, much must take place.

*Comment*

*Mary will win the victory in our time, the same way she won the victory 2000 years ago, by sacrificing her son, this time, the Pope. This will be a moment of a great and new outpouring of the Holy Spirit and a gigantic change of events in human history.*

August 31, 2011
# 91. The Effects of Consecrating Russia

# Mary

Do not be afraid to pierce the mysteries because these are mysteries of life, which will bring eternal life to those who follow my words. Now, there are towers of death, powerful and seemingly invincible. These will collapse like the Communist system. My son, Pope John Paul II, consecrated a year to me and look at what happened during that year. The wall came down and Communism was toppled, without a single shot being fired and without war being declared. All of this happened before the eyes of all, on the

128

2000th anniversary of my birth, deliberately highlighted by the Pope from behind the Iron Curtain. It was for him that I did this.

Now, I will raise up another person who will do a greater consecration, the one I have asked for at Fatima. All the world will know that this has been done, completed with all the bishops and with the world looking on.

## The Collapse of Evil

Slowly, the foundations of evil will erode. There is no need to blow up a building. If the foundation erodes, the whole building will collapse. When the building collapses, then evil will no longer go forth

What will happen when the Pope consecrates Russia to my Immaculate Heart? My armies will go forth. I will call all the little ones. They will know that my great request has been fulfilled. They will say, "We are at a new moment in history. It has taken us almost 100 years but at last, the request has been fulfilled." There will be a new hope and a new spirit. All those who worked so hard to bring this about, will experience unbelievable joy. They will have a new power. They will know that their Queen has finally been proclaimed and that I finally am placed on the lampstand. This will not just be a mental reality. I will send my presence all over the world. My army will experience that I am with them. Then, they will march.

### Comment
*So many are praying for the Pope to consecrate Russia to the Immaculate Heart. When this happens, Mary's army will evangelize in joy.*

September 1, 2011
# 92. People in the Political Field

# Mary

Who realizes what is taking place? Who can see deeply enough into the true causes of things? Men are just pawns in Satan's hands, doing what he wants and moved into place because he desires. These men say, "I have gained this high place. I have come into this position of power." Really, they have been moved there by the Evil One to fulfill his purposes.

They are given power over 10's, 100's and 1000's, and even more, because he knows when and why he will need them. It is like a game of chess in which he plots his strategy, waiting to pounce on his goal, the destruction of Israel and Jerusalem. I constantly repeat this theme but this is the goal and nothing can be understood away from this.

## Mary's Stirrings

There are also gentle stirrings, people feeling in their hearts a call. This is my strategy and quite different from the Evil One's. I do not put people in place for evil purposes, to destroy or to ruin. I put people in place to build up and to protect. This is the role of my Church but it is also the role of others in key places. I will put in very special positions, those who are closest to my heart.

I know who they are and I am right now stirring their hearts. I must re-establish the moral order. I must build again an America that accepts moral values. I must have people in place whose hearts I won. How will I block Satan's evil schemes? I must have my people in place so, when he tries to pounce upon the prize, he will be surprised by those I raise up to confront him.

This time is so precious, the time before the conflict begins.

The elections. I always speak of the elections but what other time is so important for putting people in places of power? Blessed are those who work in the political field for truth.

### Comment

*Mary is clear. Satan has people in high places but Mary also has her people.*

September 2, 2011

# 92a.  Seeking Heaven's Help

# Mary

How long a road this has been – this road into darkness that mankind has walked. Now, the darkness surrounds the earth on every side and it seems as if there is no escape. The Evil One, for centuries, has enticed man to come into his house, a house of evil and suffering.

He always knew what was needed to entice mankind, what would get world leaders to take his path and what would get the people to follow. There has been one step after another, but always along his road.

Now the pace quickens. He believes that mankind has passed the point of no return, that it is locked into his path. He has convinced man that there is only one way to solve its problems – to look at their own resources and their human solutions. He has cut off the access to heaven, knowing that if he battles an isolated mankind that he will win. He can easily trick men and use them for his own designs.

## Confidence in Technology

Are there no heavenly solutions? Indeed there are. Heavenly solutions abound but they lie useless because man does not seek heavenly solutions. "We can figure this out on our own," they say. "We have the technology. We have everything we need." O mankind, you do not realize who your adversary is and how he will use the very solutions that you put forth so as to entangle you. You will die by your own swords unless you seek the help of heaven.

Yes, right now, you must seek the help of heaven. Let the cry go up, "We must seek the help of heaven." Let it be placed in every heart, "We must seek the help of heaven." Let it become part of the nations' consciousness. Let it be ingrained in the nation's soul. Let large crowds gather. Let stadiums be filled. The ones you built for all your entertainments and for the gods that you worship on your sports fields.

Let the crowds gather to worship my Son and to seek the help of heaven. Then, you will find heaven's help in the midst of all your darkness.

### Comment
*Satan loves it when mankind does not seek God's help. He is the inevitable winner.*


September 3, 2011
# 93. Room in the Ark for Everyone


# Mary

I will open my heart wide and allow all the streams to pour forth from the heart of a mother. Yes, I am the mother, the mother of God and the mother of the Church. However, for so many, I cannot act as a mother because they do not know me and those who do know me do not come to me. So, on this first Saturday, I open up my whole heart. I share all my treasures, so I can truly be mother to all.

Some of my children are close to my heart. How I treasure them and protect them. I keep them safe from the Evil One and he cannot harm them. Now, I call out to all my other children. There are many empty spaces close to my heart. There is a place for you. I, personally, am inviting you to take the place I have for you. It is yours. I have reserved it for you. There, you will be freed from all your anxieties. You will find a place of refuge and, especially, you will no longer be alone. You will realize, "My mother is with me. I cannot fail."

## Accomplishing Great Works

I will go before you in all of your enterprises. I will keep your enemies far away and

131

unable to hurt you. I will teach you how to love and to build up your family relationships. I will send you on great missions, to accomplish great works for my Son, Jesus. I will make you stouthearted. Others will find in your heart what you find in mine. This is my plan. Many will see in you what you see in me and all will be drawn into my heart.

I always speak of my heart. It alone is the Ark of the New Covenant, established by the heavenly Father when he placed his Son in my womb. He knew what he was creating, not just a place for his Son but a place for all the world.

Let this word go forth. I am the Ark of the New Covenant and all are welcome. Within this Ark, all are safe (like Noah and his family). Outside of the Ark, all will perish. For in the days of Noah, they were eating and drinking, buying and selling. Does that not sound familiar! You know what happened next and you saw their foolishness. The floods will come but the world need not perish. My Ark has room for everyone. Come. Come. My motherly heart does not want you to perish.

### Comment
*We do not know what is ahead but Mary says there will be a flood*
*and we must be in the ark.*

September 4, 2011
## 94. When the Woman Spoke to George Washington

## Mary

So many do not see or understand. That is why I must speak so clearly. Like a wall that is built slowly, so has the wall of evil been put in place. When the wall is finished, Satan will believe that he has an inevitable victory, but it will not be so. There will be a way out of his wall for all who follow me. Now listen, so the divine light will show you the way.

### The Secular Man

These themes I repeat often but they must be learned well. There are unimaginable problems ahead. The world has seen only a few, the previews of what is to come. There will be a great shift of power away from those nations that used to call upon me. Yes, I must say it, "that used to call upon me." Long ago, they left the Church. They left the side of my Son. They adopted different values and put on a different garment. Now, they are Christian in name only. Their building still stands but they have no foundation. Their people are not united in faith. They have nothing holding them together. The secular spirit only responds in prosperity and abundance. It dissolves when faced with catastrophe. "Every man for himself." This is the cry of the secular man. "How can I

132

preserve what is mine?" are the thoughts of his heart. Where does that leave a nation in the time of crisis? To whom can they turn, when all are seeking their own interests?

America still breathes. It still has life. It still remains my hope. If only I can cure it of its sickness, it will regain its strength. Even more, it will regain its purpose, the noble purpose for which I brought it forth. Let me define the purpose of America.

## George Washington

O America, I appeared to your first president when he was still a general at Valley Forge. I told him of three moments in the history of the republic – the present moment in which he found himself, a future moment when brother would kill brother, and a moment yet to come. Go back and read those words. They are recorded by your historians. See what I said about the first two moments that have already happened. Then, you will believe my words about the third moment which is about to happen. More important, you will understand that this republic came about through my hands and that your nation has always been in my hands. Then, you will turn to me.

### Comment
*Mary is speaking of her appearance to George Washington at Valley Forge, which has been publicized widely.*

September 5, 2011
## 95. The Greatness of Medjugorje

## Mary

I will open up doors that have been closed from all eternity, special doors of saving graces that have never been seen before. At first, many will not believe. They will question, "Can these graces really be from heaven?" This has already begun at Medjugorje but many still question. How can I appear every day for years and still the world does not believe or listen to my messages? Even when people know ahead of time the very hours of my coming. Even when the visions are filmed for all to see. Even when the seers lead perfect lives of sacrifice and service, still the world does not believe.

Possibly the village is too remote. Oh, it is a village close to my heart, a perfect village dedicated to me and fervent in spirit. That is why I chose it. Even in its remoteness, millions have made their way there and have climbed the mountain of the cross and the mountain of apparitions. Miracles have flowed, especially the graces of conversion. Yes, the village is remote but the effort needed to get there and the determination to go prepare the soul. The remoteness of the village and its distance from large cities makes it the

133

perfect setting for the soul to enjoy the quiet needed to hear my voice. And how many have heard my saving voice in that village among the mountains, mountains which encircle the village in my love and kept it far from what would destroy its innocence.

## The Future Mighty Ocean

Now, let me continue. Medjugorje is my light, a light set on the mountain for all to see. From there will come forth a saving stream. Yes, let all eyes and ears be upon that little village because from it will come those words that are important for all the world to hear. Let the village become even more known and loved. The streams of grace which I have planted there are deep, and only the beginning waters of grace have, as yet, gone forth. Do not say, "We have tasted of the waters of Medjugorje and they have not provided all that we need." Go back to those waters, read my messages. Pray and repent. Above all, prepare. Soon, so very soon, Medjugorje will no longer be just a stream. It will be a mighty ocean covering the world with a knowledge of God and of events which come from his hands. Do not wait. If you prepare your hearts, you will receive much. If you do not prepare, you will have broken cisterns that hold no water.

### Comment

*Medjugorje has been a source of religious conversions since Mary began to appear to six children in 1981. She still appears daily. Millions have gone there and have been touched. Some have experienced the deepest conversions. Yet, all of that is as nothing compared to the graces that will flow from Medjugorje in the future.*

September 6, 2011
# 96. Simple Truth Overcomes the Complicated Lie

## Mary

Mankind does not understand how complicated they have made everything. Once a person tells a lie, they must tell another one to cover up, to make the story seem true. Lies are always complicated, needing many words to explain what is not true. Much also happens within the person when sin is committed. The person lies to himself. He rationalizes and marshals arguments to defend what he has done.

The way to simplicity, to straighten out the complications of modern life is truth – to tell the truth to one another and to live the truth in your personal life. Truth is the only way and I lead my children by the way of truth. If you wish to live in truth, then read on. If not, then you are wasting your time.

The Progress of Truth

Truth begins by believing in God, that he created you and sustains you, providing the earth with all its resources, even the very air which you breathe this moment. Truth continues as you thank God. Stop for a moment and give thanks to him for whatever comes to your mind.

Truth grows when you accept your responsibilities to God and to others. Where have you failed? Whom have you not served? These are questions of truth.

Truth continues as you realize that God has given you a task to fulfill, a portion of his garden to cultivate. Look into your heart. What stirrings do you find there? Have you responded to your call? Where is truth leading you?

Truth clears away all that is not true and when you break God's commandments you are living a lie and your garden is filled with weeds. These truths are simple but they must be placed firmly in your heart, otherwise you will have no foundation.

Do not compromise truth, especially your inner truth, the person whom God is calling you to be.

*Comment*

*Mary speaks about society which has become complicated by lies.*
*This brings about simplicity.*

September 7, 2011
# 97. Wisdom from On High

## Mary

All around there are pieces of evidence to show the existence and nature of God. The mighty oceans show his power and the sun shows his love. The plants and animals show that he brings forth life. But, especially in human beings can you see the evidence of God. Human life is saturated with a spirit that can easily be missed.   There is a spirit of love, of sacrifice and of service. There is a spirit of bonding, helping, forgiving and of repaying favors received and of giving favors without being asked. There is a spirit of helping the weak and going the extra mile with those in need. We call this the human spirit and man frequently takes credit for this human spirit. But just as human life comes forth from God, so, too, does this human spirit which bonds man to man and makes an unknown person your brother or sister, even for the short period of their need. This is a great mystery, a proof of God, which people overlook.

Often, there is a great spirit among brothers and sisters. Do not the parents deserve credit for installing the spirit of thoughtfulness?

The Teaching of Jesus

In spite of all this evidence, man could not come to know the fullness of God without the teaching of my Son. Man's intellect could not climb into the bosom of God, so my Son came down from heaven to teach the hidden truths in the clearest of images. Pick up the Gospel stories. In a few minutes you will learn more than your years of trying to gain wisdom.

### *Comment*

*A person with faith understands much more than a person with a gigantic intellect.*
*The Gospel stories can be read by all.*

# LOCUTIONS TO THE WORLD
## PART 3

### SEPTEMBER 8, 2011 – OCTOBER 26, 2011

# TABLE OF CONTENTS
## PART 3

September 8, 2011
# 98. Birthday of Mary, the Mother of God

## Mary

All creation rejoices today, the creation that came forth from the Father's hand but then was tainted by sin, its vast order interrupted and the darkness beginning to cover the earth.

Today, with my birth, the Father began his plan for a new creation, a complete reestablishing of divine order by the sending of his only begotten Son. This is my teaching today.

What has happened to the Father's plan? Did not everything come forth perfectly from his hand? Did not the first creature come forth perfectly? Did not I come forth perfectly? Did not his only Son come forth perfectly? What happened to these gifts? When they leave the Father's hands, they are perfect, but when they fall into the hands of men, they become marred. Mankind does not understand this truth. Everything placed in the hands of men becomes tainted, twisted, manipulated, misused, and sometimes totally destroyed, worthy only to be rejected.

### The Two Streams

What began with a noble purpose is used for an ignoble one. What was meant to bless all, blesses only those who selfishly control it. This is the stream of human history and the Father had to begin another stream, a new creation. Now the two streams flow side by side and mankind has a new opportunity. It can say to the heavenly stream "Flow within me. Let us flow together. Bring your power. Purify me. Make me go in the right direction. Straighten out my twists and turns. Send me to the fields that need my water and will be fruitful." This is what the Father intended when he began this heavenly stream, through his Son.

But, what took place? Mankind rejected the Son. The stream of man did not want the stream of God to cleanse and direct it. "I will flow in my own direction and gain my own goals." What has resulted? Look at the mess! Who can save mankind? I weep over what I see about to happen. I come so that it does not happen. This heavenly stream has great power and can act quickly. The catastrophes can be averted, but man must act quickly. Yes, man must act. The Father has already acted. His stream is already flowing. Man must act. He must accept the new stream. Will he do this when for so long he has rejected it? Can there be a new day envisioned by the Father when he created me to give birth to his Son? That is the

140

question which faces mankind. All the other questions will be answered when man opens himself to the new heavenly stream.

### Comment

*Through Mary have come the riches in Jesus Christ, but man must accept these riches.*

September 9, 2011
## 99. A Surprising Outpouring of Repentance

# Mary

Suddenly, before all these events happen, there will be a gift from heaven, given without man's earning it and even without his asking, decreed by the heavenly Father. The stream of heaven will overflow into the stream of mankind. Divine power, divine cleansing and divine light will suddenly invade the mind and heart of man. Yes, I say "invade," because man makes no efforts to save himself, no efforts to cry out to God. Yet, the heavenly Father sees what is ahead. He sees the events stirred up by the Evil One. He sees the destructive powers that his minions have acquired.

### Heaven with Earth

So, he will decree that the blessings of heaven be poured out, that the heavenly stream begin to mingle with the stream of mankind. He will not even wait for man to ask or to invite. He will do it. Heaven will mingle with her. People will receive heavenly gifts without asking. What is important is that man accept these gifts and see them for what they are – the Father's final helps, the last chance to survive what is to come.

How difficult to describe these gifts to a world that understands so little of heavenly life and powers. However, I will try to explain in simple words.

### A Miraculous Catch of Fish

First, there will be a spirit of repentance, widescale repentance coming from heavenly light arising within each person. People will see what they have done. How they have walked away from the faith of their childhood, how they have walked into the darkness and chosen earth over heaven. In this light, they will repent, saying, "I must return to the faith of my childhood. I must take up what I have cast aside." It will be like the miraculous catch of fish. The boat of the Church will be overflowing and the pastors will need to call for other boats to hold the crowds.

All will be amazed. No great preacher arose to stir the people. No great event happened to bring them to their knees. This is a gentle, hidden light placed in the hearts of those who still retain the basic elements of belief. This is where I will begin. When the Churches notice a spirit of repentance among their fallen away members and a return to active practice, they will know that greater graces are about to be unleashed.

*Comment*

*Many retain some aspects of faith. These are the ones who are somewhat prepared to receive the spirit of repentance.*

September 10, 2011

## 100. An Unswerving Will

# Mary

Why do I speak and why do I ask you to record my words? Because my words offer life and an opportunity for those who listen to them and act upon them to be saved.

O reader, do not just read these messages from curiosity, to discern the future events. If you read them with your heart, they will be like a seed planted within you that offers new life. Let us begin.

The Woman

I was conceived by the heavenly Father as the Woman Clothed with the Sun. This was his goal and why he poured out such precious graces into my soul from the very beginning. I was to belong to him as no other human person, totally his. Yes, from the very beginning, I was his.

There was a path which I was to walk, a clear path, always doing his will. Amid all the possible decisions in every single moment, I saw his will and I chose his will, like a compass which always points to the north.

Unswerving Will

My life was filled with sorrows, yet I never swerved. Whatever the heavenly Father wanted, I wanted. What he did not want, I did not want. My free will never swerved. Yet, it remained free because that alone gave glory to God. My will never swerved because he surrounded me with so many graces. These same graces are stored in my Immaculate Heart. They were placed there by the Father and since I always accepted every grace, absolutely none was lost.

I stored them up for you and I am ready to pour them out on whomever asks for them. They have only one purpose – to unite your will to the Father's will, just as my will

142

was so united. This is the greatest gift. It will last forever. In heaven, the will of every angel and every saint is perfectly in tune with the divine will. By pouring out these graces, I give you two gifts. On earth, you will fulfill your call, the reason God created you. In heaven, you will be perfectly united to God, to me, to all the angels and saints.

Let me teach you a simple prayer that will be so effective because it seeks these graces.

O Mary, in your Immaculate Heart, are stored up all the graces of divine union. If you place these in my heart, I will always do God's will. Amen.

### Comment
*Each person would like many blessings from Mary. Her greatest gift is*
*to have a free will like hers, always united with God's will.*

September 10, 2011
# 101. The Coming Election

## Jesus

I told you that America chose the darkness. In the Bible, when Israel went against the voices of the prophets, they chose their path of darkness. I let them walk their path until they repented and turned back to me. The same thing is happening in America. The economic scourge is like the Babylonian invasion of Jerusalem, the result of their sins.

### Pro-Life Democrats

The economic weakness results from their choosing the darkness of abortion. They elected a leader and a political party that sacrifices the unborn children for their political life. I must bring the Democratic Party to repentance. The few pro-life Democrats have no great effect upon the party. This year there will be a ground-swell against the Democratic Party. It will be motivated by the economy and will sweep the Democrats out of office. It will decrease their numbers so they might listen to the pro-life voices in their midst, that these would gain a greater voice. Then, there will be signs of new life.

The Republicans are trying to ride the horse of the economy to the victory line. My interest is not in the economy but in the life of my people. These are the candidates I will bring to the foreground, some of them surprisingly. Even though the electorate will see them as candidates who create jobs, I will see them as candidates who protect lives.

*Comment*
*God has an intense interest in who leads America*
*but God's goals are often different than the people's goals.*

September 11, 2011
## 102. The Spirit Comes upon the Virgin

## Mary

I gather your heart into my heart and there I reveal my secrets so all the world can understand. Nothing will be hidden from you so you can reveal all to the world.

When a person begins to be touched by these words, they will hunger for more. Then they, too, will be on the same path into my heart. I want the whole world to come into my heart. Only there will all be safe. Facing the world are years ahead of destruction and disruption of normal life. All the world will be affected. Some parts will directly experience the destruction. Other parts will experience disruption. Normal life, so to speak, will not exist. It will be a time unknown to the human race, of which the destruction of the twin towers is an image and an example of future trials.

### The Only Refuge

Long before this, people must have learned of my Immaculate Heart and the truth that I always put forward. I say it over and again. The only place of refuge will be my motherly Immaculate Heart. There is a place there for everyone, of any faith and of any denomination. The urgency is so great, that my heart will remain open until the last minute but no one should wait. If they do wait they might find themselves far away and unable to arrive on time. At some point my heart must close, like the doors of the Ark. Otherwise, the flood waters would enter and destroy those who are within. What do I mean by all these images? What does it mean to enter my heart? I will explain.

First, you must know me. I am the virgin mother of Jesus. I say virgin, so you know that the Holy Spirit came upon me. He prepared not just a place for Jesus but a place for all the holy ones. All are conceived in my womb. This was proven at Pentecost, when the Spirit came and began the Final Age. All the disciples were gathered with me in that upper room.

You enter my heart by faith. You say, "Mary can save me. Mary is the Ark of the Covenant" (Rev. 11:19). If you wish to know what is happening, if you wish to interpret these events, then read the Book of Revelations, Chapter 12. I am the Woman

144

Clothed with the Sun. Even in the greatest darkness, I will be Clothed with the Sun but you must know who I am and how urgent it is to enter my heart.

*Comment*

*On this 10th anniversary of the destruction of the Twin Towers,*
*Mary uses that event as an example of future trials.*


September 12, 2011
## 103. Preparing for a Journey


## Mary

All must begin now to prepare. "Prepare for what?" you will ask. This is the great question. "How can we prepare when we do not know what we will face?" Parents see what is ahead but they do not tell the children every detail. Would this not fill them with fear and would it not be useless? No, they tell the children little parts. They give them small hints, just enough to alert them. It is the parents who prepare. The children just trust that the parents will keep them safe.

So, there is no need for me to reveal all that is ahead. I must just reveal little parts and give little hints. I will prepare. You must trust and listen. Let us begin.


Take Little Baggage

When there is a journey, you take only what is needed. Otherwise, the baggage you carry will be too heavy for you and you will never complete the journey. So, you must grow detached. Many will mourn their losses saying, "I used to have this. I used to have that." They will spend valuable time in trying to salvage what is useless. Think of yourselves on a journey and prepare for a journey, taking all that is needed but only what is needed. I will give you the wisdom. Do not live as those settling in, providing yourselves with every possible luxury. See yourselves like those on a journey and you will survive.

Second, draw close to one another. Do not wander. Do not separate. To spread out and to go your own way is a luxury of settled existence. On a journey, all must stay close because nothing is settled. There are always new questions and last minute decisions that must be communicated to all. Many have chosen individual life styles, having the luxury of independent living. They go off. They isolate themselves and immerse themselves in things. On a journey, things are a burden. People are an asset. Having others to help you is what gets you to the end. Recapture the family relationships. Recapture the extended family. Come back home. Gather again. This will prepare you for the trials ahead.

*Comment*
*The image of a journey is easy to understand. Some will be prepared by close relationships to set out together. Others will be isolated. Everyone can begin to prepare by believing these easy to understand words.*
*The "family" can also be the Church family.*

September 13, 2011
## 104. A Summary of Her Teachings

## Mary

Do not just read these words. Inscribe them in your heart and live them in your life. They are words of light for the darkness that is coming. I will summarize my teaching so you can easily recall the light I have given.

1. The time is short. Many disasters will befall mankind. Some are already evident, the problems which are seen and felt by all. Other problems will be new and unexpected. Together, they will squeeze the heart of mankind, which will feel sorely oppressed, unable to respond and be filled with hopelessness.

2. By these words, I am preparing my children (and all can be my children. They need only to accept me as their mother). This is not a preparation of one day nor can it be done at the last minute. The time is short. Prepare now.

3. To prepare, you need to begin with the ancient truths, the basic truths that are already in your heart. These are the saving truths. There are no others.

4. Take these truths and make then the foundation of your life. Begin now. In this way, when the trials begin, they will be your foundation.

5. Gather with others. You cannot stand alone.

6. Observe the Lord's Day. This is the foundation of the foundation. By observing that day, you will find all the riches that you need. There are many hidden riches, buried in that precept. Only those who seriously try to keep the Lord's Day will discover those riches. How clear can I be?

7. In all decisions and in all events, think of my Immaculate Heart. If you do this, you will realize the truth I have been teaching. Go to my heart and find every solution for your problems. Go to my heart and find every consolation in your suffering. Go to my heart and find protection in every difficulty. This truth means nothing unless you act upon it. Once you act, you will experience the reality of my Immaculate Heart and the help which is always available.

*Comment*

*Mary sums up the main themes of her teachings.*

September 14, 2011
## 105. Look into Your Heart

## Mary

Why look around for answers when the answers lie within each person's heart? Yes, the heart must be true. If the heart is true, the person can see what is in their heart. This is where, O reader, you must begin.

Look into your heart. What do you see? Do you see the basic elements of faith? Do you see a belief that God exists? That you have responsibilities to God? What are these responsibilities? Can you list them, or at least some of them? Do you fulfill these responsibilities? Where do you fail?

Look again into your heart. What have you accomplished in life? What were your dreams and your talents? How have you fulfilled your dreams? How have you used your talents?

Look again into your own heart. Who are the important people in your life? What are your responsibilities toward them? Have you fulfilled them?

Look again into your own heart! What is sinful? What destroys you? What lowers you? What do you want, crave and seek, even if you must break God's law to get it? What is your hidden secret? What would you not want anyone to know about you?

Look again into your heart. Do you find any hope? Do you see any stirring of your heart that says, "I will arise from here and return to my Father's house"?

Look again into your heart! Do you find me there? Does my presence fill your heart? This is the easiest part. If you do not find me, then invite me. Use your own words. I will listen. As soon as you use my name, "Mary," I will come. If you ask me to stay, I will stay. If you invite me to go deeper into your heart, I will go deeper.

Recapture your own heart. Get it firmly into your grasp. Then you will be free to enjoy my words.

*Comment*

*Mary offers so much, but a person who cannot control the desires of their heart cannot profit from Mary's help.*

September 14, 2011
## 106. Dangers to Israel

## Jesus

There is a small group, tightly knit, which stays hidden. They gather money and resources and plot against Israel. Someday, they will inflict damage upon Israel as they did against the Israeli embassy in Egypt. As they draw closer, Israel will have no power to push them back because the buffers of protection have been taken away. It is a difficult and perilous time for Israel. Few know how close the destructive forces are to breaking through the Israeli defenses.

### Comment
*Each day the news reveals less protection for Israel.*

September 15, 2011
## 107. A Future Full of Hope

## Mary

Why do I come in this way? Why do I speak? Because my children are about to be covered in darkness. This is not a darkness of the individual but a dark state of the world. All will be covered in darkness.

What do I mean by the phrase, "covered in darkness"? It will not be a physical darkness, at least in this hour, but a social darkness, an inability of the structures of society to provide for its people. What people took for granted will no longer be there. Institutions will be washed away in the floods of bankruptcy and mismanagement. People will search for other alternatives but nothing will be ready. No one has prepared adequately. Life for many will be very different. Parents will worry about their children and how they will provide for the future. Anxieties will increase and, in some places, even panic and breakdowns of social life will occur. What do I have to say about this darkness? What advice can I give?

### Who Will Survive?
There will be a time of testing. Those who survive will not be the strongest or the richest. Riches will only allow them to avoid some of the difficulties. They do not insure survival. Survival will come only from faith that life still has a purpose, from hope that the heavenly Father will provide sufficiently as Jesus promised, and from love which binds people together, each one looking out for the other.

As institutions fall and as the other sources of help are ineffective, faith, hope and love will bind people together. There will arise a new, living set of relationships

148

composed of people who refuse to give up and are determined to help each other, just as Jesus taught his disciples.

This will be a time akin to the deportation of the workers in Jerusalem to Babylon (597 BC). They did not give up and they forged new lives, just as Jeremiah urged them to do.

To these faithful souls who will endure the darkness, I speak the words from Jeremiah which they must always remember, "I know well the plans I have in mind for you, says the Lord, plans for your welfare, not for woe! Plans to give you a future full of hope" (Jer. 29:11).

Yes, in the darkness, I have plans for a future full of hope and my children must believe that those plans exist.

### Comment
*What can be said in the face of worldwide unrest?*
*Mary gives as clear an answer as possible.*

September 16, 2011
## 108. Preparing for the Floods

## Mary

The evidence is everywhere. Look around. What is in order? What is stable? What will continue to exist? Everything is in question. What is not in question is the instability of the world and the frightful consequences that are so very near. These will burst upon mankind like a dam suddenly unable to hold back the flood waters.

So often I use this figure of a flood but the image is an apt one. Before a flood, life goes on as usual. No one is aware. Then the rains come. The waters rise. People are on edge. They do all they can to protect their city, hoping that this will be enough. However, the ultimate outcome is beyond their power. They cannot control nature. They cannot determine the amount of rain or how it will gather. When the floods come, everything in its wake is destroyed. Nothing is spared. Whatever is present is swept away. Only those who looked forward, who heeded the warnings, who removed their possessions, are spared from the devastating power of the flood.

### Storing Up the Virtues

This is what I teach my children. You cannot determine the place or the scope of the flood, so seek the high ground, that special relationship that I offer you. Let faith, hope and love lift you high. Only these will save you and, if you ask, I will pour them all into

149

your heart. These are not powers received at the last minute. They must be stored up now.

This is my invitation, rejected so often. In these troubled times, when all can see that unforeseen difficulties lie directly ahead, many will be open to this invitation.

"How should we prepare," they ask, "when we have no idea of what we will face?" Faith, hope and love prepare for every trial. They bind you to me. In the flood, I will be your mother. Regain your religious spirit and you will be prepared. When the floods come, your heart will be able to receive the helps I will pour out.

*Comment*
*Even though the future problems are unknown, the preparation is clear.*
*You must regain your religious spirit.*

September 17, 2011
# 109. Describing the Present Moment

## Mary

I give you little pieces that fit together into a clear picture of all that will take place. I also tell you underlying causes and what man needs to do. Although my word goes forth, few heed it. I make the teachings simple and the advice easy to fulfill, but so many ignore it and turn away. Let me try again in easier words and clearer statements.

1. The world is in a special moment, a precarious moment. All the economies of the world are closely tied together. A nation cannot withdraw. They cannot say, "We will save ourselves." All are interconnected. The fall of one will damage the others.

2. There are weapons of mass destruction that will fall into the hands of those who want only death and destruction. They seek to build no nation or to protect no vital interest. Their goal is satanic – to inflict death and suffering upon as many as possible.

3. Add to all of this, the political unrest, the feelings of the people that their leaders do not serve the national interests but their own. The toppling of dictators is not the only political unrest because leaders have no solutions to the problems.

### The Conclusion

Where does all of this lead? What should be mankind's conclusion? They should awaken to these worldwide problems. Their eyes should be open. Instead, they put their political solutions on the table, knowing full well that they are as useless as putting paper over a fire. Quickly, the fire will devour the solutions and even feed on them.

Who can debate me? Who cares to contest my statements? Who can say that all of this is not true? This is the state of mankind, but no one listens to me. My saving word goes unheard. It is put aside until it is too late.

Return to my Son. Return to the Prince of Peace. Return to him who alone can reconcile you to one another. He will pour out a different Spirit upon you. Yes, he will pour the Holy Spirit upon you. Yes, he will pour the Holy Spirit upon the whole world. He will again pour out that holy fire. Which fire do you want, the holy fire of love or the satanic fire of destruction? Take your pick. You have no other alternative. Secularism has no fire.

### Comment
*The locutions come to a new clarity and a new moment of decision.*
*Which fire does the world want?*

September 18, 2011
## 110. Three Unwanted Gifts

## Mary

I open up my heart to you for you to distribute the riches contained there. Distribute these riches to all who are worthy. If the unworthy want the riches, give it to them, also. The riches will make them worthy.

Unfortunately, the riches I want to give mankind, man does not want. Let me list theses riches which are scorned and rejected.

1. I would give purity of heart and freedom from lusts but man turns aside. He wants his lusts. He enjoys the fires of passions even though they control him and destroy him, even though they lead him into destructive relationships and ruin his family. Yet, I will give purity to whomever asks.

2. I would give truth, but man wants to retain his power to lie, to turn to his advantage what would not be so. He wants to tilt the table, to gain the upper hand even if he needs to lie to do so. Yet, I will give truth to whomever asks.

3. My greatest gift is the desire to sacrifice yourself for others, to lay down your life in service. How I like to distribute that gift and how I love those who want to receive it. These I bless more than any other because they are like my Son who gave his life for many. I give them every blessing because I know they will bless others.

I give them money because they will use the money for others. I give them strength so they can continually give of themselves. I give them wisdom so all they do is exactly what needs to be done.

And when they grow tired and discouraged, I draw them close to myself so I can send them out again. These are my messengers, my servants, the carriers of the life that I want for the whole world.

So, I ask, "Who wants these gifts?" Just ask and you will receive. Seek and you will find, knock and it will be open to you. These are my Son's words, but mankind so often turns away from the gifts of my heart.

### Comment
*God's plan is to give divine favors to all his children to make then holy,*
*but man's free will must want them.*

September 19 2011
# 111. Receiving the Fullness

## Mary

I rejoice to see those who have my gifts but I sorrow that I cannot give them even more. I will explain what causes this sorrow. I give great gifts, but people accept only a portion. I want to give even greater gifts, but only a portion of what I have already given is used. Does a mother put more food on a child's plate when he has not eaten what is already there? This is the problem which I will address. Let us begin.

### Divided Hearts

My children come to me with divided hearts. Oh yes, they are my children. They are even religious and priests. They are good and they desire eternal life. They want my gifts and would never want to be counted among those who reject me. They even join religious orders or participate with religious groups. How I would bless them! How I would use them as great instruments in the coming darkness! Yet, I cannot use them for the great tasks that lie ahead because of their divided hearts. They want me but they also want their personal life. They want the kingdom but they also want the world. They are satisfied with a portion of my gifts.

If only they accepted the whole gift, the full gift, I want to give them new and greater gifts, but they do not seek the fullness. When a person wants the fullness, their heart expands. Their capacity grows. They bulge at the seams, like Peter's boat in the miraculous catch of fish. Peter had to summon another boat. Peter never said, "Lord, you are sending too many fish." No, he accepted all the fish and made provision that all the fish would be taken. After that, Jesus gave him the great task. He would be the "fisher of men."

Notice that the task came only because he received the full gift. He opened his heart to all that Jesus wanted.

Oh, devout soul, come to me. Leave behind your other desires. Empty your hands of what you grasp. Empty your heart of what you desire. I will fill you with divine favors, fill you to overflowing. Your capacity to receive will multiply. Then I can use you for the great tasks. Otherwise, you will be limited to smaller and unimportant works. If you want to do great works, open your heart fully to my favors, turning away from everything else.

### Comment
*Mary's desires for all of us are unlimited.*
*We limit everything. Enter into her idea for you.*

September 20, 2011
## 112. The Road the King Will Use to Come Again

## Mary

I begin where I always begin – in my Immaculate Heart. This is the heavenly Father's secret, his plan for the salvation of the world. He has placed his Son in my heart. His Holy Spirit has come to abide in my heart. These are the secrets that I am trying to reveal so all might know of this treasury. Some misinterpret this doctrine. They think I am speaking of my own powers and my own prerogatives. Rather, I am speaking of God's powers and where to find them.

Am I not the Mother of God? Did not Jesus, true God and Lord of all, dwell in me? Did not the Holy Spirit overshadow me? These are the realities that I speak about when I proclaim the importance of my Immaculate Heart. "He who is mighty has done great things in me." I am revealing what God has done by his own free decision. Just as he decided to abide in the human nature of Jesus, so he has decided to make my Immaculate Heart a place of his abiding and a place where all can find him.

People search for Jesus. They look, but so many times they do not find. He is in my heart. He abides there. He dwells there. For this reason, the Father wants all the world to honor my Immaculate Heart. This is the easiest place to find his Son, Jesus.

He came the first time through me and he will come the second time through me. If a king is coming by a certain road, cannot the citizens go out to meet him? Surely, they can stay home. Yes, the king will certainly come. Yet, the wise citizens say, "We need not wait. We can go out to meet the king." They only need to know the road that he will use to come to their city.

153

Everyone knows the road that Jesus used to come the first time. This is without dispute. My revelation is so simple, "The road he used the first time, he will use the second time," and those who understand it can go out to meet him. They can find him before the others, who have no interest in meeting the king or do not know which road he will use. Now you see the importance of these revelations of my Immaculate Heart. The king is coming and you can be the first to greet him.

*Comment*

*This clear truth is taught by St. Louis de Monfort. Jesus will come the second time exactly as he came the first time. Why would he confuse his people?*

September 21, 2011

# 113. To the Disillusioned Person

# Mary

You have taken the wrong road. Oh, how many paths lead astray and so many walk them, delighted by what they see at the beginning, but disillusioned by what they discover along the way. If only you had listened, you would have been spared the suffering of walking a fruitless path for which you have nothing to show.

The paths of the world are filled with promises and the human heart feels itself drawn. The sights are set and they begin. Soon, their hearts feel entrapped because they were not made for this road.

Do not be afraid of this moment of your disillusionment. It is a grace to see that you have taken the wrong road. It is a time of opportunity.

My path is different. It is entered by faith. As the person walks, they experience a joy, a realization that I will not disappoint them. Can you not begin again?

Will I not reveal my path for you? You will surely find it. Let me teach you what to do.

## A Place

Find a place, possibly a church, where you can be quiet. Go there often, because it is not in one day or one moment that light is given. The light will come slowly. Be faithful to these visits. I will be there. Call upon me.

Gradually, I will turn your heart to what is of value. I will cut away the false hopes and empty promises. You will see what is of lasting value which you set aside as unimportant. You will pick it up again. You will say, "What I have spurned is really what I should have chosen." Take it up again. This is the path I have for you.

*Many make wrong decisions. Yet, Mary always holds out hope of finding the right path.*

September 22, 2011
# 114. Listening to the Prophets

## Mary

The stars, the sun and the moon are all on course. It is only mankind who has lost its way. How far off course is the human race and how serious are the results? I cannot stop everything because man will always remain free, the ultimate chooser of his destiny, but I can offer light, and those who walk by my light will be safe. Let us begin.

No one knows all that will happen in the future. Much is hidden. However, to some whom I have chosen, I have revealed enough that, if people listen and heed the messages, I can prepare them and bless them. Why do I choose this method?

This is the method chosen by the heavenly Father. He sends the prophets with their messages. Blessed is that community which has prophets in their midst. Blessed especially is that community which listens to the prophets.

### The Prophet's Task

The prophet does not say everything. The prophet points out a road of blessings, a road of light. As the people walk that road they find the blessings and the helps which God had in store for them. The prophet does not provide the blessings. He only points them out. Many are disappointed with the prophet's words. They want signs and wonders. The prophet is not God. He is only sent by God. He can only say what God wants him to say.

Many are disappointed. The prophet's words are true but they do not act on his words. Other people find light. They act on his words and find the blessings that God provides. They know the words are true because they have found God's help through the words.

Let me bring forth one prophetic word. If you act on this, you will find God's blessings. "Do not trouble yourselves with future events, like 'What is to happen this year? What will happen next year?'" Focus instead on the daily reception of the Eucharist. The daily Eucharist will give you the light that you need. You will see your whole word in a different way and you will be prepared for this year and for next year.

### Comment
*Mary tells us how to make good use of God's helps.*

155

September23, 2011
# 115. Light Entering Your Heart

## Mary

I lead you along this path so that others can know that there is a way of salvation. Mankind must be given a ray of hope. Otherwise, all would be darkness. A ray of hope does not cast out the darkness but is given even during the darkness. It is timely. Available at the urgent moment. This ray of light cannot wait. It must arrive when the need is greatest. That is why I give these words now. They are urgent and must be delivered as saving hope to all who will listen. Let us begin.

I draw near. I am close but man does not realize this. So, I must speak, "Here I am. I am at the door of your heart. I am not far away. Just open the door a little bit and I will come in and bring my light with me."

If there is light in your heart, even if you are surrounded by darkness, you will be safe. Now it is just the opposite. The light surrounds you but darkness is in your heart. I must reverse this. If the darkness comes and there is also darkness in your heart, then all will be dark. You will have no light to walk by. So, this is an urgent task.

### Knocking at the Door

How does light enter your heart? Is it hard to find? Must you search diligently? Not at all. I am at the door, knocking hard with all my might. I speak boldly to you. "Open the door and let me come in. I am your mother and I have come to save you. I know what is ahead and I know that you are not prepared. You have no spiritual thoughts. Your will is weak. You have even set aside some religious practices. You are entangled in the world. You are confused and anxiety has begun to enter. This is your inner state. Your outer state is shaky. You do not know what the future (which once was quite rosy) holds in store. You are frightened and you do not know where to turn for help. That is why I have come to you. Yes, through these words, I have come. I am at your door, knocking at your heart. Call upon my name, 'Mary.' Let my name be always on your lips. You will see its power and what I will do for you."

*Comment*
*This is simple. Let "Mary" be on your lips and you will witness her help.*
*She is at the door.*

September 24, 2011
## 116. A Help in Sorrows

## Mary

I do not try to pierce the great mysteries because many would not understand. Instead, I speak of simple truths which all can grasp. In this way, people can take these easy steps and move into the Divine Will without even knowing where I am leading. Let us begin.

I speak today of sorrow. How many sorrows burden human hearts. If only they could throw off these sorrows or gain some relief from them, then they would thank God. So, this is where I will begin. I am the Mother of Sorrows, so I am well acquainted with sorrowful burdens and how to carry them.

### Mary's Sorrows

I carried sorrows all of my life, beginning with the prophecy of Simeon that a sword would pierce my heart. Even after Jesus rose from the dead, I carried the sorrows of the Early Church as I saw his disciples martyred in his name. Violence was everywhere in my life even though I am the Queen of Peace.

I suffered disruptions. The trip to Bethlehem because of the census. The flight into Egypt because of King Herod's anger. So, I am filled with sorrows, and what words can I offer to you who are also afflicted? Listen carefully.

### Source of Your Sorrows

Some of your sorrows come from your own free will. You have chosen the wrong road. You have acted selfishly. You have turned your back on the good and have chosen the evil. Examine your present state. Go back to that fatal decision that set you on this path of sorrows. There is always the door of repentance, of going back to where you made your mistake and righting the wrong. Go back. I will help you.

Others sorrows are beyond your free will. They come from the circumstances of life – the death of a loved one, the loss of a job, the breakup of a relationship, the many things that go wrong. To you I say, look to me. I am the Star of the Sea. I see your little boat on the ocean of life. Call upon me. I will come to you in your sorrow. I will guide you through the waves until you come upon calmer waters. Do not despair. I am the mother of hope. That is why I speak to you.

### Comment
*Some sorrows are in our hands. Others are not. Mary offers words to both.*

September 25, 2011
# 117. Nuclear Proliferation

## Mary

You do not know where I lead you until the door opens and you enter. Behind each door is a gift which awaits you and which you receive in faith. Let us begin.

The reason I come to you is because of the perilous state of the world, which I constantly point out. I also come because mankind is not prepared. It has walked away from the Age of Faith. So, there are two problems – the perilous state of mankind and the lack of any faith in God's Providence. All of this is a dangerous mixture for despair. Even now, this despair has begun to grip people's hearts and brings about a paralysis.

The forces of destruction will continue to multiply as atomic weapons proliferate and fall into the hands of terrorists who are committed to the destruction of the West and the rise of the Muslim faith. This will present new and more dangerous situations. The resources of the West will be stretched thin, easily able to be penetrated. So, what can be done in the face of these mounting problems?

Crying Out to Heaven

If my people but ask me, heaven will respond, but their crying out to me cannot be sporadic. They must set aside their endless hours spent on entertainment and gather in intercession as never before. The time is urgent and the stakes are higher. The weapons are more powerful and more proliferated than ever before. So, the intercession that reaches my heart must be louder and more extensive.

During World War II, did not my people gather in the churches? Did they not fervently pray for the safe return of their loved ones? Did I not bring the war to a conclusion on my feast day? Did I not guide America?

So it will be. What happened in the past can happen again! I repeat. There is no need for mankind to go down the road of nuclear war, but the time is short and people must realize the urgency.

Do not wait! Do not wait! Gather now in intercession. Begin in the home. Move to the parish and then spread everywhere. Hands must be lifted in intercession.

### Comment
*Prayer can change everything but people must have the faith to pray.*

158

September 26, 2011
## 118. The Need for Just Systems

## Mary

The forces continue to grow like yeast placed in the dough. They are hidden but show their power in their effects. The evil is like a fungus that spreads everywhere. Who can stop its growth? Men use their human means. They believe that if they kill a few of the enemy, that they will limit the problems.

Yet, the death of one leads to others taking his place. The victory is not won by force. How many times mankind has gone down this road, a road of the multiplication of weapons and their distribution to others (seemingly friends) who later become enemies. Is this the only road? Is there not some other solution which man should try? Let us begin.

I will teach man a new road, the path to true peace. This path has not been hidden but man has shown no interest. Man claims, "I will bring about peace." Then, what does he do? He takes up weapons of war, not realizing that he is contributing, not to peace but to violence.

Man says, "What else are we to do? We must respond. We must confront the adversary." Yes, at times, the innocent must be protected and kept safe. However, you have neglected the more important aspects of peace. Peace is the fruit of justice, and justice has for such a long time been ignored.

Go back. Build just systems. Begin now. Do not say, "It is too late. We should have done this years ago." Certainly that is true but if you begin, if you change your priorities, if you begin to shift, I will be with you.

You will claim the hearts only of those people whom you have treated fairly. Do not think that the secret pacts are secret to me. I see the just man. I see the uprightness of his heart and his attempts to be fair to all. I bless the just man. I bless his labors. This is what is needed. The just person sitting at the bargaining tables. The just person setting the nation's priorities. The just person trying to bring peace. This is my promise. I will bless just men and women. Go forth now in justice.

### Comment
*God sees the secret negotiations. He sees every decision of man.*
*All must be done in justice.*

September 26, 2011
## 119. Jerusalem – The Center of World Peace

159

## Jesus

At the center of my heart is Jerusalem. This was always true but even more so now, because my blood sanctifies its soil. Anywhere that a martyr has been slain, the blood sanctifies that soil. The heavenly Father notes all of those places. Rome is holy because of the blood of Peter and Paul and so many other Christians.

In some places the blood of martyrs still flows. There are pilgrimages and devotions on that ground and even miracles. In other places, no devotion occurs and the blood, so to speak, does not flow.

### The Blood Shed at Jerusalem

My blood was not just shed at Jerusalem but it was meant to flow continuously. Yet, look at the history, all that has happened there. Indeed, some pilgrimages take place, but in so many ways my blood does not flow from Jerusalem as it should. Today, Jerusalem is seen as a political place, controlled by Israel. That is not its importance. My blood anoints its soil and I want my blood to flow out to all the world – to Jews, and Christians and Arabs. They must gather in Jerusalem and there will be peace in the flowing of my blood. Jerusalem is at the center of my heart because there I will gather the nations for world peace.

*Comment*
*Few see Jerusalem as Jesus sees it.*

September 27, 2011
## 120. Closing the Doors of Death

## Mary

The ways of God and the ways of men are quite different. God's way is a way of life, where true life flourishes and the instruments of death are set aside. Man's way is a way of selfishness, of seeking what can please himself. Man does not intend death, but if something gets in his way, he does not exclude it. For him, the death of another is an alternative. He never shuts the door. He never says, "I cannot take that road." So, in the back of his mind, there always lies the alternative of death.

This brings uncertainty. Those who are weak and dependent are never sure what those who are powerful will do. They are helpless. They know that death is always an option.

There can only be a culture of life when man obeys God who has said so clearly, "Thou shalt not kill." The direct killing of another is a door that must be kept forever

160

closed. It was first opened by Cain and, since then, it has introduced untold miseries to the human race.

## Renouncing Violence

Who will be the first to close that door forever? Who will be the first to renounce violence and choose the way to peace? These will be the peacemakers of the New Age. This was the path which my Son chose when he told Peter to put away his sword (Mt. 26:52). This has been the path of everyone who truly followed my Son. They always closed the door of death, even if it meant their own death.

The world will cry out, "We cannot do this. There is violence everywhere." Begin where there is no violence. Is the child within the womb violent? Does he attack anyone? Why is the door of death so open to him? Close that door first and a new gentleness will settle upon America. Your eyes will be opened to other doors of death that can be closed. Most important, you will not be opening new doors of death that have, until this moment, never been opened before. You cannot open one door to death and think that you can keep the others closed.

### Comment
*Mary is so right. Opening the door of death of the unborn leads*
*to uncertainty and ultimately to opening all the doors of death.*

September 28, 2011
# 121. Living in Truth

# Mary

The way of truth lies open for everyone. All can walk it, but man covers it over. He pretends that he does not see what should be evident. He wants to walk his own path, the directions that he chooses. He does not realize that truth is God's invitation. Even if a person does not believe in God, they still understand truth and if a person would just walk the way of truth (which they understand) they will arrive at a personal God and Savior (whom right now they do not understand).

No one can say that they cannot find God. Let them live in truth and they will quickly come to him. That is where he awaits them. Even if they have never heard the Gospel of my Son, they will come to know him in the truth of their lives. He will be there, although still hidden because they do not yet believe his story. If they continue in truth, they will begin to ask questions. These questions always lie deep in the human heart, not surfacing because too many other concerns are piled on top.

## The Deeper Questions

But a person who seeks the truth begins to go deeper. He asks, "What is true? What is firm? Upon what foundation can I build my life? Does not everything shift? What I thought was important in my earlier years has disappeared from the scene. What I thought was important even last year is no longer my goal." He grasps that all human life changes and he seeks what is lasting and true. The surface things can no longer hold his affections. He is restless within, but it is a good restlessness of searching for the truth.

O reader, if this describes you, then pick up the Gospel stories. Read about my Son. He is the truth. In your searching, you have really been looking for him. Now you know where to look. You are thirsty and he is the living water. When you will drink of this water, you will not be disappointed.

### Comment
*Where does secular man begin his search for God?*
*God has placed a desire for truth inside every heart. Begin there.*


September 29, 2011
# 122. How to Gain the End of the Road


# Mary

I want my children to persevere until the end. Then, I can greet them and welcome them into their heavenly home. What good is it to begin a journey, to make all the preparations and all the effort (even for years) and not arrive where joy and celebrating take place? This is why I speak, why I give these daily words. My children need daily words so they persevere until the end. Yes, I will speak every day and they must look for my words. Let us begin.

The burdens are too great. That is the problem. The commitments and the entanglements are too complicated. To persevere to the end, modern man must simplify his life and cut the many strings that bind him.

## Too Entangled

Let each of my children look at their life and ask this one question, "How did I get entangled in all of these obligations?" Let them go from there. Let them cut away what is so evidently useless. Regain your life.

Mankind has heard too many voices. Gone down too many roads. Reached for too many pleasures. Yes, life is filled with so many pleasures, so many things to distract

162

and entertain. Each of these entails time and money and more complications.

Man must say, "Enough! I must stop. I must slow down. I must gain control of my life. I have a long way to go. I cannot keep up this pace." How happy he will be when those decisions are made and he has chosen a different course. Then he can feed his inner life, his spirit that is thirsting within. He can deepen his relationships with those who accompany him on his journey.

This is the secret to persevere to the end – carry little baggage and walk with others in deep love.

### Comment
*Modern life presents multiple opportunities to persevere.*
*Man must reject many, retain his inner freedom and deepen relationships.*

September 30, 2011
## 123. Mary Is Always Seeking You

## Mary

These words come like a little stream of life. They do not overwhelm but invite people to drink of their waters. They are a gentle invitation so even the most fearful will not be afraid to come and drink. Yes, I want all, saint and sinner, to come. Let us begin.

### Always Inviting

In the beginning, I invite. To those who do not come to me, I continue to invite. What other words can I say? First, they must choose to be with me. This choice is very important. I cannot force myself upon them. Yet, I will never, never leave them. I will not go away. I will not withdraw. Even to the last moment, at the hour of their death, I will still be there, inviting them to come to me, asking and pleading that they would accept what I have to give – eternal life.

If they had heard my voice earlier, I could have given them greater blessings. They would have had time to receive. The seeds of life would have grown within them. But that is not important. There is still time for the important seed of eternal life.

This is what I want to say to everyone in the whole world. I am the Mother of God and I am your mother. My name is Mary and I conceived by the power of God's Spirit. I have been chosen by God so he could enter this world by becoming flesh and dwelling among us. I was the woman chosen as God's path to man. I am also the woman chosen as man's path to God. That is why I will always be with you. I will always stay close.

Always Seeking

Wherever you go, even if you take the paths of sin, I will follow you. Even if years pass by and you never call on God, I will still be close to you. No matter what you do, what sins you commit, what refusals you make, I will be there. You can never go anywhere that I will not seek you out. This is called the Secret of Mary and it must be revealed.

I need only one thing from you. I need you to say the words, "Mary, help me." Say them now. Say them from your heart. I am waiting to hear them. After that, all will change.

### Comment
*This is a great secret. Many think of themselves as abandoned by God (which is not true) but they are never abandoned by Mary.*

October 1, 2011
## 124. Four Clear Points

## Mary

What do I ask of you who read these words? I ask that you move forward, that you see these words as a true light by which you can walk. When I light a path, I invite you to walk upon it. Otherwise the light is of no avail.

You cannot stay where you are. You must move ahead into safer ground, to a higher level, so when the problems come, you will have already been lifted above them. This is a clear image for acting now. Some will hear these words, but will delay. Then they will forget them altogether. What good then are these words? They have fallen on deaf ears. So, let us begin.

All with eyes are able to see but they do not grasp the cause of the problems, the extent of the problems, the closeness of the problems, nor the way to escape the problems.

Let me speak of all of those. First, the cause of man's problems is his withdrawal from the heavenly Father and the giving of himself to totally secular goals. Because of this, the safety factors that any father would place for his children have been removed. Like a child who wanders into dangerous territory, the human race has walked into a perilous state.

Second, the extent of the problems is enormous. What part of creation is still safe? Only those parts which have remained under the heavenly Father's protection. In these groups and in these places, the safety factors are still in place. These children have not wandered into perilous fields. What are these safety factors? How does a father protect his children? The safety factors are the Ten Commandments. A father protects his children by his words and he sees that they obey his words.

Third, a child can wander and disobey the father. Sometimes, they escape unharmed and nothing happens. However, if this goes on too long and if they wander farther and farther, the chances of total ruin grow greater. This is the current state of the world.

Fourth, how to escape? The answer is obvious. Stop wandering from the heavenly Father. That is the only choice to escape total destruction.

*Comment*
*The four points are extremely clear.*

October 2, 2011

# 125. Immoral People in High Places

## Mary

The task I give you is to record what is deepest in my heart so my secrets are known. Why must they be known? So, light is given and at least those who hear these words can be saved. Yes, my words are saving words, words of life and hope, which invite all. Let us begin.

A new army will come forth for which the West is not prepared. They do not realize that Satan has not revealed all of his strengths. The West thinks they are prepared. They have put in place their homeland security and have shared all their spying intelligence, as if they could know what is hidden in Satan's mind and heart (for that is what they are facing). They are not facing a human intellect but an angelic intellect that is far greater than theirs.

He probes, not just from the outside but from the inside. He knows people in high places whom he can corrupt. He has them in his back pocket. They lead sinful lives and are open to blackmail and extortion.

### People Entrapped by Vice

In this age, when my Son's teachings are set aside, many have corrupt hearts, unable to overcome their passions. They are given to vices that they must keep secret. Satan has a hidden army. They do not even know that they belong to him. However, when he needs them to fail in their duties, they will not be free to resist. They are compromised men and women, yet they hold sensitive positions and are entrusted with important secrets. This is what I call "Satan's Hidden Army."

165

So, I say to the West, your safeguards against terrorism are not as strong as you think because of the immoral lives of some of your people. Do not overlook goodness of life in selecting those whom you trust. Return to the practice of knowing a person's moral life before you raise him to a high position. Begin to cleanse your ranks. Purify your members. Weed out those who could be compromised. Otherwise your system of self defense will not defend you at all.

### Comment
*Mary points out what only she can know, namely, who lead sinful lives and will betray the West because of these secrets.*

October 3, 2011
# 126. The Waves Beating Upon the Shores

# Mary
All proceeds on course, hidden from the eyes of men but seen clearly by your heavenly Mother to whom the secrets of the Most High God have been revealed. All is clear in my sight. Let us begin.

There are waves of evil, like the ocean hitting upon the shore. Each wave has its time and leaves its effects. People forget the evil that has come and gone, but the effects are lodged in their souls and in their memories. They forget the ways of the past, the ways of faith. These have been washed away and replaced. Everything is weakened and weakened and weakened, made ready for a complete and sudden collapse.

The waves will continue to come and pour upon the shore, eroding what seemingly was so strong and irreplaceable. So many things have been replaced – the family life, the dignity of the unborn, the role of motherhood, the sanctity of marriage. These were the foundations of true life.

## Restoring American Life
Who will rise up to restore these to American life? Who will see the clear need to reestablish these foundations? Is there anyone who can say to the sea, "Stop beating against the shore and stop eroding our foundations"? This is a Herculean task that is beyond the power of man, even of those in high offices, but it is a gift I will give to the nation if it just calls on me.

I will again clad America in the modesty that used to protect its young people, and in the innocence that used to prevail in its entertainments. Oh, how far these have eroded; how far out of sight are the standards that used to guide the filmmakers. This was the Age of Innocence for America, when censorship was not a dirty word and individual expression was limited for the good of the community.

Now, all has broken loose. All is freedom of speech and constitutional rights. Look at what spews forth and even the youngest children are touched by the filth. Now you understand, America, why I weep when I see what you have dome to the children I have given to you.

Comment

*Mary sees our history. There have been so many waves that have removed barriers of decency, that children are inevitably touched by evil.*

October 4, 2011

# 127. God Does Something New

## Mary

Let the whole world come to me. There is room in my heart and food for all. Everything that is needed for all of humanity is held in my Immaculate Heart. All are invited. All can be cared for. So the word must go forth. Come to the banquet. Let us begin.

The world is filled with frenzied activity. Man is ever active, seeking first this and then that. He arrives at his goal but quickly sets out again, discovering that he does not have enough of this or of that. He is restless, more than any other creature. How restless is the human heart, unable to be content in created goods, made for the infinite, living on earth but seeking the heavenly home. This is why man is restless. Earth can never satisfy him. No earthly kingdom is enough. His heart is greater and bigger. Earth can never fill it. All that earth can give, with all of its kingdoms, are like the tiniest drop of water placed upon the thirstiest of tongues.

When will mankind understand that its heart was made for God? Now I reveal my secret. God has created another heart, my heart. There he has dwelled. He has blessed my heart and made it a place of refuge, a station of life along the way. I am not God but I am the mother of God and he has stored all of his treasures within me. He has also given me a task. He has said, "My children are lost. Go and find them. I have placed in your heart all that they will need for the journey. In this way, they do not need to walk because you will carry them. They will not grow hungry, because you will feed them. They will not get lost, because you know the way."

This is the secret. I am God's way-station, a refuge which he has created for all the world to be saved. Whoever finds me, finds life. Whoever comes to me is safe. Let the word go forth. God has done something new. He has made a creature his own mother and he has given to the world a new Eve. These are my prerogatives and all must know so they can be saved.

*Comment*
*God never had a mother until Jesus was born.*
*He wants all the world to be blessed in her, his new work.*

October 5, 2011
## 128. A Purified Humanity

## Mary

I do not speak these words in vain because as the person reads them, I am working within their heart and bringing them to fruition. This is my goal, lives that are changed by repentance. I want a purified humanity which is able to hear God's voice and see clearly what he expects. Then, there will be new life upon planet earth.

Mankind seeks life, expanding all it energies to gain the highest level of life. But the greatest and highest life is a life of purified love, when selfishness is purged and the person sees others who need their help. A purified humanity – that is my goal. That is also the goal of the heavenly Father and of my Son, Jesus. We are of one mind and one heart. We want a purified humanity which has life at the highest level.

But how will we bring this about? This depends on the choice of mankind. Yet, what options does mankind leave us? I offer to mankind the most gentle way of purification – by obeying my word. If he listens and follows me, I will take him by the easiest of paths, where he experiences ever new joys of personal freedoms, freedoms which he has never known, freedom from unruly passions, freedom from overwhelming guilt, freedom from haunting memories. He will have the "glorious freedom of the children of God" (Rom. 8:21). All this comes from just listening to my word.

The other option to purify humanity I do not even want to describe. It is a harsh and dark road, a road of pain and humiliation, when the secrets are openly revealed. The Father has already done this to some whom he had to bring down. Read the Bible. Read the history of Israel. Read the book of Revelations. These tell the stories of those moments, past and future, in which the Father purifies mankind by chastisements. This is always his final choice, when mankind leaves him no other option. I do not want that to happen. It is too terrible to describe. So, I offer you, O reader, these words and this path of light.

*Comment*
*Who would not choose the path to freedom over the path of chastisements?*

October 6, 2011
## 129. The Election Process

# Mary

Why do I speak this way? Because my heart is filled with sorrow as I see people scattered in so many directions. No one can unify them and draw them together in their common concerns. They are scattered sheep without a shepherd. Many try to be their shepherd and to claim the crown of leadership but no one succeeds. All have their little following, those to whom they appeal, but none can gather all together for a united front. This is the situation in the Republican Party.

Meanwhile, the Democratic president continues his policies that have been so ineffective. However, he is locked into them, unable at this point, to adapt to the changing situation.

As a result, events carry the country along and events will continue to decide the path, not leadership. No one arises to say, "This is the way we should go," even though that path should be clear. Instead, there are political compromises or political stalemates. America suddenly looks old, burdened with a tax system which is anachronistic and counterproductive.

Such is the state of America as it turns the corner and begins to face the early primaries straight ahead. These come closer and closer. States are always changing their dates, trying to be more in the limelight. This only confuses the process even more, forcing the candidates to run a race different than what they foresaw.

From all of this mix, will the right person emerge? One who can lead this country in a sound direction? How many things can go wrong! How much can be bought with money! How many elections can be stolen! Suddenly, the wrong leader, the one whom so many people do not want to see, is able to put together a winning coalition, piecing together what is needed to be elected. This is why I weep – at the frightening sight of such a man once more gaining the presidency. However, if America does not seek me, if it continues to turn its back, then nothing can be done. Pray, America. Fall to your knees. Your own efforts are worthless against this darkness which you have chosen.

*Comment*
*Mary is consistent. She said America chose the darkness. Now, it might choose it again.*

October 7, 2011
## 130. Our Lady of the Rosary

# Mary

Today, so many will call on me and remember me in both my joys, my sorrows and my glory. Yet, so many do not know of the power of this devotion to the rosary which can save the world.

When I came to the children at Fatima, I carried the rosary. I taught them to say it fervently and I told Francisco, in particular, that he had to say it properly. He responded with great fervor and said the rosary daily with great devotion.

My servant, St. Louis de Montfort, wrote "The Secret of the Rosary," which all should read. It is a small book but will inculcate devotion. He writes that he does not know why, but the rosary is the most powerful of prayers.

Let me take you back in history to the famous Battle of Lepanto (1571) when Europe could have been overwhelmed by the Muslims. So many in secular Europe forget their history. They do not realize how only those with faith saved the Western civilization from being totally wiped out by the Muslim attacks. Only the papacy continued to rally the forces of good. Many others, caught up as usual in their selfish interests, would not cooperate and would not turn their eyes to the threat. Only the Pope and those whom he could stir were interested in this vital battle.

Although outmanned and really no match for the Muslim fleet, the papal forces won the victory and the West was saved. This naval battle was reinforced by the many who recited the rosary, and so this feast was established, (by Pope Pius V), as an annual reminder of the power of the rosary.

O reader, learn the true history that has been taken from you. The Muslim threat is again at your door. This time, new methods are used, very effective and powerful. You, on the other hand, are asleep. You do not realize how soon will be the day when America will be attacked, an America that is so unprepared to respond, an America that is willing to compromise the truth. The Muslims have no desire to compromise. They seek only conquest. Do you want your children and your grandchildren to live under Muslim rule? Then wake up. Take the rosary in your hands and begin to pray it, today and every day.

### Comment
*Many extraordinary circumstances surrounded the Battle of Lepanto.*
*Read the story and say the rosary.*

October 8, 2011
## 131. Seeking the Right Help

## Mary

I pull back the veil for all to see the great conflicts of man, because much is hidden from the human eye. Even though they see, they do not understand. So, I reveal the deeper truths, especially the future that man sees only so dimly.

In man's heart, there resides a great fear, because he sees that what was once secure is now in jeopardy and what he placed his confidence in is quickly melting away. Mankind has lost its way and it has lost faith in God. I come to restore both, if only man would listen. Let us begin.

Sorrow looks to the past and weeps over what has been lost. Hope looks to the future and what can be claimed. So, mankind has a choice. It can sorrow over what has been lost or it can hope. I do not speak of a false hope by which man says, "We still can reclaim the past," but of a true hope based upon faith in God. Yes, even at this hour, God will help man. It will not be the help that man seeks (a restoration of his riches) but it will be the help which God, in his love, truly intends. If man would seek this help, God would gladly give it and more besides.

1. Seek a purified heart, set free from selfish desires.
2. Seek a purified mind that sees clearly what is of value.
3. Seek restored relationships that offer comfort and solace.
4. Seek to help those in need, for they will be your blessing and gain what you need from the Almighty.

When you seek these, you will awaken from your slumber of avarice. You will be a changed person. That is God's greatest gift. You want a changed world, but God wants a changed you. What blessings can be given to an unpurified heart and mind, to someone who lives only for self and helps no one? Whatever God would give would be spoiled and ruined. Purify your life so you can receive the blessings. I will help you. Let us begin now.

### Comment
*Mary's advice is sound. Do not worry about a world you cannot change.*
*Change yourself and God can bless you.*

October 9, 2011
## 132. The Most Unique Moment in History

## Mary

Time does not stop. The clock always ticks away. History moves on. There are various people and different scenes on the stage of life. Every day, a drama takes place and another scene is completed. The next day, the world wakes to resume the story. All of this will continue until the end of time, when history is completed and my Son will come in glory to gather the elect from the four corners of the world.

Anyone can see that nothing stands still. All is in movement. And what are the forces that shape the narrative? Is the script written ahead of time? Are men and women just actors who speak lines and perform deeds that have been plotted out ahead of time? Not at all. Each has their assigned role but each person is free to accept their great call to be a part of God's story or to rebel against him and create their own story – a story of death and tragedy.

That is what is happening on the human scene. People have set aside the original script, the original story that was meant to unfold into a story of life and of happiness. Instead, a story of death comes forth and now two stories are intermingled. The story of God is life. The story of man, written apart from God, is the story of death.

How evident all of this is. Human history is a mixture of life and death. Life given by God. Death introduced by man.

Which way will the story go? Here we come to the modern era. Oh, the question has been present, in every age. But, now the story comes to a climax. Yes, I say, a climax and all are witnessing the beginning parts of the climax. This is no longer the same question as in past centuries. Certainly, there were wars and collapses of empires. There were plagues and famines, but these only involved sections of the world. Now all the world is intertwined. The economies are global. The weapons are atomic (or worse). The ability to truly conquer the whole world does lie in the hands of man. See this clearly. Everything is on the table. Everything. All of history. All of human life, the whole world as you know it. That is why I speak and why my words are so vital. Can I make myself any clearer?

### Comment
*Mary's words are evident to all. Mankind has never been at this moment before.*


October 10, 2011
## 133. Building Systems without God's Wisdom


## Mary

Why do the nations march according to the wrong tune? This is due to earthly wisdom which is no wisdom at all. They do not have the Spirit of my Son. They do not begin their meetings with prayer and they do not seek divine wisdom. As a result, their conferences yield little because each nation is ready to yield little. They go into their meetings with one purpose – to preserve (or even to enhance) their own interests. Little is accomplished while time moves on.

I say this. Events will not wait for your time schedule. The powerful events will just move on and catch you unprepared. Everyone has their hands in their pockets or their arms folded, caught up in their national interests. "Is there any other way?" you say. "Is not this the way of international cooperation, that each nation sees to its own good?"

This is what I say to you, O rulers of the world. Because you do not call on my Son, you are severely limited. You have only earthly wisdom. You measure by earthly standards. You say, "This is what our people expect. They elected me to preserve the national interests." I say this, "Your people are like yourselves. They, too, are caught up in human wisdom and all will go down together, people and leaders." The events are coming. They are built into the systems that you have constructed. They are your systems, not mine. For years, you have been putting them in place. You have made decisions without consulting my Son, without asking, "What would the Lord God of hosts want us to do?" You have banished divine wisdom and now you have your systems that will soon collapse.

Is it too late? Oh, the changes that must be made! Everyone, leaders and people must turn their hearts to God. Only when your hearts have turned back, will you see the true light. All must turn. All must say, "Let us seek divine wisdom." I will help you, but it is very, very late. Some parts will still collapse. However, some can be salvaged.

### Comment
*The world systems have been built for decades (and centuries) upon human selfishness, so their corruption is deeply ingrained.*

October 11, 2011
# 134. A New Spiritual Greenhouse

## Mary

Time is running out and no one can control the timing of all the events. All that mankind can do is to prepare because the seeds are sown and will come to fruition in their time.

Can new seeds be sown that will come to fruition quickly? Let there be hope that there can be new seeds and new fields of harvests, new generations and new beginnings. These are always possible and all can share. Never do I say that it is too late.

Where are the new fields? In the hearts of my young who have not consecrated themselves to evil and in the hearts of others who are willing to receive the new seeds. Do not say, "It is too late because time is needed from planting until harvesting." Do not say that. I can plant one day and have a harvest the next day. I can take a fallow field and bring forth a new harvest. All that is needed is to sow the seeds in faith. No seeds will mean no harvest. No harvest means that only the seeds of destruction will flourish. What are these new seeds? These miraculous seeds that can spring up in one day and be harvested the next day? Where will they be found? Where should they be planted?

Let me reveal this new mystery. It is an important mystery of hope. The pace of world events is always quickening and the children of this world are more quickly indoctrinated. There is no longer the leisure of childhood innocence. The sins of the adult world are known to the youngest children. They are broadcast daily. Children become sophisticated, hardened and satiated so quickly. They have no time to mature. So, I must do a new work.

I will give a greenhouse where the spiritual seeds are planted one day and bloom the next, where maturity, true maturity, springs up overnight. Where saints are made quickly and easily. Where sinners repent and are filled with the Holy Spirit. This greenhouse is my Immaculate Heart and for those who choose to live in my heart, I will shorten dramatically the time needed to prepare. I do this because time is running out. I will explain much in future locutions.

*Comment*
*We are so far behind. It seems impossible, but in Mary's heart*
*saints can be made quickly.*


October 12, 2011
# 135. Disturber of the Peace


# Mary

The boiling pot will continue to overflow and there will be events that attract people's attention. Yet, once the event is over, once the destructive powers no longer grab the attention of the mass media, the event slides into the darkness of forgetfulness, and life continues as usual. This is what mankind wants, a life that continues as usual, that flows along with little disturbance. Mankind would even say to me, "Do not disturb us by your words. Do not speak the way you do, always reminding us of dangers and evils. You are a disturber of the peace. Let us alone."

Yes, I am a disturber of the peace but it is a false peace based on total illusions that mankind can continue on this path and have no repercussions. I come to awaken the world and to offer solutions to the problems. Either listen to my words or suffer the consequences (not from my hands, because I am your mother, but from the hands of those who hate you and would destroy you). Let us begin.

I will describe the problems with great clarity and I will describe steps that can be taken to avert the collapse of Western society. My words must go forth and millions must believe them. Millions must say, "We must walk a different road because this road will lead to our destruction." Those who turn off this road and walk in my paths will come under my care and I can save them. Those who reject my words and do not want to be disturbed, I cannot save.

My words must lead to decisions, to concrete decisions which are made today, not tomorrow. So, I do not speak to the millions, I speak to you who read these words (hopefully there are millions of you). Read my words every day. Light will come to you. The words mean different things to each reader. For example, I say, "Turn away from what is destructive." In each life, what is destructive varies. When each person reads these words, I will give inner light, revealing what I mean for each one. Every message that I give points out one part. Only by reading all the messages, each and every day, will I be able to form your mentality and draw you away from the illusions of the modern world. Be faithful to reading the messages.

*Comment*

*Mary's wisdom contradicts the world's illusions.*
*The person learns this wisdom only by daily reading.*

October 13, 2011

## Mary

Why do I hold Russia in my heart? Why do I ask for a consecration of Russia to my Immaculate Heart? Why do I single out that country, which spreads from East to West, and is composed of so many peoples?

When I first mentioned my request to the children of Fatima, Russia was in the ascendency. It was not ascending to holiness but to power through a demonic strategy. What was hidden on this day (94 years ago when the miracle of the sun took place) soon became manifest to all. A demonic power called "Communism" was about to commandeer an entire nation and use that nation to attempt to build a world-wide empire dedicated to Communistic principles. Russia was not Communist. Its people were believers in my Son. However, this demonic evil chose to attach itself to this nation and to use it as its instrument. The harm that resulted, the millions who were killed and the millions who were enslaved by Communism's spread is known to all. In the year dedicated to me by Pope John Paul II (1987 – 1988) Communism began to be toppled. Yes, the external walls were removed. The system was dismantled and new freedoms and structures arose. But the demonic has not been cast out. The peoples' hearts have not been set free. The darkness still remains at the center. I do not have a purified Russia. The evil still lingers. The demonic is still in its blood. Russia does not belong to me.

So, I must stress this again. I want the Holy Father to consecrate Russia, in union with all the bishops of the world, to my Immaculate Heart. Then Russia will be truly mine and I will begin to work signs and wonders. Both the West and the East will see what I am doing. Everything will go forth and all will begin. This will be the first act in the new drama.

*Comment*

*October 13, 1917 was the great miracle of the sun at Fatima, Portugal, seen by 70,000 people and reported in all the newspapers. At the same time, Communism was taking over Russia.*

October 14, 2011
## 136. The Coming Economic Collapse

## Mary

When everything begins, there will be many surprises. Those who were thought to be strong, will fall quickly, while those who seemed to be weak will persevere because of their faith. How will people handle this adversity? First, let me describe what will happen, so that those who read my words can prepare. I will lead them but they must not wait.

The relationships of faith must be made strong. This is the way to survive. People must strengthen their ties to others, the bonds of their faith. When the tragedy first hits, people will be shocked. How could this ever happen? There will be great turmoil and the leaders will be scrambling to come up with answers. But those who have placed themselves in my heart will not give way to useless anxiety. They will have a firmness of heart. They will know my words. This is my promise, "I will provide. I will take care of you." As a mother says to all of her children in any crisis, "Stay together. Stay close to me. Do not wander. The road is too dangerous."

The great problems will not be in the beginning. In the beginning, there will be shock and wonderment. There will be anger. "How could they allow this to happen?" I am talking about the economic woes that will come upon the West, and even to America.

Who will survive these drastic changes? Not those with resources (for these will whittle away) but those who bond together in faith and who seek ways to help each other.

This will be a time of great sacrifice. The individualism of America, sparked by the decades of affluence, will be reversed. People will need each other to survive. Families will be reunited by the need to put together their incomes. New forms of helping others will emerge. Where the churches are vital and alive, the people will coalesce and the church will again become a focal point for the community. The teaching is clear. Where relationships of faith and love are already in place, people will be better able to respond and survive. That is my teaching. Begin now to form relationships. Come together. Gather now, even when you do not know why. Later, you will see how important are these steps.

### Comment
*There will be some economic collapses that surprise America.*
*In that new situation, those who have others to help will respond best.*

October 15, 2011
## 137. The Satanic Control of Russian Leaders

## Mary

The wars that are ahead will be much different. There will be no clear lines, nor any taking of land. They will be wars of destruction, like the world has never seen, fought quickly but then lingering on, with no clear winner. This is Satan's goal. He stirs up nations to think that they can easily grab a prize, but when they grasp it, it clings to their hand and nothing is resolved. So, the fighting just continues, draining each side and causing untold suffering.

Suffering is what he wants. He rejoices in his demented fashion when everyone is suffering, even those who have put their lot in with him. Yes, there are nations dedicated to him, even though they are not aware of whom they are serving. They even think they are serving God, but they are serving Satan in their military endeavors.

This is already happening. Wars go on far beyond the expected deadline. The enemy finds new life and new sources of supplies and soldiers. It is endless and will remain so until Russia is consecrated to my Immaculate Heart. Then the heavenly Father will give peace to the world.

Many will say that Russia is not the problem but I see the truth. I see what happens behind the scenes. Why does anyone trust that leader whose heart is so ambitious to have Russia regain its military and diplomatic powers? He saw these taken away and he wants to regroup them. He is already acting, trying to draw the neighboring nations into a unity which he will use for his demonic plans. Who confronts him? Who opposes him? He acts without any opposition. He is no longer seen as the sinister force. He has changed his costume, but not his heart. Keep your eye on Russia. Do not allow him to expand his influence.

The West is relaxing. They are saying, "Russia is our friend. Russia is no longer a problem." How foolish can you be? The heart of Russia's leaders still belongs to Satan. Do not be fooled by the seeming lack of resources. Satan possesses his heart and he can arm him in a second. What do you think Satan is doing in Iran? Does not Russia delight? Does he not participate? Russia is not on the sidelines. They are active participants. Wake up! I want Russia consecrated to my Immaculate Heart before it is too late. It is already very late.

### Comment
*Read the news and you will see that Our Lady speaks the truth.*

October 17, 2011
## 138. The Jerusalem Covenant of Blood

## Jesus

At Jerusalem there was the covenant of my blood followed by my death. Today that covenant is celebrated throughout the world (the Mass). Look at Jerusalem's history, the many years when that covenant of blood was never celebrated there. Look at today. The covenant of my blood is celebrated but the crowds are few, and often it is for pilgrims. Know my heart. I want a Jerusalem where Mass is the central act, where thousands gather and the life of Jerusalem centers on the covenant of my Blood. I rejoice when lips receive my Blood but I rejoice most when Jewish lips partake of my Blood. There will be peace in the world when the covenant of my Blood is central to the life of Jerusalem.

Look at what is happening. Jerusalem is endangered. It is the target of the Muslim terrorists. If it is destroyed, or if it falls into Muslim hands, then the Covenant of my Blood will not be celebrated at all in Jerusalem.

The opportunity would then be lost for centuries to come and the light that I intend, the light of world peace, would be cast aside. There would be darkness.

The protection around Israel is being stripped away. The natural protections are being removed. A time will come when Israel will have no natural way of protecting itself. At that moment, I will save Israel and then the Covenant of my Blood will become the central act. The Church will be enriched by Israel, and all will see that the Catholic Church is the true Church, when Israel and the Catholic Church are one.

Satan sees the importance of Jerusalem. His eyes are on Jerusalem to destroy it. My heart is on Jerusalem to protect it.

*Comment*
*The teaching is so understandable. The Eucharist began in Jerusalem*
*and Our Lord would want its celebration to flourish there.*

October 18, 2011
## 139. Explaining the "Events"

## Mary

Begin now to prepare. These are always my words. "Before it is too late." These words I always add. Place them in your heart and do not lose a single day. Every day is important and that is why I speak on a daily basis.

From now on all the events will speed up, with no interruption. One event will still be going on and another will begin. At times, two or three or more events will be taking place. What do I mean by an "event"? It is an action of Satan, stirring up people to disrupt, to tear down, to destroy, to turn the hearts of some against the hearts of others.

Some would object. They would say that issues have to be confronted and that changes have to be made. Read my words. Do I not say the same thing" Do I praise the status quo? Who wants change more than I do? Am I content with the world in its present state? That is not my point. Listen to my teaching and you will gain wisdom.

Satan exploits these areas of society where there are grievances. He sees each of these as an opening into which he can place his demonic fire. Yes, that is what he does. He sees the injustices and he sees people who experience these injustices and he places there his demonic fire. At first, the people feel a warmth so they accept this fire into their hearts, but after a while the fire burns them, turning them to anger, even providing them with intelligent direction. However, the direction is always destructive. People are pitted against one another. The problems are drawn out. Nothing is solved. The second state is worse than the first. Nothing constructive results.

Oh, the people he uses can point to certain truths. These provide credibility. But these are half truths which blind people to the other side of the coin. Their actions serve Satan's purpose and in the end, nothing is accomplished except his goals. This is what I mean by the "events." When you see them happening, one after the other, you will know that the force behind them is Satan. There is always disruption, chaos and destruction. Nothing truly positive and lasting is brought about.

### Comment

*We have seen many events. The Middle East uprisings and the Wall Street uprisings. We will see many more.*

October 19, 2011

## 140. A Return to a Non-Nuclear Age

## Mary

As far as the East is from the West, so is the distance now between the heavenly Father and mankind. The human race is hurtling down this road which it has chosen. The speed picks up and the distance from God grows greater. So, I come to search and to confront, to speak and to urge. I am the final barrier protecting mankind. I must stop him in his tracks and turn him around so that the ultimate forces of destruction are not released.

It seems impossible to mankind that these forces will be used. For decades now, mankind has lived in an atomic age. At first, this caused great fears but as the years went on and as these bombs were not used, mankind learned to live in an atomic age, as if the span of years guaranteed that the bombs would never be used.

How foolish this is. Has man ever invented a destructive force which he has not used? Does not a moment come, when someone, in desperation, does not resort to the final weapons at his disposal? Are these weapons not at the disposal of so many? So, what precludes a use of these nuclear arms? And if one atomic bomb is used, will it be the last one or only the first one, as other nations unleash their nuclear might in retaliation? The result is too devastating to even imagine. No nation would have the resources to come to the rescue and to offer even the minimum of help.

I paint this picture so as to confront mankind as he hurtles down this road away from the heavenly Father. (I will say this). The weapons exist and the enmity between nations exists because of Satan's hopes and plans. He has engineered all of this, raising up people who have brought this about, stirring up hearts that selfishly looked to their own prominence in the world. Now the world is an armed camp. What can be done?

There must be a nuclear melt-down that removes the power of these armaments, which makes them ineffective, where nations will want to destroy these weapons forever. There will be no lasting peace until every atomic weapon is destroyed and man returns to the simplicity of the pre-atomic age. Can this ever happen? It is the only solution. These arms cannot continue to be in man's power and never be used. Can man return to that moment when these weapons of war never existed? I hold that grace in my Immaculate Heart and I await the consecration of Russia.

### Comment

*This promise of Mary is extraordinary, that we will return to a non-nuclear age. Yet, her other statement is certainly true. If mankind stores up atomic weapons, they will inevitably be used.*

October 20, 2011

## 141. Feeding the Desires of the Spirit

## Mary

I open up all my secrets and I place before the world all that they need to know to walk the right road and to head in the right direction. All of this demands a choice, a turning around which is not accomplished in one day. Therefore, I speak each day. Slowly my words will penetrate the heart. The person hears my voice saying, "Come this way. Leave the road you are now on and take another path." O reader, if this is happening to you, then listen carefully to my words. These will make it so much easier because I am asking you for difficult sacrifices.

I do not want superficial changes. These will not be enough. I want deep conversions, a turning away, a new style of life, even new friends and new interests. To ask anything else of you would be to deprive you of your rich inheritance and to mislead you. Eternal life is the great prize, the pearl of great price. A pearl must be received fully so it is not lost. So, eternal life must be taken into the center of your heart, or it is in jeopardy. Let us see what is required.

Everything begins with an inner stirring, an interior restlessness, a call, a voice within saying, "Seek and you shall find." You do not know what to seek or how to find. That is why I speak and instruct you.

Listen to that voice and soon you will see opportunities to find life for your spirit, chances to nourish the spiritual cravings within you. This is the secret which I reveal. Your restlessness comes from your spiritual cravings. Your spirit is reaching out. Your spirit is crying out within you. Nourish these spiritual appetites. Feed them and they will grow. Then, you will "hunger and thirst." When you have physical hunger and thirst do you not know how to satisfy them. So, when you experience great spiritual hunger and thirst you will not need anyone to teach you. You will know what you need. You will know where to go to be fed. I will be waiting there for you.

*Comment*
*Each person has spiritual desires. As these are fed, they grow*
*and the desires themselves act as a guide.*

October 21, 2011
## 142. The Coming Hour of God's Intervention

## Mary

In the very beginning, I revealed the mystery of the Fatima revelations which set the tone for all that followed. Now, let me set everything in context, so that people can see clearly, even if they do not understand everything.

This is an age of the great intervention by the heavenly Father into the history of the world. At Fatima, I did not just come to three children. I spoke of world events. I spoke of the ending of World War I (and it would have ended much sooner if man had not interfered with that flow of graces). I also spoke of a future war, World War II, that would happen if mankind did not turn to the heavenly Father. That, too, has now happened.

Therefore, no one can say that these revelations were just personal ones to the children, or that I appeared at Fatima just to stir up Catholic devotion. My appearance at Fatima was the clearest sign of the heavenly Father's intention to intervene in history and to offer mankind an opportunity to avoid the disasters that lie ahead. Fatima is the final barrier against the destructive forces which Satan has planned for so long to unleash upon the human race, his great hour of triumph. That is what he foresees. He foresees his hour, his moment, and he is carefully and methodically moving to that point.

However, the heavenly Father has a different plan. This will not be Satan's hour. This will be my hour, the hour of the triumph of the Immaculate Heart. It will certainly be my hour. There is no doubt about that. The heavenly Father has already decreed that moment. The question is "Will it also be your hour?" Will you share in my victory? Will others share? How many in the world will share? That is why I enlighten the whole world to the events that are taking place. This is not the time to be neutral. There are two armies in battle array. You must choose. Please share with me. It is my hour and I want you in my Immaculate Heart.

*Comment*
*Mary gives a clear overview and offers a clear invitation.*

182

October 22, 2011
## 143. The Coming Economic Scandals

## Mary

I am trying to bind mankind to myself, like a boat that must be tied to the pier in the middle of a storm. Otherwise, mankind will just be taken out to sea, lost amid the coming economic storm.

So much will be blown away. So many financial institutions that once stood strong will be swept away in the flood of debt, victims of selfishness and greed. The question arises, "What can be done at this moment when so many forces have already been released?" Let us begin.

I will not speak of economic policies. Those that are needed are well known. The economists know how to put things in order. They know well the measures that need to be implemented. The problem is not knowledge. The difficulty is to get everyone willing to implement the fair decisions. However, no one trusts. All are suspicious. Financial stability is gained only by constant policies that do not change. When people trust, the system is solid. When selfishness enters, then people change the system, wanting rules that favor their interests. The trust is broken. The problem is this, "How do you put together a consensus when everyone is splintered?"

How do you get splintered? What happened to the broad-based consensus that would put aside selfish concerns for the common good? What has allowed this selfish greed to go unpunished? Who or what has brought about this current situation where even the powerful are helpless (or too busy enriching themselves)?

I will call the perpetrators into my courtroom of justice for all to see. I will call elected officials before the people and expose their hearts. I will call owners before the public. When all is revealed, they will call it scandalous. So, when scandals abound, when the secrets are made public, when greed and avarice are uncovered, know that I am trying to provide an atmosphere that is clearly a help to the economy and can be put in place. Unfortunately, scandals are needed to correct greed.

*Comment*
*As Mary says, only scandals cause people to change economic practices.*

October 23, 2011
## 144. In the Middle of a War

183

## Mary

Upon all of the events, I will place my hand and Satan's power will be quelled. I do not say extinguished but the full evil will not pour out. Satan would seek a total destruction of all creation, an end to human history before my Son returns in glory. This is his jealousy. Satan sees my Son exalted to the Father's right hand and there is an eternal competition which will last forever. He did not submit to my Son in the beginning as the Word of the Father, and he does not submit to my Son as the Word made Flesh.

By my accepting the role of being the Mother of Jesus, I was placed in the very middle of this conflict, which has raged from the beginning and will rage forever. In truth, all human beings are also caught in the middle of this eternal war. This is the problem with all of human history. This is what I have been trying to describe over and again. Let me place this in easy words so all understand.

In the beginning, before material creation, God created the angels and revealed to them his divine plan, that he would bring about a material creation and that his only begotten Son would take flesh and would be the Lord of all creation, spiritual and material. In this way, both angels and men would be united forever with the Father. In Lucifer's heart, a jealousy arose because he was the greatest light among the angels. Now a greater light would come from the Father's side, and even though he would share in this light, he would not be the greatest creature. Instead, a human nature formed for a woman, would take precedence. His pride rebelled. Under these conditions, he would not serve and war broke out in heaven.

Michael cast out Lucifer and all who had adopted his spirit of pride. He cast him down to earth, the very earth where this humanity would be formed. This was his greatest torment, and he is totally committed to the destruction of the human race. Every human person is caught in the middle. What can be done? I also am in the middle and I offer to all the only safe haven in the middle of this war – my Immaculate Heart.

### Comment
*By understanding that we are in the middle of a war, we can*
*grasp the need for Mary's help.*

October 24, 2011
## 145. Needed: A Public Turning to God

## Mary

Before going any further, stop a moment and realize what I am saying to you. I tell you clearly that mankind is at the edge of a precipice and does not realize how perilous are these times. He sees no need to call upon heaven for help, even though heaven is so ready to come to his aid. In fact, the Father has sent me to give that very message, "Heaven is anxious to help." The Father does not will the destruction of life. He would lead man away from the edge. Even the slightest turning to God will be rewarded. This is the message. Turn to God and very quickly the blessings of safety will be given. Let us begin.

First, mankind must believe that the reversal of all the powerful evil forces is possible only if man turns to heaven. Otherwise, he will follow the same path and will go off the precipice, falling into irreversible destructions. I say, "destructions" because it will not be one gigantic moment but a long series of moments, one leading to another. A chain of events will be triggered by one defining moment. Then will come reactions to that moment and then counter-reactions. From this clear description, you see that the disasters do not fall from heaven but they take place on earth and are the product of man's decisions. This helps you to see. Man is not helpless. His future lies in his own hands, but if the future stays in the hands of mankind, it will be a future of destruction.

Man needs God's helps. The Father is ready to offer even extraordinary helps if only man begins to implore heaven. There must be a public turning to God, where all the world knows that a man has decided to say, "We need the help of heaven. Let us implore that help." When all the world knows that it is calling on God, he will act so the world will see the connection and will know who brought about his rescue. This is why the Consecration of Russia to my Immaculate Heart must be done publicly, for all the world to know. Then, when the whole course of human history is changed, all will recognize that it has come from heaven. I will speak more about this later, exactly what will begin to occur when man seeks God's help.

### Comment

*Mary fills in the picture. The future evils happen at the hands of men,*
*by a series of events, but all can be avoided.*

October 25, 2011
## 146. Picking the Vice-President

## Mary

Evil grows in darkness. There men do not see or realize the forces that shape events and the powers that drag them in the wrong direction. Let me explain.

In the beginning of a project, men have good ideas. These offer a genuine hope for the welfare of the earth, but inevitably, the original idea is corrupted. What was meant to serve many soon becomes a source of great evil.

So it is with the political systems. Originally they were established to bring about good order and allow the voice of the people to be heard. But, these political systems have been corrupted. Officials are bought off. Bribes are paid. The good of the people is set aside. Politicians need large funds to gain office. The system labors under gigantic weights that sap its effectiveness and burdens the people with extraordinary taxes. Good people try to reform the system, but vested interests destroy any attempts to recapture the original purpose.

This is so true in every sphere of political life that the entire system is weighed down and is about to collapse. The money will not be there to support the system. Federal and state governments are in debt. No one can shake out the system and rejuvenate it. How long can Washington continue in this way before everything collapses? The warning signs are everywhere, but people think that things will go on as usual.

So, I say this clearly, Washington, you are much, much closer to financial collapse than you can possibly imagine. It is right around the corner. Yet, you do nothing – deficit after deficit, always making the building higher and paying no attention to the foundation that can no longer sustain your debt.

Who will come forth? Who will the American people trust? Who can secure the economic future of the American government? He is there but you do not see him. He has held back. He has not put his name forward. He stays in the shadows. Is there anyone who will see and go to him and pull him into the limelight? Even if he is just second on the ticket, he will be high enough up to bring about the needed reforms.

*Comment*
*Mary speaks of America's greatest need, a person as the vice-president*
*who has the skills and the courage to get the financial house in order.*

October 26, 2011
## 147. Having No Poor in Your Midst

## Mary

I place you in the middle of all these events, so you can see clearly the will of the Father and the perversity of man who would take all glory to himself, and turn everything to his benefit. This is not how the Father acts. From the very beginning of creation God has done everything for man's happiness. All blessings pour out from the Father and can be received by man according to the Father's wisdom. However, man substitutes his own wisdom and loses the blessings. This is what I want to describe.

The world is filled with blessings. There would be even more, but man has ruined parts of creation and has deliberately set aside other parts (as when fields are deliberately left fallow). What was meant to be a mighty flow has become just a little stream. As a result, many are deprived. This has happened for centuries and scientists will soon uncover more and more evidence.

However, I am interested in the modern age, so we will begin there. With the production of modern weapons and of modern technology, the ability of man to destroy creation and to cause human shortages has multiplied. Everything is done with a view to profits and little is ever done to bless mankind. Who thinks of the hungry mouths that need to be fed or of the wounds that need to be treated? Who oversees the flow of destructive arms? Who plans how good water is made available? Who sets aside ten percent of their resources to help the needy, as the Bible so clearly teaches? This is my teaching today. Do not say that when people go to Church, they should give 10%. Everyone, in every part of society, should set aside 10% for the needy. Companies must set it aside. Families must set it aside.

People say, "The government takes care of the poor." Really, there should be no poor. If everyone thought like the heavenly father, people and companies would look around to see who they can help. When companies go to poor countries, they go to rob that country of its resources without even thinking, "How can we bless these people? How can we lift them out of their poverty?" Instead, they leave the people worse off than before they came.

What always happens? People do not set aside 10%. Companies and other institutions do not set aside 10%. The government raises taxes to care for the poor. The politicians pocket the money and distribute what is left over to those who vote for them. You can see how many social and political ills would not exist if charity happened where it was supposed to take place. All who have income and profits should set aside their tithe to help those who sit at their doorstep. I will bless these families and these companies, in good economic times and in poor economic times. However, no one listens and all is done with a view to profits.

### Comment

*Mary speaks about a gigantic change in the social structure,*
*coming about by setting aside 10% for the needy.*

# Locutions to the World
## Part 4

October 27, 2011 -- December 17, 2011

# TABLE OF CONTENTS
## PART 4

October 27, 2011
## 148. Inviting Mary onto the World Stage

## Mary

In the power which the heavenly Father has given to me, I walk into the middle of every storm, and I quell it, removing its power. These storms of destruction come from the Evil One who loves to stir up strife and violence. When I calm the storm, I defeat him and set my children free from his grasp. This is the lesson I want you to learn today. So, let us begin.

God created man to live in a tranquility of order and enjoy relationships that lift up the human spirit. Adam was created in a paradise where all is in order. He notices only a loneliness in his heart, the need for another. When Eve is created, he sees her as a helpmate and a companion. She is, "Bone of my bone, flesh of my flesh."

Tranquility and peace are God's plan. Discord, strife, violence and war are Satan's plan. Learn this well. Whenever you see hatred, lust, anger and violence, know that the Evil One is at work. These are the tell-tale marks of his presence and power.

In the midst of strife, you must say, "The Evil One is at work," but even more, you must say, "I will invite Mary, the Woman, the sworn enemy of Satan. She will defeat him." Yes, just ask me to come, whenever there is strife. I will come and the sting of Satan will have no power. The issues can be resolved in light and the solutions will be lasting ones.

This is why I ask that Russia be consecrated to me. I am waiting and waiting to be invited. I wait in the wings waiting for my cue to come onto the world stage. When I come, I will overcome the Evil One.

Why do I wait for the whole church to invite me? Why do I want the Pope and the bishops to do this publicly? When a couple invites me, I come on the family stage. So, when the whole Church invites me, I come onto the world stage. By this public worldwide invitation, all will know, "Mary has been invited." When invited, I will release all my powers and the fires of hell will be quenched. Then, man can solve his disputes according to right reason.

October 29, 2011
## 149. Mary, the Fundamentalist

## Mary

In the world there is always movement. Things are always changing. One thing fades and another comes into prominence, like a show on a stage which moves from one act to the next. Yet, man does not perceive. Each scene leaves behind its effects. This is what I want to describe.

People forget the way the world used to be, how people obeyed God and lived in his light. This was the Age of Faith, when God's law formed the culture. Then, one thing after another came onto the stage. Need I list them? Divorce, contraception, abortion, homosexuality, in vitro fertilization, Playboy Magazine, Viagra. The list goes on and on. Fashions change and modesty is thrown away like an unwanted coin. These did not come overnight. Each one appeared slowly on the scene, one after another. What will come next? You can see what I mean. What people would never accept if introduced quickly, they gradually accept as it is presented to them little by little. Life is forever changed because they forget the way life should be. Now, all these forces are released in society and children who are born come into quite a different world, a darker world, a world filled with darkness that did not exist before.

How can this society be purified? Anyone who preaches is called radical, a fundamentalist. Let it be known, I am the deepest of fundamentalists. I see clearly the will of the Father. I see how he views all these changes that have moved mankind away from his law. I see the total disregard for the Lord's Day. I see the scourge that has happened to your children by the introduction of drugs and pornography. I see and I speak so you might see. Open your eyes to what has happened to America! Look at your children. Are they the same as you, or has society stolen them from you and erased their religious values? Do they see life as you see it? Is their faith as deep as your faith?

What can be done? See the situation for what it is. Awake from your blindness. Cleanse your home. Purify your family. Say to yourself, "My family and I will walk a different road. I will find other families who will walk with me. We will come together to foster the ancient truths and the former values." I will be with you on this long and arduous quest.

### Comment
*When the culture was healthy, families were healthy. Now, the family must resist the culture.*

## Jesus

Many persons and institutions are hollow, having no inner core of truth. A time of judgment, different for each one, will come. Those persons and institutions built upon a lie will be removed from office or they will collapse. They will be replaced by people of truth and by institutions built on truth. In this way, when decisions are made, the darkness will be put aside.

These people and institutions of darkness, allow the powers of darkness to spread and grab hold. They see absolutely nothing wrong with the darkness. They even agree with the darkness. Because darkness is part of their agenda, they foster the darkness instead of removing it. This must change.

October 29, 2011
## 150. The Real Face of the Arab Spring

## Mary

The time is ripe for rebellion and the overthrow of dictators. However, what happens after he is removed? What forces fill the vacuum of power that is left behind? Those who took the initiative are forced out of the way and the forces lurking in hiding know that it is time to come forth. And come forth they have! Now the true face behind the Middle East uprisings is seen, the dark face of radical Muslims who are quickly taking advantage of the situation as I told you months ago. Now, I will speak about what will take place in these nations which are plunging into a greater darkness which could not be seen by the West.

The radical Muslims will quickly strengthen their hold. They know how to organize. They know their goals and how to attain them. Others will sit on the sidelines, confused and not knowing how to respond. These Muslims will do what they always do. They will show one face to the West, the face which the West wants to see, but they will act for their own goals in a secretive and hidden manner. Some reports will leak out, but these will be set aside in the West because the West wants to see this as the Arab Spring, a fiction which the radicals will use and will even pretend is happening. O West, do you think that human rights and human dignity will win the day? You do not want to look. You will not examine beneath the surface.

You did not plan these revolutions. They sprang up from the power of darkness, from Satan who used the legitimate aspirations of the people for freedom from a dictator for his own goals. Now, he has taken control over these nations and he will use the people and the resources to fuel his fires. I say "his fires" because that is what you will see.

Do you believe that he is limited by national boundaries? Does he not set fire in one country, so that it would spread to others? Do you think he is content with claiming Muslin countries? That is not his goal. His goal is Israel, and now he has taken the surrounding nations and is tightening his grip. And you call it an Arab Spring.

*Comment*
*In these locutions, months ago, Mary warned about the forces of darkness taking control. We see them in Egypt and will see it in Libya.*

October 31, 2011
## 151. Safeguarding the Other Children

## Mary

I wait and wait, never giving up hope that all would turn to me and be saved from the coming chastisements. I plead with the heavenly Father to delay his judgments and to set aside the chastisements which man truly deserves. Is this not the normal approach of a mother, to plead for mercy and forgiveness? I plead like no one else, and the Father sees that I have attained this role by standing at the foot of the cross and enduring my Son's passion. Yet, how long can I plead and how long can I keep back the scourge of God?

Evil cannot just be passed on. The more that God delays, the more he must allow evil to continue without being removed by divine intervention. This is the dilemma. People commit sin. Out of mercy, God delays in punishing them. Yet, this same mercy allows the sin to continue and to contaminate others. God cannot just look at the individual. He must see how the individual sin adversely affects others and leads them into sin. Yet, I plead and ask man to seek another path. This is what I preach. Mankind must quickly take the other path. They cannot delay. It is unjust for the Father to postpone punishment when others who are innocent will be caught up in the unpunished evil.

Do not say that God's chastisements are unjust. He must care for the other children who are in the house. Can a father leave an eldest son's sins go unpunished when the other children will quickly follow suit? No. He must move against the evil, choosing the best method to correct his sin and destroy the evil. No one would call him an unjust or merciless father, when he has other children to protect.

This is the position of your heavenly Father. However, when I see what he needs to do, I plead with him to gain more time for repentance. Yet, I can only hold back the chastisements for a short time. Then, the righteous anger, fueled by the sins of mankind, will pour over in ways too horrible to describe. In those moments, I will weep for my children but I will not say it is unjust or not needed. I will resign myself to what has been destroyed and move on to those whom I can help. Yet, this need not happen. If only you would listen to my messages.

*Comment*
*People wonder why God punishes. However, without chastisements,*
*sins are passed on to God's other children.*

November 1, 2011
## 152. Lanterns in an Emergency

## Mary

All the world is in my hands and I have been told by the heavenly Father to protect all those whom I can and to make it easy for them to find the right road in the coming darkness. The Father wants to provide for his children. He is like a father preparing for a coming disaster. He sees what Satan has in store. He sees totally what will happen (even though he will not cause it). He knows every moment and every situation of every person in the coming darkness. He prepares ahead of time, not wanting his children to be lost. So, he provides lanterns of light that will be put along the road. All who see these lanterns will know where they can walk in safety. They will not be lost.

The Father has prepared many lights. They are all available, but Satan would cover them over. If anyone listens to my words, this cannot happen. They can return to my words again and again to gain the needed light. So, listen to my words.

First, never fear because fear destroys hope which is needed as the darkness continues and people see no end in sight. When a disaster happens, people seek actively for solutions. However, as time goes on and the problems grow, they give up hope. The Father has entrusted these children to me so that they never, never lose hope. In the darkness, keeping alive hope is the key to survival.

Second, love one another. Stay close to one another. Help one another. Sacrifice yourselves. In this way, something will happen within you. You will find yourself unbelievably strong. Great heroism will be released within. You will see storehouses of inner strength that you never knew that you had.

Finally, believe these words, "I am coming." Yes, time and again I will come to you. Whatever you need, I will provide. At present, you believe in me but you do not experience my presence because you do not need this now. The darkness has not come yet. When it comes, I will come. It is like the emergency lights that never shine until an emergency happens. When the darkness comes, I will come. Blessed are all those who have learned to call on me. Goodbye, my children.

*Comment*
*The heavenly Father will use Mary to light the path in darkness.*

November 2, 2011
## 153. The Responsibility of Parents

## Mary

I watch over the world like the most loving mother watching over her sick children. Is there not a special love that goes forth from a mother when a child is sick? Does she not always think of the child and even want to absorb its pain? Such are my feelings toward the children of the whole world. I see all their ills and have a constant desire to bring about their good health.

I see those who are causing them to be ill, who care nothing about God's law or whom they lead into immoral behavior. They do not fear to scandalize the little ones or to invite them into the worst of sins. Can no one see the evil power of scandal? Can no one see the responsibility for the children? Do you want me to list what happens every day? How the children go unprotected?

Let us begin with the parents, the primary teachers of their children. They think nothing of the literature that comes into the home. They think nothing of the television programs they watch (which means their children watch them also). They think nothing of the products that are advertised. Sometimes, they think nothing of the language which they use, including my Son's name. They pretend that their children do not see or do not hear. Or, they think that they do not understand. I say to you. They see. They hear. They remember. They understand all too well, even better than you do. Their hearts are innocent and the evil makes a deep impression. There are memories they will never forget. They will always remember your words and actions in your home. Do you not remember what your parents did and said? Did this not deeply affect you? Now it is your turn. This is the way that God made the human family. The parents mold the children. God created them and put them in your hands. "How can I fulfill this responsibility?" you ask. Let your own heart be pure and chaste and right with God. That is where you must begin. Purify your heart and you will purify your home.

Nothing is more important. I will help you.

*Comment*
*A purified home is the parent's greatest gift to their children.*

November 3, 2011
## 154. Avoiding Foolish Choices

## Mary

I see the flow of time, the stream which the Father began and which will continue until my Son comes in glory. I see that each person comes on the scene and remains just a short while until all the events of that person's life are completed. Their choices are forever present in their souls.

They were free and they made their decisions in freedom. Some were wise and chose what would not pass away. Others were foolish and chose the things of earth. They did not realize that the stream of time moved on and what was of earth would pass away. They did not know that they were made for eternal glory and for a life that would be forever and ever. Let me teach on this point – the foolishness of man and the wisdom of God.

Man begins foolishly. He is deceived by his surroundings. He sees the beautiful things that God has made. However, a moment must come when man's eyes are lifted up. When he looks among all the beautiful things of creation and says, "Although these are beautiful, they will not satisfy me. I am not made for what God created but for God who did the creating." At this moment, man is being saved from being consumed by desires for created things. He begins to live a new life. He has found his goal. "O Lord, my heart is made for you and it will not rest until it rests in you." (St. Augustine)

*Comment*
*Without divine wisdom, we are condemned to a lifetime of foolish choices.*


November 4, 2011
## 155. The State of Egypt

## Mary

The fires burn brightly but they are not the fires of hope. They are the fires of destruction. At present, these fires burn only in the hearts of those who would destroy Israel. These fires are fanned by all the new developments, especially the instability of the region. This opens new doors to them and they seek to consolidate their foothold. What will happen and why?

As the euphoria dies down after the fall of the dictators, the people will survey the situation. What will they see? What is the second state of their nation? Is it worse than the first state? In truth, some repressions have been removed and the people no longer fear a dictator. But has their state, their daily way of life, gotten better? Do they see their economy humming? Do they see cooperation among all the elements of society? Do people share the same goals? Of course not. They shared the goal of overturning the dictator but, after that, they share no unity. They are diverse, splitting into a hundred parts, with no established leadership, except among those groups that existed before the overthrow – the army and the radical Muslims. These are the two groups which are poised to take control. Who will confront them? Will there be more demonstrations? That is all that the people seem to do well together. Yet, a nation is never built by protests.

So, what will happen in Egypt? The radical Muslims, with their tight knit unity and their Sha'riah law, will make gains, step by step, because they have a clear goal. They know what they want and they have wanted this for decades. They will not change, especially now that the great prize is closer to their grasps. They will unite even more. They will harden their positions. They will demand concessions far beyond their numbers. When they gain what they ask for, they will begin to ask for even more. This is your state, O Egypt. You thought you were gaining your freedom. Instead, you have only gained a different dictator who will impose greater burdens upon you.

Comment

This is a clear prophecy about what will happen next in Egypt.

November 5, 2011

## 156. Understanding the Kingdom of Darkness

<u>Mary</u>

I walk with you in a great intimacy and I share with you the secrets of my heart. I want to share these secrets with all of the world and I will use you as my secretary. So, record well the sentiments of my heart. Let us begin.

When all of the events begin, many will be confused. "What is happening?" they will ask. They will not be able to read "the signs of the times." They will see these events only by natural eyes. Their mind has never accepted the reality of the two kingdoms, the kingdom of light established by my Son and the kingdom of darkness which belongs to the Evil One.

Satan controls this kingdom of darkness. He rejected the light that God gave to him. In the beginning, he saw the light in his own being. He was called "Lucifer" meaning, "the one who bears or carries the light." Indeed, he carried the greatest light, but he

199

made one mistake. He thought that he owned the light, that it belonged to him and that he could always claim it. Really, the light belonged to God, who out of love, filled Lucifer with this light. When he chose not to serve (for that is what he said, "I shall not serve"), the light was taken from him and he fell into complete darkness. This is the origin of the kingdom of darkness. His kingdom grew as other angels also said, "I will not serve." They, too, lost their light and entered into darkness. You can see that his kingdom is always growing. He constantly adds new members, people who say, "I will not serve God." These people join him in darkness. However, while they still live on earth, they can change. This is why I always speak of conversions, when a person says, "I will serve God." At that moment, they no longer belong to the kingdom of darkness. They have passed over into the kingdom of light.

From this easy explanation, you can understand what is going on. Satan, who used to be Lucifer, wants everyone to rebel and to refuse to serve God. Then, they belong to him. Those who experience a religious conversion do not belong to him. His kingdom is always causing disruptions. Then people blame God and ask, "Why did God allow this to happen?" I am teaching you that God wants no harm to come to man, but if men choose not to serve him, then they enter into darkness and immeasurable harm can result. I hope this is clear to all.

### Comment
*A rebellious spirit that wants to say "I will not serve" exists in all of us.*

November 6, 2011
## 157. Why God Is Misunderstood

## Mary

I want the whole world to know of the burning fire of love in the heart of the heavenly Father. He is not known because my Son, who came to reveal him, is not known. The Father chose me to be the mother of his Son and to pierce the mysteries. He has revealed everything to me and he has made me the woman clothed in the sun. He has placed all his secrets in my heart and has told me, "Teach these to all my children so they will see as you see and love me as you love me."

So, look with me into the heart of the heavenly Father. What do you see? Do you see an angry and unjust Father who selfishly chastises his children? No, not at all. You see a Father who created you and wanted you to exist. He formed earth to be your temporary home and heaven to be your eternal home. This is his plan. The plan also included man's free will, the ability to cooperate and share in the Father's will. You can become

200

like God, blessing others, bringing forth new human beings, and helping others to gain the heavenly dwelling place. This is the source of all man's problems – a free will that does not share in the Father's plan.

By this free will, man creates a different world, a harsher world and even a demonic world. This world should perfectly reflect the Father's loving heart. Instead it reflects the demonic hatred and the selfishness of man. All of this obscures the Father's loving heart. So, he sent his Son, Jesus, saying, "If they can no longer see my love in the world I created, they will see my love in the Son whom I have begotten." Jesus came in love. He preached love. He lived love. And, what did the world, the demonic world do to him? They killed him upon the cross. Look at the cross! See how twisted is human life and how it is a distortion of the Father's heart. That is my message. Too many judge the Father's heart through their daily experiences in a world that has become demonic. Judge instead by my words. That is why I speak every day.

### Comment
*So many people suffer bad experiences and judge God by what happens each day.*

November 7, 2011
## 158. Casting Out the Demonic Lie

## Mary

The world is like a maze, a puzzle with many parts which no one can decipher. Such is the confusion caused by a diabolical intelligence. He creates confusion and has mankind seek after solutions that cannot work and do not matter. In this way, time is lost and the great problems go unattended. Then, mankind awakens to dangers and threats which it never imagined and to which it had given little attention.

To gain wisdom, you must step back from the maze, set aside the superficial events, stop looking at the surface and go to the center of the difficulty.

The center is this. The Evil One controls so many hearts. Besides these hearts, many others allow themselves to be caught up in the demonic schemes (for their own purposes). Only a few truly see the central forces. They are alert and save themselves. However, this is not enough. I must alert every heart. All must see the demonic presence and they must rise up and say, "We must cast out the demonic. We must not tolerate his presence."

That is the problem. People tolerate the demonic presence and power in your midst. All who read these words must see and act. Let this cleansing begin in each one's heart and home. Let the cleansing spread to the public scene. Because of conflicting views, not everything can be accomplished. Yet, much can be done.

I will tell you exactly where to begin. Satan is the Father of Lies. Begin there. Do not tell a lie and do not let anyone else. Live in truth and make others live in truth. No lies, at any time or for any reason. In this way, you cast him out.

(Everyone must tell the truth. What a different world it would be if the president told the truth, if the lawmakers told the truth and if companies told the truth.)

Hold yourself to this high ideal. Do not stray from it and you will see a great purification. Much of the world you cannot control. Many, especially in high places, will continue to pour out their lies. I will purge them from the scene. For you, the future must always be a way of truth.

### Comment
*The devil always lies. The child of God never does.*

November 8, 2011
## 159. The Israel-Iran Nuclear War

# Mary

What is deep within comes to the surface. What is sown in the field comes forth in the harvest (good or bad). This is the law of nature and it is also the way of the kingdom, except for one thing. The Father wants to intervene. He does not say, "Look at mankind, he has sown evil; I will let him reap evil." No. He wants to destroy evil. What is planted can be torn up. Even though man has sinned for centuries, even though he has sown evil seeds of terrible destructive power, seeds that are beginning to break through the surface, there does not need to be a harvest of evil and destruction. This is why the Father has sent me, the final preacher, the final word of warning to mankind. He has sent me because although evil seeds are about to bring forth an evil harvest, the Father can and will intervene, even at this last moment, if only mankind repents of what he has done.

All of this seems impossible. There have been so many sins for such a long time (so many abortions for so many decades). How can, at this last minute, the harvest of death be avoided? Yes, that is what man has sown, a harvest of death, and that is what man is about to reap, a harvest of death. Not at the hands of the heavenly Father but at the hands of man himself.

Satan has stirred up nation against nation, peoples against peoples. He has armed them with the most destructive weapons (and he is continuing to arm them at an alarming rate). The nuclear arms are being moved into place. Soon they will be aimed at Israel. All the world just watches, as if it has seen this before. Did not India and Pakistan gain nuclear arms to defend themselves (as they said)? Yet, these arms have never been used. Iran is not arming itself for self-defense. Satan owns their hearts. From the very beginning, they had their target, Israel.

How imminent is this confrontation? Will it not draw other nations into the conflict? Will it not touch a match to all the oil spread throughout the Middle East (I deliberately use that image)? Once that fire it lit, how will it be contained? I say clearly, the hour is late. The great harvest of worldwide destruction is about to come forth. Yet, even at this hour, the Father will intervene but no one calls upon me or listens to these words. I am God's final preacher.

## Comment

*The world has gotten so used to nuclear proliferation that it views Iran as just another country gaining atomic weapons, but Iran is different.*

November 9, 2011
# 160. Satan Uses People

## Mary

I lead you even deeper into these mysteries of destruction, the fires that are already burning in the hearts of men who just wait for the opportunities to destroy human life. Why are they waiting? They need to wait until it is the moment of decision. This decision is not in their hands, even though they think it is. This decision is in the hands of Satan. He decides the time and the place, just as he decided to have Pope John Paul II shot on May 13, 1981 in St. Peter's Square. This was to be his greatest moment when my son, the Pope, would shed his blood in front of all these people.

That moment came. The situation was just as he wanted. The Pope was so near. The gun was fired. Yet, death did not take place. I preserved him so he could serve the Church for all of his remaining years.

So, I look into the future. I look into the forces of satanic evil and I see all the other events which he plans. He has already chosen whom he will use (just as he chose Ali-Agca years ago). He knows their expertise, as he knew Ali-Agca's marksmanship. He knows the evil in their hearts and what he can use to lead them to act. He knows their spheres of influence. He does not need to move someone into a different culture and setting. He has people in every culture and in every setting whom he is easily able to stir to violence and destruction.

What is holding him back? Why does he wait? Because there is a right time to strike, when the most will be gained for his advantage.

If he needs to start a fire in Egypt, he has an Egyptian. If he wants to destroy America, he has an American. Each person is perfectly suited to his purposes. They know how to destroy and what methods to use. I am not just speaking of outward violence. I am speaking about diverse fires that destroy an economy, or a given company, or a person who would do good. Look at the assassination of President Kennedy that ripped apart the very fiber of America from which it has never recovered. That is what I mean by the fires of destruction. Satan owns thousands of people. They belong to him even when they do not believe he exists. They are his finest instruments. They think they see clearly and are more clever than others. They see themselves exerting a gigantic effect over human life. They envision themselves as "game changers." That is why they are willing to risk everything. They are in his grasp and he will use them at the right time.

Here is the question. Can I touch their hearts so that nothing happens? Can I touch their hearts so that they are no longer in Satan's hands? I say this to someone who is reading these words, "You are in Satan's hands and you are ready to inflict great harm. Call upon me and I will come. I will change your heart and remove the destructive power that you hold in your hand. Yes, you are powerful. You have great destructive power, but if I change your heart, you will not use it and you will be saved and live eternally. Otherwise, you will destroy yourself and others.

*Comment*
*Someone who has read this message is now being given the grace to turn back from evil. Is it you?*

November 10, 2011
## 161. The Satanic Fires Consuming America

## Mary

As the fires continue to burn and spread, people will ask, "What can be done?" I tell you that it is late. Much time has been neglected and wasted. These fires were fed and nourished. "We need not pay attention to them," people said. They went about their normal life, just as if nothing was happening. Yet, a fire was burning, more than one fire. There were many fires of destruction, all set by the same hand. Satan is an arsonist. He burns and destroys everything that is standing and he is always searching for new targets. Nothing is out of his reach. He would burn the whole earth and make it like his hell. That is what the earth is facing. Nothing will survive. Never has the human race seen anything like what Satan wants to bring about.

Right now, he is enkindling his fires. He carefully guards them and allows no one to put them out. He has enticed the whole world. He has friends everywhere. Decades ago, he set the fire of abortion and released it upon the world. Suddenly, laws that for centuries had protected the unborn were swept away by a single stroke of the Supreme Court's pen.

Any attempt to put out that fire is met with swift and powerful opposition. "The woman has a right to choose," they proclaim. They do not understand that they are friends of Satan, protecting his fire of destruction that has killed millions and gained great profits for Planned Parenthood abortion providers.

Do you not see? People protect Satan's fires. Attempts to stamp them out are fiercely opposed. Is this what you want, America? Do you want Satan's fire? Every day you are choosing his fires and I say to you, "His fires will burn down your house. It will burn your fields. It will burn your institutions and it will even burn your Constitution. You will become a despoiled America, an America that is torn apart and divided. I tell you that if you do not put out the satanic fire of abortion, your house will not stand. The decision is yours. Which fire do you want, the fire of Satan or the fire that comes from my Immaculate Heart? The fire of my heart contains all the unborn. If you reject the unborn, you reject my fire and choose his."

*Comment*
*People are totally unaware of Satan and his fires. They protect a fire*
*which they should be putting out.*

November 11, 2011
## 162. The Forthcoming Failure of the Super Committee

## Mary

When I give you the words, you record them for all to know. In this way, I extend my influence over human history. Yes, I must influence all of history or else mankind will plunge into the greatest darkness. This has already begun. The signs of darkness are everywhere, in every part of the world and in every facet of human life. The forces of destruction and disruption pour out freely, going wherever they wish because so few are aware and so few even know how to confront them. So, I will speak again of the true sources of these fires and what must be done.

These fires pour out from the belly of hell. They enter into human life through the hearts of those who seek their own interests. Hell gladly fills them with intelligence and power. Yes, those are the two qualities you must look for. Who are both intelligent and have power? Into these, hell pours its fire because through them, this fire pours out into all of society more quickly.

People turn to those in power. They elect them. They feel that these leaders will protect them and guide the nation well. These are the very ones whom hell fills with its fires. As the people sense that their leaders are taking them astray and when their policies are making things worse, the fires of hell fill the intellects of these leaders with clever words. They are able to divert the people's eyes and to blame others. They put the clever spin on what they are doing. They paint a false picture and divert attention. The fires of hell use these people's powers to destroy the nation and their intellects to confuse the people.

I ask you. Have I not clearly described what is going on? America is in the flames of debt. Yet, the leaders multiply the spending. They do nothing to put out the fires and cast the blame on others. These actions and these deceptions come from the fires of hell. Do not expect rational powers to solve this crisis. Do not think that super-committees will come up with solutions. I have constantly preached the same message. "Your problems, America, are demonic and only the power of God can save you, but you have turned away from him. Turn back and I will give you true solutions."

*Comment*

*Some leaders are led by Satan. These powerful people have great intellects which Satan gladly enlightens for his purposes.*

November 12, 2011
## 163. The World's Structures

## Mary

Do not grow tired of recording my words because my words are life and light. They carry powerful gifts to lift up my people in this time when so many parts of society will collapse. Yes, that is what you will witness, a total collapse of many parts of the social structure. Like the parable of the two houses, one built on rock and the other on sand. Both looked strong but when the floods and the winds came, the building built on sand collapsed.

So it is with the world's structures. I say "structures" because it is not just the economic structure which is built on sand but all the structures are all built on sand, the political structure, the educational structure and, especially, the family structure (which is really the "structure of the structures," the one upon which all the others are built). What is to be done now? For decades, the family structure, which supports all the rest and from which good citizens are meant to come forth, has been seriously weakened. The true values have not been communicated and when the children become adults they do not have the moral fiber of their parents (who often abandoned them and sought another relationship). These are now the adult children who are staffing the economic and educational structures of the country. They look the same but they are not the same as those who went before them. The tight, moral fiber is gone. The idea of right and wrong is twisted. The role of personal responsibility is absent. All is relative. There is no solid truth. There is no God to whom they feel responsible.

There is a sea of relativism. Can you build systems upon a sea? Can you have firm foundations when no one agrees on what is true? How many police can you hire and how many courts can you build, when the human person does not police himself and does not hold himself responsible in the court of his own conscience? You have banished God, America. You have banished his commandments. Fine! You have external laws, but you have citizens without consciences that should tell them to keep your laws. Your buildings are about to collapse. They have no strong foundation. This is why I plead with you. If you listen to my word, we will begin to salvage what can be saved.

### Comment
*What is wrong with America? Mary says it clearly, people need to have consciences and live by moral laws.*

November 13, 2011
## 164. A One-Sided War

## Mary

I watch over all who call upon me. I protect them from morning until night. They are never out of my sight. I want to keep everyone safe, but if people do not believe in me and do not look to me for help, then a wall exists, placed there by the Evil One. A darkness surrounds people and covers their eyes, so they cannot see their heavenly mother and be guided by her. This, too, is the work of the Evil One. By these words, I try to remove the wall and scatter the darkness. If this happens, then the fullness of my protection can come to each person. Even in Satan's greatest trials, I will provide an escape. Let us begin.

The Book of Revelation speaks of Satan's plots against myself and my child and when these are foiled Satan goes off to wage war against the rest of my offspring "those who keep God's commandments and witness to Jesus" (Rev. 12: 4-17).

This is what is taking place. He has gone off to wage war. The war is raging and the signs are everywhere. They are totally misinterpreted by the world which wonders what is going wrong and which believes that man can solve these problems. The longer these misconceptions continue, the more headway the Evil One can make. This is a ridiculous situation. One side has declared war and is ravaging the countryside, plundering the treasures and killing the inhabitants. (How many have died because of drugs? How many babies have been killed by abortions?) Still, no one realizes that war has been declared. There is no awareness. There is no call to arms. There are no strategies because people do not even know that a war is raging.

That is why I give these messages. You are at war! Yet, for you, it is life as usual. You take your vacations, spend your money (which is not yours) and you do not listen to the voice that would save you because I say, "Prepare!" Will the whole land be ravaged?

### Comment
*When only one side wages war, the other is bound to lose.*


November 14, 2011
## 165. The Forces of Chaos


## Mary

Problems break out all over and the human race can no longer adequately respond. The forces of chaos grow stronger and now are overwhelming the powers of mankind to keep order. All of this goes back to creation, when God brought order out of chaos.

Now, the chaos that was conquered by the breath of God is reasserting itself. It is coming to the surface. Man has never learned the first lesson. Any human life without God returns to chaos. Only God sustains creation in its goodness. This is the basic lesson I have repeated so often. Beauty and order, goodness and peace are not innate qualities of human life. They are gifts from above. In man, there are powers of chaos that are always at work and only a purified mankind can sustain the balance of peace and the tranquility of order.

Instead, man turns to himself, thinking that he can subdue the chaos. His efforts are feeble and unavailing. He runs to solve one problem and a greater one breaks out. There are revolutions, disturbances, economic breakdowns and even defaults. Pause a moment. Look at what is happening on your planet. The Father gave it over to you. God set Adam in the Garden of Eden "to cultivate and to care for it" (Gen. 2:15).

It was meant to be a partnership, a working together of God with man, a covenant in which both sides had important interests. God has not walked away from the Covenant. He restored it with Noah (Gen. 9:9) and continued it with Abraham. Then he sent Jesus who established a New Covenant in his blood.

You, mankind, have set aside the covenant. You have tried to destroy it and to rip it asunder, but God will never let you go that far. What is the solution to your chaos? Return and renew the Covenant. Become God's partner again. Only then will the chaos be overcome by God's holy Breath.

### Comment
*Creation is very dynamic, ever moving towards God's order or returning to chaos.*

November 15, 2011
## 166. The Coming Supreme Court Decision

## Mary

Those in power lay truth aside and pick up lies instead. Armed with lies, they believe that they can easily conquer and deceive the people. Their lies are spread out before them, as in battle array. They know which lies to send out first (to soften people up so to speak). Then, they can bring out the hard lies that will shake people's convictions and have them give up what they hold on to as true.

This is the political game which Satan, the father of lies, orchestrates so that people whom he controls can gain power. But, I know his game. I see his strategy and I know what needs to be done to foil his plots. So, let us begin. This is what I will do.

I will take the people whom he holds in his grasp and I will publicly strip them of all credibility. I will use the truth, the truth that reveals their hearts, their misdeeds and their evil intention. When you see this happen, one after another, when one after another of your political leaders and those who share their power are exposed by the truth, then you know that I am working to bring about elections that will be held in the truth.

The great moment of exposure will take place when the Supreme Court passes judgment on the health care. This will force all the truth to the surface. Nothing will be able to be hidden. It will all gush forth for all to see. This decision will be so much in the limelight that no hidden powers (the behind-the-scenes powers) will be able to cover up the darkness that took place. When this decision is handed down it will level off the playing field. Truth will have a chance to emerge.

In all of this, you can see that your heavenly Mother is doing all she can to make this election an election of truth. But all must do their part. Live in the truth. Demand the truth

209

from your leaders. Propagate the truth by every possible means. There will be surprising moments and unbelievable revelations about what has happened. I am the Mother of truth.

### Comment

*The Supreme Court decision on the Health Care Law will reveal much that is hidden.*

November 16, 2011
## 167. Earth Detached from Heaven

## Mary

What is the road that lies ahead? The Father knows and sees but he does not decide. Man decides. Man chooses. However, at some point, the Father intervenes, entering into this process in many ways. At every moment, the Father tries to hold back the evil deeds from flowing forth. Sometimes, he stops people in their tracks. He even brings about their deaths so they do not continue to destroy and ruin.

Every single day mankind makes choices. Decisions are put in place and changes occur. Every day, the state of man is in flux, often like the herd of pigs which went over the hillside and into the sea. Such is the state of man, hurtling toward moments of self-destruction. Why does the Father not stop mankind? Why does he allow the destruction to occur? Because mankind has free will.

Learn this lesson. Heaven is the Father's house. In heaven, all will be exactly as the Father wants it to be. Earth is different. At one time, it was perfectly attached to God. Then earth said, "I will detach myself from God. I will have my own life and go my own way." This was man's choice and in that moment earth no longer belonged totally to the Father.

In the fullness of time, the Father sent his Son, Jesus, so that earth could once more be like heaven. However, earth killed him and the Father raised Jesus from the dead, establishing him as the great high priest, the bridge, the unifier of earth with heaven. Jesus is the one who will restore creation "as it was in the beginning."

So, I say this clearly. Mankind has chosen to separate from God, to withdraw earth from heaven. This is the source of all the problems and will be the source of greater problems. The Father wants to prevent the disasters. He has intervened in my Son, Jesus and now, he has sent me so earth can be united again with heaven.

### Comment

*All the problems occur because earth is separated from heaven. The Father has tried to reunite earth with heaven by sending Jesus and now sending Mary to preach.*

November 17, 2011
## 168. The Middle East Powder Keg

### Mary

I tell you the truth. I reveal the secrets that lie behind the turmoil and even how those events will unfold if there is not an intervention of heaven. It is difficult to speak of those future events because there will be so few good results. In a war, there is much destruction, while a few people practice heroic virtue. These are the heroes but what are they compared to all the people who have fallen, all the families that have been ripped apart and all the people who have acted selfishly in the middle of the conflict? When there is war and destruction the proportion between evil and good is totally out of balance. Moreover, when war begins no one can foretell what will happen. Secret reserves of destructive power are released on both sides. The conflict cannot be contained and those on the sidelines are helpless. That is why I speak. My words will be on the mark. I will not mince words.

### Armed Conflicts

The world is facing armed conflicts, such as never have been seen before. These conflicts will obliterate the memories of two world wars (which should never have happened), so great will be the devastations. These wars are not far away. They are at your doorsteps. Some shots have been fired but, at this point, no one understands. Only looking back will anyone see the unfolding of events and how, what was seen as isolated events were not isolated at all. When a match has been placed to a line which leads to a keg of dynamite, have not the explosions, in a sense, already begun. So, the fire has been set and the events need only to run their course.

Is everything predetermined? Is the world helpless? Not at all. But there must be new leadership, people who understand the Middle East and see the Middle East for what it is. The Middle East is a powder keg. The fire has already been lit by the Egyptian uprising (what the West calls "the Arab Spring"). Do you think that a war in the Middle East will be contained? Do you think it will touch only a few nations? No one is paying attention. That is why I speak so clearly.

### Comment
*Although Mary has often spoken about the Middle East, these are the*
*clearest words she has ever given.*

November 18, 2011
## 169. The Coming Muslim Menace against Israel

# Mary

These days are so important for they will be filled with many crucial decisions which will not be seen at first, and only later come to light. These are not decisions of light but decisions of darkness, all following and consolidating the basic decisions to overthrow the dictators months ago. These decisions will not be made in public. They will not be made with the knowledge and consent of the people. They will be made in secret by those groups which have their own self-interests at heart. They will be announced to the people, who will realize that their resolutions did not place power in their hands but in the hands of radical Muslims. These Muslims have a clear agenda and are acting quickly to make sure that their influence is solid and that it can grow in the future. The doors are opening, not to the freedom which the people sought, but to a new darkness that will seem small at first but will quickly spread.

## The West and Israel

The West is helpless, standing outside of the situation. Israel is threatened, placed right in the middle of the turmoil which will continue to spread to other nations that help the United States. Where and when will this end? It will end in the great confrontation (for which I am trying to prepare all those nations which call on me). It will come quickly, much sooner than anyone can now conceive.

## Gathering for Years

These forces have been gathering for years, like dark clouds on the horizon. They are now filled with the rain of terror and destruction. The darkness is coming and it does not come like a thief in the night. It happens before your very eyes. Oh, it comes in disguise, under the mask of a supposedly legitimate government. Do not accept that legitimacy. Do not be fooled. They are wolves in sheep's clothing, covering over their true natures so no harsh measures are taken against them until they get close to their prey, Israel. Then, they will take off the mask and claim that they have perpetuated the acts of destruction. But, they do not know my response and how I will use their acts to bless my Church and to bless Israel. This is the great mystery which is about to unfold.

### *Comment*
*Mary expands on the correct interpretation of the Mideast uprisings.*

November 19, 2011
## 170. Spreading the Message from the Housetops

## Mary

Why do I shout from the housetops? Yes that is what I am doing. My words go forth by every possible means. So, why do I shout from the housetops? The time is short. I have said this again and again. The possible destruction is vast. This, too, have I said many times, "Much can be done." That is why I speak. Otherwise, I would be silent.

"What can be done," you ask, "when the destructive powers are so great and spread throughout many nations?" Little can be done at the last moment but much can be done if people begin now. This is the message I speak from the housetops.

### The Light on the Mountain

I will place a light on the mountain. My people will see the light and be drawn to it. People will come from every side. When they gather, they will know that I have brought them together. They will ask each other, "How did you come here?" "We saw the light," they will say. Then all will realize that I am doing something special. They will continue to search. "What does Our Lady want of us?" they will ask. Some will walk away, when they see that there are no immediate answers. Others will continue to search out the meaning, the purpose of the light and why they were drawn together.

I allow some to walk away but not to discourage them. Later they will realize that this experience prepared them for future light. I need people at the core and center of this divine gift to be people of the deepest convictions, who will realize the greatness of the gift and who will be willing to sacrifice themselves so that this gift of light will go forth.

### Someone to Carry the Message

How can I speak from the housetops, when I have no one to carry the message of light and hope? That is what these people will be. That is why I call them together. What is the light on the mountain? It is the messages themselves. These messages will attract people. They will see them as true light. They will ask, "Why did Mary gather us together in this light?" They will realize, "We are called together to spread this light. We are to take the messages to everyone, by every means. Our Lady wants to speak from the housetops. We will be her messengers." So, I speak to you who are reading these messages, "How did you find out about them? Who told you? With whom have you shared the messages?" How many of you are deeply interested to find your call in these

213

messages. This is what you are to do. You are to gather together with one purpose, that you will spread these messages in every possible way. Right now, I call you to this and I give you my full permission.

## Mary's Housetop

You do not need to be learned or clever. I place this gift in your hands. Just give it to others. Let your numbers increase. Many will find light in these words. Some, besides finding light, will want to spread the light. Let them join with you so that you grow in numbers. I will provide the teachings. You will be my housetop from which the words go forth.

### Comment

*Mary gives a simple call and structure. Besides reading the messages, you are called to gather with others (even just two or three) to spread the messages by every means.*

November 20, 2011
## 171. The Penn State Scandal

# Mary

The time of accounting is at hand, when all of the debts come due. This is not the will of the heavenly Father but the will of the devil who has accumulated so many IOU's. A time comes, when he calls them in. Many people are in his debt and he gladly lets them run it up very high. But he is not an easy taskmaster. He is a tyrant, who plots and plans how to ensnare the children of men.

Many have chosen his ways of foolishness and consider themselves wise. They have what others do not have. They move along in life. They break commitments so they can move on. All of this is inspired by the Evil One. The people think they are riding high with not a care in the world, far above others. Really, they are ensnared and Satan just waits for this moment, the moment that always comes, to destroy the person and all of those around him and all those who in any way were involved with him.

## Satan's Entanglement

This is the issue at Penn State and now it is all too clear – the years in which Satan allowed someone to flourish. All during those years, Satan allowed more people to become entangled, good people who were puzzled by some actions but did not see the core of the evil. Then, when his net was as full as it could be (because he did not want to

214

waste any more time), Satan allowed the evil to explode upon the scene, destroying so many, with many more to also be included in the final counting.

## Mary's Teaching

I use this example, known to all, so I can give my explanation. Satan sees your vices. He feeds your vices. He wants them to grow. Seemingly, he is blessing you, but really he is entrapping you. You must stop now. The evil that lies ahead can be avoided. Your family can be spared the embarrassment. You can retain your dignity. See your vices for what they are. They are Satan's opportunities to destroy you and everyone associated with you. Many look at Penn State with disgust. You must see it in a different light. Your own vices, if fed and nourished, will entangle you in the same manner. You do not want to arrive at that point. So, turn back and I will lead you to a life of truth and freedom.

*Comment*
*There is so much we can all learn from the Penn State scandal.*

November 21, 2011
## 172. Globalization and the Demonic Virus

## Mary

In time past, there have been many evils. Often these have spread and made the body of mankind very ill. Yet, there were other forces that sprang up and destroyed the evil enough to allow the body to continue.

This has been the constant state of mankind, a body which is partially well and partially ill. The Father has so constructed the human race that it was spread out. For centuries, people in Europe and Asia were unaware of the New World or that the human race inhabited these unknown regions.

## The Full Body

Now, all of mankind is drawn together. No place in the world is unexplored. Mankind knows the full extent of its body. More important, the parts are all joined. The body is one, so to speak, fully aware of all its members. This should serve the body. The health of one part can be communicated to the other. Unfortunately, the opposite can and does happen. The illnesses are communicated. The healthy traditions are destroyed and moral sickness becomes contagious.

Who will win this battle? All can see that the human race has entered a totally new stage. By learning the extent of all the members and by unifying those members, much good can result. However, great evil can also quickly spread. The safeguards have been taken down.

## New Blood Stream

Mankind calls this new stage, "globalization." It represents a condition with which man has no experience. By globalization, events happen quickly and are instantly communicated to the whole world. Man now has a technological blood stream that flows to every part of his body. Whatever enters, good or bad, goes everywhere and affects every member.

This is why I speak. The Evil One sees his opportunity. He needs only to find a few cells of the body (people whom he controls) to inject them with his viruses, and then to let nature take its course. Soon, what he inserted into these people begins infecting the whole human race. I am the antidote to Satan, knowing his infectious codes and understanding what will kill these viruses. Without me, the human race will fall mortally ill. Yet, it need not happen.

### Comment
*Mary makes excellent use of this image of the human race being one body.*

November 22, 2011
# 173. A Mankind Which Is Lost at Sea

# Mary

People work hard. They toil all day long, thinking that they will accomplish great things. Then, as the years go on, they realize that they have toiled all night and caught nothing. This is the way Satan confuses people. He places goals in their minds of great accomplishments. He tells them that they have great talents and can bring about great things. He gets them off the track. He points them to goals that they can accomplish with their own talents. Let me describe the problem.

The world today is so complicated and contains so much power over people's inner lives that man no longer perceives correctly. There is a total disorientation of man's thoughts and feelings. The rational word, the logical conclusion and all the appeals to the mind, are of little value. All is disordered. Logical truths had power when man was seeking truth. Now, life is disordered. The immediate gratification takes precedence. The latest sensual images, these are the lord of daily life. I say this again. Man's life on earth is in such a disarray that approaching him with logical truths has little appeal. Those truths cannot touch his heart. They are too far away.

They are like the shoreline to a man who is drowning in the middle of an ocean.

I have chosen another way. I come as a mother. I approach. I come close. I speak. I warm the heart. I attract. I give hope. Man's heart experiences a new power, a new attraction. Later I will give the logical truths. They are like the beach for a man who has been rescued. For now, the beach is too far away and man is being carried out to sea. I say this is for you, O reader. If you find yourself at sea, call upon me. I am the star of the sea. I will come to you and we will make our way to the shore.

### Comment
*The logical truths of the Catholic Church provide the firmest foundation,*
*but right now modern man needs a lifeguard.*

November 23, 2011
## 174. Satan's Mistake

### Jesus
*(Note – "Rise" means that Satan's kingdom is coming out of hiding*
*and is becoming more evident in the worldwide problems.)*

Satan's kingdom is rising and taking shape for all to see. This is what I call the rise of the satanic kingdom. The question is this. Why is his kingdom rising? Why has Satan chosen to become so visible when he is making such progress by being hidden? What causes this? People will soon see the worldwide spread of satanic power. They will see the worldwide darkness and, for the first time, will conclude that all this darkness is beyond the scope of merely natural powers. But why would Satan want to rise up and be seen? First, he is making a mistake, just as he made a mistake in stirring up those who killed me and gave me the victory of the cross (1Cor. 2:18).

He is impatient and would have greater results if he had stayed hidden. He is proud and wants to assert himself before the proper time. So, as his kingdom rises up and people begin to bemoan this evident show of demonic power, you can rejoice because Satan is making a mistake.

### Comment
*People believe that Satan always acts intelligently when really he*
*makes lots of mistakes. God uses these for his purposes.*

November 23, 2011
## 175. Cairo – Satan's Stronghold

# Mary

Cairo is the center of the demonic forces. From there, the disturbances will continue to spread. There is no peace in Cairo and there will never be peace. Satan has set up his stronghold. He owns so many people – the military, the Muslim brotherhood, and by the spread of violence, even those who oppose the military. He holds all in his power, some directly and others indirectly. The city has entered into a darkness that no human efforts can lift.

The struggle will go on. The casualties will grow. More and more will turn against the military but it has been strengthened by billions of American dollars. It is well financed and well armed. Nothing else in the city can compare with its might, not even the Muslin Brotherhood.

## The Military Decision

This situation is quite different from a dictator who spent years in power and had a history that the people revolted against. This history united the people. They had all lived through it. But the military control is new and they are not just one family. They come from different sectors and enjoyed a great popularity during the revolution. Now, all is changed. They have made decisions inspired by Satan. He has now taken Cairo to his second step.

## Revealing Himself

As I said before, he fulfills his plans secretly and only when they are in place does he reveal himself. Now, through the army, he is gradually revealing the full depth of his plan. He has chosen Cairo as his center. He has a firm hold. There will never be peace. He does not want it. There will never be reconciliation among all the groups. He ferments only hatred and division.

What are his future steps? Why has he chosen Cairo? These answers will be revealed in the coming months. The situation will worsen. People will see the nightmare that comes forth. They have already killed my Coptic Christians because Satan wants them removed. Other elements of Christian presence will also disappear. This should be a sure sign of the evil that is taking hold of Cairo and sinking its roots. The poor people. They sought only their freedom and did not discern the forces behind the revolution.

### Comment
*Mary is very direct and clear. She predicted these events months ago.*

November 24, 2011
# 176. The Year 2012

## Mary

All will readily agree that these are not the usual times. But what are the causes of these tumults, of these destructive waves that hit upon the shore? This is what mankind cannot see. They cannot get to the bottom of things. As the tumults continue, man begins to lose hope that there is any answer at all. He sees that the answers are beyond his resources.

### Satan's Strategy

This is Satan's strategy. He wants to lead mankind into a total state of despair, the despair that exists in hell. He wants to turn earth into a hell of confusion, hatred, violence and hopelessness. The signs of these are already appearing. As a rash appears on the skin and warns of some deeper unknown illness, so all the signs are appearing in human history. This is a time when the inner illnesses of man are making themselves evident for all to see.

### Compare 2000 and 2012

Who would challenge these words of mine? Who would claim that the world is better and safer than at the year 2000? Was there not a worldwide euphoria with the beginning of the new millennium? However, I saw what lay ahead. Now, you yourselves have seen eleven years of this century. What are your thoughts? Has not human life shifted drastically? Does not the year 2000 look peaceful compared to the problems of 2011? The year 2000 was the very recent past, just a decade or so ago. Look at what has happened in these eleven years! What will be the future?

What will 2020 look like? Do not even bother to look that far. The gigantic problems are at your doorstep. Dare I speak about 2012? Dare I reveal the chaos, the destruction and the collapse which will happen in that year? Will you be giving thanks one year from now? How changed the world will be!

### Satan Revealing Himself

Satan now has no qualms about manifesting himself. He has thrown off his cover. He has come out of hiding. Why has he done this? For two reasons. First, he is able to act more freely. Acting in a hidden way limits the scope of activity. It means acting only behind the scenes. Second, he wants the human race to fear, to panic and to fall into

219

despair. He can only accomplish this by great, external signs of disaster and destruction. So, he has chosen to come out of hiding. It serves his purposes to have people acclaim his handiwork and to admire what he has been able to accomplish in destroying mankind. He thinks that he will be seen as more powerful than God. He will be seen as the inevitable victor and people will give up all hope.

These are serious words and I speak them so that everyone knows ahead of time that I have told you. In this way, you will hope in my Immaculate Heart. When these things begin to happen, you will say, "Our mother told us that this would take place."

## The Flames of Mary's Heart

But I will not end my words here because the history of mankind will not end with Satan's victory. I will not allow this to happen. However, I cannot save anyone who does not come into my Immaculate Heart. Yes, the world will be aflame with destruction, but my heart will be aflame with salvation. I give you this prayer, "Mary, draw me into the saving fire of your Immaculate Heart." Say this and I will save you.

### Comment

*Who can argue that gigantic problems have come upon the world since 2000?*
*Who can argue that 2012 will not be a year of destruction?*

November 25, 2011
# 177. A World without Wine

# Mary

I watch over my people and those who turn to me with sincere hearts. I do not reject anyone. So, reader, whoever you are and from whatever background you come, you are totally welcome to receive all the blessings that flow from my Immaculate Heart. I do not ration them. I pour them forth for all to receive. There are more blessings than all the world can receive. Now, I will explain why these blessings are so important at this time.

## No Wine

At the end of the wedding celebration at Cana, there was no more wine. Without the joy of wine, some would leave early and their celebration would end. Others would stay around, but the joy would be missing.

This is the present condition of the world. Joy is being replaced by desolation and sorrow. People will soon be saying, "There is no hope. No matter where we look there are no solutions." You are like the young couple. No matter where they looked, there was no more wine. Suddenly, the headwaiter is calling the groom. "You have saved the best wine until last." There were suddenly large stone jars, filled with the best of wine. Who had done this? How did it happen? Only the servers knew, the woman of Cana.

I am the woman of Cana, my role hidden up to now, but no longer. I am the woman of Cana who desires full life for mankind. I am always working for this life (now more than ever since this life is threatened). My workings are deep in the hearts of people and at the center of human history. God is revealing my role, so people will invoke me. The world must invoke me. The Church must invoke me. Families and individuals must invoke me. It is not too late. The wine of wisdom will flow out to leaders. The wine of hope will flow out to those in despair. But these are not the greatest blessings. Invoke me and I will turn events around. I will confront the deadly powers of the world that limit life and I will confront the demonic powers that will destroy human life entirely. I cannot speak any more clearly.

## Comment
*Mary saved the wedding couple very quietly. Now, she proclaims her power to save the human race.*

November 26, 2011
## 178. The Economic Shaking

## Mary

Why do I speak this way, lecturing a world that will not listen but inviting everyone to come? Does not a mother act that way towards her children? Some will listen and others will not. My heart is stirred with the deepest of emotions. Never have I seen so many swept into sinful life styles, never so many abandoning the faith which they received from infancy. The great tides are sweeping them along. They are pulled out to sea, far from the safety of land, far from those who could bring them to safety.

### People Adrift
We have a world of uprooted individuals, who have been beguiled by a world that promised them everything. They have lost their faith. They have only superficial relationships with those who do have faith. They are truly adrift and so many waves come against them. Yet, they do not see their plight. They are without a clue about their situation. I must speak now, so what happens in the future will guide them back to shore and not push them further out to sea.

## The Shaking and the Calm

The world will begin to shake. What was thought secure and certain will be seen as toppling and collapsing. This will cause panic. It will be followed by a short period of calm, when things seem to settle down. Do not be fooled. The original tremors are a warning signal calling people to turn back to their faith. The time of calm is given so decisions can be made and the faith relationship can be restored.

I must insist this time of calm is not to be wasted. Otherwise, the final chance will be squandered. After the calm, comes the collapse. Every institution not built on solid rock will go under. All of the weaknesses built into the economic system will become evident. Trust will vanish. People will say, "Why didn't I see this coming?" Despair and fear will grip many. Earth is all they have and their earth is collapsing.

## A Regained Faith

But those who used the time of calm to strengthen their faith, those who again sought the blessings of the Church and returned with their families to regular worship, these will find the light and strength that they need. Their newly-regained faith will be their light in the darkness. I cannot be any clearer.

### Comment

*So many have abandoned (I will not say "lost") their faith. The economic collapses will be a sign to them to return to their faith. They will have a short period of time to do this.*

November 27, 2011

# 179. Open Your Eyes to Russia

# Mary

I open the doors to the future for all to see. Some do not want to see because they must change their lives. Others will not believe my words, thinking that they cannot be coming from the Mother of God. Yet, the words are true. They come because I love mankind and because the Father has asked me to be his Final Preacher. Should not the Final Preacher use the clearest words, so easy to understand? Should that preacher not talk about the problems of the world and how the Father wants to help the human race?

Let us begin again as I continue to open the door on the future, so mankind is alerted and repents, turning away from all that is destructive. Do not read these words from curiosity, seeking to know what will happen in the future. Read them with a religious spirit. Ask, "How can the messages help me? How can they bring me more faith and a persistent hope that will allow me to perdure?" Let us begin.

## The Evil Dismantled

By the grace of God, Alaska was purchased from Russia, otherwise that nation would have a foothold in North America. A few decades ago, Russia's influence was at a peak until I began to dismantle it.

The popes made numerous dedications and whenever a dedication was made, I showed my response by great blessings. Yet, my request for the Consecration of Russia to my Immaculate Heart to be made by the Pope in union with all the world's bishops has not been made. The evil has not been attacked as I directed, so it still resides in the heart of this country which is so expansive.

## The Evil Returns

As a result, the evil has grown back; the Cold War confrontations are being resumed. More important, the evils behind the scenes are multiplying. All of this is clearly known by President Obama but is being hidden, as far as possible, from the American people. A foolish treaty has been signed that is useless and restricts America.

Have not the American leaders learned by now? Treaties with Russia do not lead to peace. Evil lurks in the hearts of those leaders and treaties are just instruments of their evil designs.

## Coming Back into Prominence

Now, the stage is set. Russia is clawing its way back into prominence. The goals are clear, the same goals they have always had – to destroy other nations and to co-op other nations by circumstances so that they become a world power. Of itself, Russia does not have the resources to dominate the world, but if they entrap other nations (as they did with the Iron Curtain), then they can lift themselves to prominence.

## The New Tactics

The situation is new. An Iron Curtain will not work because there is too much communication. But other systems can be used. There can be a different binding and tying together. What would connect nations? The answer is selfish interests that look to the destruction of other nations. Evil has a great power to unite. When evil interests are shared by nations that are looking to rise to power, then the bonds become very strong even though the nations themselves seem very different. This is what is happening behind the scenes. So, open your eyes to Russia.

### Comment

*On a few occasions, popes have made dedications and consecrations that have been*

223

*followed by clear divine intervention. Now, Russia is involved in Iran's search for atomic weapons. It has recently threatened military operations against the United States' efforts to deploy a defense shield in Europe. Other Russian cooperation with evil will be reported.*

November 29, 2011
## 180. A Few Coins Trying to Repay Massive Debt

## Mary

If anyone desires the way to truth, I will lead them through these words that come from my heart. Everything comes from the heart, good or bad. From an evil heart come the fruits of evil. From a heart of love come gifts of love of every kind. The time ahead is filled with evil, sown for so long in the hearts of men. Reason will not put out those destructive fires. Treaties are like paper for the fire. I say this over and again. God has established one antidote; "Fight fire with fire" is the saying.

The fires of destruction are burning powerfully. They have been stoked for centuries. They have claimed many hearts and are now claiming many nations. They are becoming evident and man has no power to contain them or to extinguish them.

Yet, another fire exists. It, too, has burned for centuries and is now becoming manifest, open for all to see. I constantly speak of this fire in my Immaculate Heart. I have revealed it at Fatima. I have spoken about it at Medjugorje. I have spoken to many others of the flame of my Immaculate Heart. Many know and practice this devotion. These I will keep safe but the others, the rest of the world, I must also save. So, let me begin my teaching.

O mankind, you have no defense against the demonic flame which is now sweeping world history. You do not even know the true source of all your problems. You are like a man with a few coins in your pocket trying to pay a bill that amounts to trillions. How futile are your efforts. You switch money from one bank to another, from one country to another. You sell bonds that are worthless, and constantly downgraded. People riot when austerity measures are imposed. One nation is entangled with another. Solutions are short-term, just buying some time but never solving the problem.

Do you not see? The problem is not with your accounting but with your hearts. The destructive fires are planted in the hearts of the people and of the leaders. Nothing is accomplished because of Satan's fires in your hearts. I have another fire and it is in my Immaculate Heart. I would gladly place this fire in the hearts of everyone. In this way, I will destroy his fire. How long will you wait? How long will you allow the

224

destructive fires to hold sway? I have spoken clearly. Your hearts need my fire and I will gladly give it.

### Comment
*We forget that all the economic problems begin in the hearts of people.*

November 30, 2011
## 181. True Devotion of St. Louis de Montfort

## Mary

I move about the world, always trying to make my presence felt, inspiring those who turn their hearts to me and filling them with divine wisdom so they make all their decisions in the light. What I am doing by these messages is to offer this light to all. A person does not need spiritual sensitivity. By these words, they know my thoughts. They do not even need to be seeking me. By these words, I seek them. This is the extraordinary purpose of these words. The help that I give regularly to devout people I give now to everyone who reads these messages.

Yes, O reader, I want to influence you. I want to enter your life. I want to guide you. I am your Mother, even if you do not yet know me. Even if you have not yet awakened to the woman who would bring you forth to birth and nourish you at her breast. I say "would bring you forth" because for some this has not yet happened.   Let me explain.

Everyone has a physical mother. All spent months in her womb and came forth from her womb. Concerning this, you had no choice. Everyone also has a heavenly mother who would bring you forth to heavenly life, but this you must choose.

So, I invite you right now to choose me as your heavenly mother. Once this choice is made, all my powers of being a mother begin. Also, as you constantly choose me to be your mother, as you ask me each day to be your mother, my care and protection over you increases. This is the secret which I am now revealing to you.

You are a child and you need to be nursed. As you grow, I will help you to walk. And as you come to adulthood, I will guide your every step. This is called "The Secret of Mary" and has been revealed, especially to St. Louis de Montfort. I call all to learn this "True Devotion," so that the spring of living water is yours. Learn it now. Do not delay. So many helps and favors are not distributed because people do not know about the True Devotion of St. Louis de Montfort. Read his books and they will open your eyes to hidden treasures.

### Comment
*Devotion is the door to Mary's blessings.*

December 1, 2011
## 182. Iraq, Afghanistan, Iran and Pakistan

## Mary

Iraq and Afghanistan have worn down the American desires. They have depleted American resources and sapped its energy. They have cost many lives and yet America has brought only temporary stability to the region. As all the forces are withdrawn, the fruitlessness of these endeavors will become evident to all. There will be a collapse of all that America has spent so much, in terms of lives and money, to build.

That the structures will collapse is evident, but the question is, "What will take their place? What will happen in this region?" There will be a growing power of Iran and of Pakistan, two countries who have or will have nuclear arms. So, the situation is quite grave and their influence will spread. This influence will be evil and destructive, and will totally change the region into a hotbed of potential violence that will not go away and which cannot be dealt with. These two countries survived even when there was a large United States military presence. What do you think will happen when this presence is removed? The field is wide open. Their enemy has left. The structures that they left behind will collapse quickly. There will be little resistance. Deals will be struck and a facade of legitimacy will be put on, but the spoils of power will go to the winners, and Iraq and Afghanistan will not be the winners.

In Iraq, America removed the source of stability, even though he was a dictator. Now, the people who hate America and hate Israel will gain uncontested power.

Where will all of this lead? Is there anyone or any group that can or wants to oppose this evil? They are nowhere in sight and those that would have some vital interest to oppose them are woefully inadequate.

Can you not see, O West? You are helpless before these enemies. Your technology and weapons have not conquered because the evil is so deep. When the troops pull out, the next chapter will be written, far worse than this present chapter. Let the reality set in, a reality that my words have tried to express so often. "The battle is between heaven and hell and because you do not seek heavenly help, hell is destroying the world." Seek heaven's help. Return to faith and belief. Invoke me and I will help you. Iraq will be swallowed up. Afghanistan will be infiltrated and eventually controlled.

### Comment
*This is what will happen after the American withdrawal.*

226

December 2, 2011
## 183. America Erases Its Name

## Mary

One step at a time. That is how I lead you so you can look back and see the path which you have walked. This is far safer than trying to look ahead, trying to see where the path will lead. So, let us take the next step as we talk about the nations.

In the Bible, the "nations" always meant those who were aligned against the Lord's anointed. Yet, there were special moments of divine actions when the nations would align themselves with God's will and share in the blessings of Israel. So, "the nations" can be both friend or foe. They can be destroyed or blessed, the object of blessing or curse. It all depends on how they line up according to God's will. No nation is prejudged. No nation is consigned to destruction. Those who listen to God's will are blessed. Those which defiantly seek their own will are destroyed, because they themselves have chosen their own path.

Every nation is on a path, a freely chosen path. Each has its national goals. Each determines its own way of life. Each nation chooses to have God or to reject God. Because many do not see the importance of that choice, I speak so clearly.

How does a nation choose? There are hundreds of choices. These include the decisions of their courts, the legislation that is passed, the people they vote into office; what is tolerated and what is rejected. Every day a nation is making decisions. The people make decisions – to worship God or to forget God. In this season, I must point out a truth. America used to be proud to highlight my son in a crib, the Nativity scene it was called. It was placed on government property and accepted by all. Now, these scenes are gone. This represents a nation's decisions. Need I go on? Christmas is now called the "holiday season." It is all too clear. America does not want my Son. We are banished. This is the decision of a nation.

How dangerous this becomes. A nation that was firmly inscribed in the book of blessed nations is stripping itself of its Christian identity. It is erasing its own name from the book of blessings. God is not erasing your name or blotting out your identity. You, America, are making the decision. Your courts, your legislatures, your president, they are erasing America from the book of blessings. How dangerous. When this action is completed, what will be your fate? Who you are and what will happen is in your own hands, America. Where will you line up? Which nations will you join? Where do you want to be listed? You are quickly moving from blessed to cursed (and it is not God who is moving you).

Another movement must stir. New voices must be raised, "We will not turn our

227

backs on God. We will not renounce our Christian roots. We will not have our identity changed. We began as a Christian nation. We prospered as a Christian nation. We will only continue to exist if we remain a Christian nation."

Stop holding back. Come out of hiding. Speak up. Confront this erasing of Christian identity. You are the majority. Your voice should be strong. Look at your numbers. All you need is a voice, my voice, saying to you, "Take back your nation. Reclaim your house, before it is too late! I will help you."

### Comment
*For decades, the wrong voice has been heard, destroying America's Christian identity. Mary wants a counter-revolution.*

December 3, 2011
# 184. Israel's Second Chance

# Mary

All over the world the tensions increase and the suffering multiplies, especially in Syria where there seems to be no end in sight. The same is true in Egypt, where the problems are deeper than anyone suspects. Today I want to speak of Israel, which to some degree, just sits on the sidelines and watches all of these developments which are so important in its national security.

O Israel, I am your security. I carry your blood in my veins. I have always identified myself as a "daughter of Israel." I will not disclaim the religious heritage that you gave to me. In your synagogue, I learned your history. I learned about the Messiah, the anointed one who was to come. I learned the names and the teachings of your prophets. In every sense, I was your daughter, in my flesh and in my spirit. I loved you, Israel, more than any other of your daughters. For you and your salvation, I brought forth the Christ. I nourished him in your faith. I taught him your psalms and your hymns. I took him to the temple and prayed with him in the synagogue. I answered his questions and formed his soul, all in the mold of Israel.

We were Jews, faithful Jews, who sought only God's blessings upon Israel. We were Jews who looked forward to your salvation, not your freedom from the Romans but your true salvation, the inner-salvation of your spirit and a re-establishing of a true relationship to the heavenly Father. That is what we sought but you rejected the gift. Time and again, you rejected us. You rejected my Son. You rejected his disciples and you still reject the Christ.

I am still a daughter of Israel and you are still at the center of my heart and the center of God's plan. Your prophets told you correctly that you were his child and he could never reject you. "Even if a mother could reject the child of her womb, I will never reject you, O Israel."

Now you have other enemies, with even greater weapons. They, too, surround you on every side. Your future is no longer in your hands. Do not trust your weapons and your armies. Your forefathers did that with the Romans and failed. Your Messiah came to save you and you rejected him. Now, I come, a true daughter of Israel. I come with my words to save you. Listen to these messages and I will lead you by a safe path. Then, I will send my son, the Pope, who will bring the gift of peace.

### Comment
*History is repeating itself and Israel is getting another chance to choose the Messiah.*

December 4, 2011
## 185. The Two Fires

## Mary

Open wide the doors! The time is short. This is a time of abundance, the abundant helps of God that man needs so desperately. Even if man does not seek me, I will come. Even if he does not call upon me, I will answer. The time is short and too many will perish. I will act quickly and powerfully, like a mother saving her children when the house is on fire.

Yes, soon the house will be on fire, ablaze in violence. When it is unleashed, who will not feel its wrath? This is not the wrath of God against man. It is the wrath of man against man, of neighbor against neighbor. It is already happening. Open your eyes. You are seeing only the first sparks of the great fire. They are coming forth so you might go and see. Yes, go and see the fire that now still burns beneath the surface. That is the fire that is coming. Look at it well. Do not minimize it. Do not say, "That section of the world has always been a tinderbox. Israel has always been threatened." This time is different. The fires will not be contained. The world will be dragged in. This is why I speak so often and, today, I speak so urgently.

The time is close. The fire is great and it will not be contained. When Satan wants a fire, is he content with one nation or one region? Does he not see himself as ruler of this world? Does he not want the whole world to become like his hell? This is his plan. He just waits until the final pieces are in place, so when he releases the fire, it will spread everywhere.

My Son has said, "I have come to cast fire upon the earth," but you have rejected this saving, purifying fire. So, you have no defense. There will be another fire, a destroying fire. This is why I speak. It is not too late. (Although at some point it will be too late for some.) Which fire do you want – the fire of my Son or the fire of the Evil One?

I will place a new fire in the Church and the bishops must be open to this fire. They must stop walking away from the messages of my Immaculate Heart. This is the fire which I offer my people and if they do not find it in the Catholic Church, then where will they discover it? Now, I am revealing my plan in more detail. Before the destructive fire is released (and this is inevitable), the Church and the people must have received the divine fire within my Immaculate Heart. Only if they have been deeply touched by this divine fire (which will bind them together) will they survive the satanic fire.

I speak to the bishops and the Pope. Begin now. You use so many other means that are useless against the satanic forces when the fire in my Immaculate Heart is ignored.

### Comment
*So many times, Mary has asked people to seek her help. Here, she shows where that help must be found, the primary place of the Catholic Church.*

December 5, 2011
# 186. The Medjugorje Visionaries

## Mary

Arise and come, so I can reveal my words and the nations will be enlightened. Yes, I can enlighten even the nations that live in darkness. My Son is a light to all the nations. If only they would walk in his light. That is why I speak. My words do not extend my light but his light. I do not speak by my own powers. The Father has sent me to extend the light of his Son to all the nations.

O nations of the world, you walk in the darkness of your own thoughts. You sign treaties, make agreements, align yourselves according to your own wisdom and your own light. You have cast aside my Son's light. "We have come to the enlightenment, to the age of reason," you say. "We have cast off the Dark Ages and have liberated ourselves. We use the light of natural reason to guide our course."

I say to you, "Is there no selfishness? Cannot the light of reason be used for evil? Does reason correct itself?" When does reason say, "I am wrong"? Only when it is too late. Only when all is destroyed. Then it must conclude, "I have taken the wrong path" (if it is even willing to be honest).

Do you not see? The wrong path is now nuclear. The stakes are too high. The mistakes are too costly. There is no room for error. How can you entrust the human race into the hands of reason when reason has led you to two world wars and constant conflicts? Why entrust yourself to reason when you can give yourselves over to your heavenly Mother?

These are my clear words. You are on the brink of nuclear war. You are helpless. Your rational approaches cannot defeat the evil that is being unleashed. Your treaties are useless. Your diplomatic approaches have failed, one after another.

I wait for you. I can lead you away from the coming catastrophes. These catastrophes I have revealed to the children of Medjugorje. They already know them. They are my ten secrets. Yet, I gave them a message of hope, but their words are muted. Many have not heard. The Church must proclaim them with full voice. How long must the visionaries persevere until the Church sees their words as so vital? Why not bring the story to the center? Why not bring the visionaries into the limelight? No longer keep them in the shadows. The validity of these apparitions is attested to on every side.

### Comment
*When nuclear war is a possibility, the stakes are high.*

December 6, 2011
## 187. Fire in the Earth's Belly

## Mary

So many events will happen so quickly and one will trigger the other because nothing stands firm. The first to collapse will naturally be those with the weakest foundation and those that are closest to the destructive fires. They will not at all withstand even the first shocks. Then, others who encircle them will not be able to resist the collapse. Then the whole world will realize that it will be drawn into the battle. This will not be a regional war, one that can be contained. The conflict will entangle all the nations.

The leaders will meet as usual to draw up plans, but the spark has been lit. The fire has been set.

Then will come a time when the conflict seems to be settled. The fire seems to have run its course, but this is only a calm for a little while. The great fire is still smoldering, but, as usual, the leaders will look the other way.

What do I have to say about these travails? These are constantly flaring fires that burst into flames, do their damage, change the state of the world for the worse, and then seem to be over, like a fire that has spent itself. They are only the symptoms of the illness, the surface reactions which should be alerting mankind but are not. So, let me teach clearly once more, always repeating the same message. There is a satanic fire (even though you do not believe in it) that burns in the belly of the earth (i.e. in the heart of human history). This fire escapes from time to time in all of the wars that constantly plague mankind. Until this satanic fire is put out, wars will always be with you. They will constantly erupt. They will grow in scale and in destruction greater than ever before with unimaginable destruction of human life.

I am the Woman and the heavenly Father has given me power over all these satanic fires. Without me, these fires go unimpeded.

### Comment
*We must turn to Mary as quickly as possible.*

December 7, 2011
## 188. Mary's Special Invitation to You

## Mary

I wait and I wait for the world to turn to me. I speak and I speak, hoping the world will listen. I search and I search, trying to find hearts that would receive all my blessings. I will not cease to wait and to speak and to search, because I have a mother's heart which can never forget the child of her womb.

Now I search in extraordinary ways. I do not limit my words to those who gather for worship. I go everywhere. I go to every nation in the world by these modern means of communication, but my messages are quite different.

When someone uses the Internet to send their message, the word goes forth for anyone in the world to read, but the person does not go forth, only their word. When my word goes forth, I accompany it. Yes, reader, as your eyes are now upon my word, I stand at your side. I touch your heart. I am already pouring out my gifts.

I am searching for you and I have found you. If only you would open your heart to me, I would enter your heart. Your heart is a very special place. There is a gate, a door into your heart which is closely guarded by your free will. No one can enter unless you are willing and no one can leave unless you eject them. This is the greatest mystery – the human heart with all of its choices.

All of your life, you have chosen whom to accept and whom to reject. This is a very special moment. You have a visitor at the gate. I stand at the door, and by these words, I knock, not just once but many times, not just softly but with great clamor. If you do not hear, I will knock louder. If you do not open, I will not go away. For years I have been searching for you. In the years of your sinfulness, I waited. In your years of questioning, I spoke. Now, at this moment, when so many of God's graces have made you ready, I come and knock.

Look at your life. Has there not been a series of graces, a gradual turning away from the darkest moments of your life, a gradual, almost imperceptible dawning of light? Now, I am closer than ever before. I am the noonday sun and I want to bring you into a fullness of light that will always remain within you. Take the step. Seek out confession. Rid yourself of your sins and you will have stepped into a new day that will remain with you, all the days of your life.

### Comment
*Mary is speaking to some soul who she has quietly visited and brought out of deep darkness. Now, she invites him/her into the full light.*

December 8, 2011
## 189. The Harshness of the Coming Winter

## Mary

How difficult is the winter for so many. The people ask, "When will the springtime come?" as they look forward to the end of the cold and of the storms which often lash out at them. Mankind cannot control the winter. Its fierceness is not subject to human wills. As the storms follow, one after another, a hopelessness sets in which is allayed only by the knowledge that spring will follow.

Is this situation of human history? Is a winter of destruction always followed by a springtime of restoration? In the middle of human destruction can someone look at a calendar and say, "I know when this will be over. It will soon be spring." The seasons are subject to God's will. Winter cannot say, "I will replace the spring." Nature has an order given to it by the creator.

Human events do not enjoy such a certainty. They are in the hands of man. They follow man's timetable and are not subject to the order of nature. The man-made winter of harshness and suffering has no calendar. It is not automatically followed by the spring. This is why I must speak. The harshness of winter has its times and its seasons but then it must give way. It has no choice. The heavenly Father has decreed that it be so. But, when man moves away from God, when man says, "I will determine the season," then there are no limits to the harm or to the length of breadth, height and depth of the destruction.

That is why I come to wrap my mantle around mankind, just like a mother wraps her child during the cold of winter. Man can begin this winter. He is free to unleash his weapons, but I am free to wrap my children in the warmest of clothes.

Satan will not harm my little ones even with the fiercest of winters. No matter how long it lasts and what devastation he plans, because I will bundle my children in the warmest of blankets. But I must say this clearly. It is not the springtime of freedom when children can run freely. It is the winter when the children must gather around their mother. This winter will be fierce. It will seem like it will never end. But, does a baby wrapped in a warm blanket and held close by his mother, even know that it is winter? Does he even think, "When will come the springtime?" or is he quite content to be held in her arms? Come to me. I would wrap the whole world in my mantle.

### Comment
*The images are easy to grasp, Satan's winter overcome by Mary's protection.*

December 9, 2011
## 190. The Endless Midnight

## Mary

The night is coming and, like any night, it comes slowly, first the dusk, then the twilight, then the darkness and finally the midnight, the total darkness. Yet, no one despairs. All know that the darkest of nights must give way. Night is limited by daylight. It has its time and then must give way. It cannot claim a permanent hold over the earth because God has made the sun. So it is with nature, so orderly, no chaos, easily able to be charted and predicted.

This, however, is not the way it is with satanic darkness, which is chaos. Nothing can be charted or predicted. There is no sun in his world that can arise and say to the night, "Be scattered, for your time is at an end. You must give way to my light." His world is total darkness and those who descend into his world have no hope of light.

This has been my clear message. The world, unknowingly, has chosen the darkness. They have said to my Son, the Sun of Justice, "Do not rise, I do not want your light." Fine. You have chosen the darkness and I will let you remain in the darkness (I have no other choice) until you realize that the secular world you have chosen has no day. (Is that not what you are always saying? "We are secular.")

Yes, you have chosen a world which begins in light (the light given by your Creator) but which moves into twilight and midnight. When you get to midnight, the clock stops ticking. You have arrived at the center of the satanic world. He has tricked you, entrapped you. He told you to abandon the light of Jesus. He gave you a false light that would quickly fade, never to return. O world, if you continue on this road, you will reach a midnight that never ends. Now, you are only in the twilight yet look at the confusion and the chaos. What will the world be when it is endless midnight?

Turn back. I offer you the Sun of Justice. You are blinded by false lights that will lead to midnight. That is why I try to call you away, and why I offer you another light. To the reader, I say, "You know the religious light that you used to have and the religious devotion that you used to practice. Go back and retrieve them. They are easily available, right at hand. I am not asking for what is impossible. Those devotions and that faith are the light. Live that faith and you will never suffer from an endless midnight."

### *Comment*
*Mary uses powerful and clear images to invite you to familiar devotions.*


December 10, 2011
## 191. A Clear Summary of the Messages


## Mary

One thing is obvious. The world cannot continue in this direction. By my words, I have revealed, as far as possible (that is, as far as you need to know), what lies ahead if the world continues on this path of self-destruction. The power to destroy the world and human life as it now exists is already in place. The fires of anger and hatred burn so fiercely in the hearts of so many. The instability of economic structures affects even those who otherwise would feel safe and above the fray. Human life is so fragile and complex, that it can easily be disrupted.

All of these things I have shown you so often because they are the first part of my message. The second part is also clear but not as much accepted. All of this could have been avoided. Mankind did not have to come to this moment. It was not an inevitable result of natural causes. This is the part that the world cannot receive, but I will say it again. Satan has brought all this about. He has used the intellect and the selfishness of man to build a world that, with a few strokes of his genius, he can destroy so that human life is changed for centuries. That is the moment in which mankind finds himself.

For so long, especially since the French Revolution when the goddess of reason was exalted, man has excluded God; the human race has been tricked by Satan and has had to deal with two world wars that never needed to occur.

Now, he has mankind on the edge of a greater precipice. The heavenly Father will not allow Satan to fulfill his plan but he has only two options. Mankind can return to

God and walk in his ways. Or, the heavenly Father can allow the divine chastisements to stop mankind in its tracks. The second is just the lesser of two evils. There will be the chastisements of heaven so there is not the destruction planned by Satan.

I have spoken clearly and concisely from my motherly heart. If mankind repents and turns back to God, I will lead man by an easy path. Do not think it cannot be accomplished.

### Comment
*Mary has said these truths at various times in these messages.*
*Today she summarizes everything.*

December 11, 2011
## 192. The First Waves of Darkness

## Mary

The world is entering a time of great darkness and it is a long road back into the light. Many will get lost and never find the light, but I promise to guide everyone who trusts in me and listens to my messages through whatever darkness they encounter. I will tell you what I do.

When a person comes to me, I first quiet and still them. They are filled with fears and believe that they cannot continue. Sometimes, it takes a long while to quiet these fears because anxieties multiply themselves. They beget images that oppress. Everything is blown out of proportion. The fears enter the deep regions of the heart and paralyze the person. This power of darkness, these lies of Satan, need to be put to rest. I speak simple words with a mother's voice because the person in this state has become like a helpless child. (But a helpless child at least has a mother while so many in the world do not know that they, too, have a mother.)

This comforting must happen again and again, because, in the darkness, fears multiply. So, I bring some rays of divine light. I recall the eternal truths to the person. The heavenly Father has not abandoned the world. He is drawing the person close to himself and he has sent me so that no one loses the way.

In this darkness, the person feels my presence. They do not see me but they know I am there. Sometimes, I give them great faith and peace in the middle of the trials. At other times, I bring about a sudden and surprising rescue from the difficulties. In both cases, the person knows that I am with them.

And so, we wait together, getting through one day at a time, surviving even amid the most difficult of times. Soon, the person grows strong in faith. They have survived the

236

initial darkness. The fears are calmed and they return to their usual way of life. They are surprised. They can function. They can continue. The first waves of darkness have not destroyed them. There will be other waves but they know they have a mother who will help them. Blessed are those who know that I am the Woman, the powerful Mother of all mankind. How unfortunate those who think they are orphans.

### Comment

*Mary does not downplay the difficulties of the darkness that is coming, but she describes how the person can gain her help.*

December 12, 2011
## 193. Fatima and Medjugorje – Preparing for a Greater Light

## Mary

Today, I pour out the deepest words of my Immaculate Heart. They are words dripped in blood. When I brought Jesus forth in Bethlehem, there was no blood. It was a virgin birth. But quickly, there began the blood of suffering when Simeon prophesied about the child and Herod even threatened the child's life. So the words I speak are words dripped in my own blood, like a mother bringing a child to birth.

Before going on, I must explain the divine plan, what is in the Father's heart. He has only love for mankind and when it sinned, he sent his Son. As it continues to hurtle to destruction, he has sent me as a messenger, a voice, the modern John the Baptist. I am not the Word of God, I am only his voice telling you to receive God's Word, Jesus, my Son. Now, let us begin.

From the beginning, God planned great glory for man, like a rich man for his newborn child. But also, from the beginning, those plans were destroyed by sin. Man became unworthy of God's glory. Sin continued and grew powerful and the likelihood that the Father's plan would ever be accomplished seemingly vanished. Then, in the fullness of time, God sent an angel to reveal to me his plan of sending His Son. I saw my role, as difficult as it would be, filled with the shedding of blood, and I accepted that role. The light of God came and burned brightly. Jesus was raised up and placed on the lampstand. But now, the power of sin repeats the original distancing. Every day sin multiplies beyond its former limits. It intrudes even into the sanctuary of the Church and touches the highest office of worldly powers.

So, the Father decided to intervene again. At an important moment, as the New World was just beginning to open up to the European explorers, I appeared to St. Juan

Diego at Guadalupe. There began the greatest moment of conversions to Jesus in all of history, a power that continues until this day.

Can this not happen again? Cannot the Father again send me as his heavenly messenger. It has already happened. The sun itself was shaken at Fatima. The visions continue each day at Medjugorje. Both of these will come into a full brilliance. Their light has not been spent. These two sites are preparing hearts but the full brilliance of my Son is still to come – soon, so very soon. Prepare the way of the Lord.

<u>Comment</u>

*God never gives up. When the darkness gets greater, he sends greater light.*

December 13, 2011

# 194. An Invitation to See

# Mary

The day begins with light but ends in darkness. So, human history begins with the light of God. It is not meant to have a darkness. The light was meant to increase as man's relationship to God grew. But, this is not what has happened. Man has turned his back on God and, even if the sun would shine seven times brighter, man would only see the darkness of his own shadow.

That is what is happening in human history. Man is turning his back on God and the shadow grows longer. So, the Father sends me to preach, to say to the whole world, "If you would just turn around, you would be filled with light." Yet, there are difficulties which I must explain.

Since mankind is not used to God's light, as it turns, there is great pain. The eyes have grown accustomed to the darkness. Mankind feels quite at home with lies, and cheating and promiscuity. Promises are given quickly with no real resolve to keep them. Accounts are juggled. The "books are cooked." All is accepted with the wink of an eye, even though a just creditor will be defrauded.

So, the call to light poses some difficulties. The actions, so easily accepted in darkness, must be put aside. The person sees with new eyes and must assume new responsibilities. Many will say that this is impossible, that the habits of darkness are too ingrained. I do not say that this is an easy process or one that will be completed quickly, because living in the light has a cost. I just say that this is possible, that I invite you, the reader, to come into this light and that I will be with you in your new life.

What is your other option? You can continue in the darkness, which will grow and grow. You will come to moments when you know you are lost, so surrounded by darkness that you can only despair. How many invitations to light can you reject and still escape the darkness? Listen now. No matter how many past invitations you have rejected, I am giving you one more. I cannot promise you that there will be future invitations if you reject this one. You who read this know what I mean because I am also speaking in your heart right now. Go to confession and in the darkness of the confessional, you will find light to see.

*Comment*
*Darkness is convenient. Light reveals our responsibilities.*
*Darkness leads to despair and light to life.*

December 14, 2011
## 195. A Return to Innocence

## Mary

No one will turn you away from the door. No one will say, "You are not welcome." No, I will hear your tiniest knock, your softest touch upon the door of my heart. I will open and see you, trembling and afraid. I will say, "Come in. I have your place all prepared." You will see all the others I have gathered, so similar to yourself, sinners but all gathered together by the Woman, all rejoicing because they never thought they could enjoy the privilege of being God's child. Yet, they find this hidden identity within themselves, something written on their hearts, "a child of God made in his image and likeness." No one knows what they have been through until they tell their stories. Then, all see that the stories are so familiar, exactly like their own story. I will recount them, giving a sense of what happens.

The stories all begin with a happiness, a joy. However, this joy is cast aside. It is misjudged as of little importance and other things are taken up instead. The person becomes fascinated with these false goals and soon they are wandering far astray, losing their way, following an illusionary goal.

Then they hear a voice within, reminding them of what they were and the way they used to be. Then they hear a voice saying, "I will be with you. Turn back." This voice leads them to the door. They recognize the door so well. It is where they used to worship the Father. It is the door of goodness. "Dare I go in?" they ask. "How can I ask for entrance after all I have done?" Yet, the attraction is so great, that they approach and knock. I am standing there. When I speak they recognize my voice, the voice that said, "I will be with you, turn back." Yes, O reader, you once lived in great innocence but you have wandered after false lights. By these words, I urge you to return to your first innocence. Regain the joys of a good conscience. I will be there to make sure that the door opens.

*Comment*

*When innocence is lost, the person always grieves. They feel that the loss is irreparable. Not at all. The door to innocence is always open.*

December 16, 2011

## 196. Why the Chastisements Are Delayed

## Mary

"Why do I wait so long? Why do I hold back my chastising hand?" These are the questions that the heavenly Father can legitimately ask. He sees the sins of mankind. He watches them flout his laws and even deny his existence. He has given mankind the beautiful earth and the gorgeous heavens. So, why does he not act? This is the great mystery, the delay, the constant delay, the pushing back.

The heavenly Father waits patiently, hoping that he does not have to act, always hoping that mankind would turn to him, so he could act with the greatest of mercies. He even raises up intercessors, who come before him night and day. These are God's closest friends, and they plead with him to show mercy. In this way, he can put aside his justice for a while. He can claim that these chosen souls are like Moses who pleaded with him and allowed him to forgive the Israelites.

This is the drama which takes place behind the scenes, which I will explain for all to understand. God has many attributes, innumerable attributes that man cannot even understand or imagine. These attributes are the ways he acts with mankind. They are the qualities of his Divine Person. Even in the Bible, God seems to have many faces. At times, he chooses Israel, then he chastises, then he promises and then he restores. God has only one face, but he has many qualities and all come into play in any relationship which God has with man. The Bible tries to catch this diversity, this complexity of God (even though he is perfectly simple).

God is not arbitrary. All of these attributes are in perfect balance and harmony. God is very predictable. If mankind repents, God will forgive. If mankind sins and continues in its sin, God will chastise.

But the question here is about time. When will God chastise? When a person repents, God forgives immediately, but it is quite different with his chastisements. He puts them off and puts them off. People even complain, "How long, O Lord, before you vindicate our rights?" This is because God stretches his mercy as far as he can, until

240

showing mercy is foolish, destructive and harmful to the human race. I must say, "We have reached that point," yet he still delays only because many chosen souls plead before his divine presence. They delay the chastisements and gain time for repentance. This is my message, "Do not put off the time of your repentance," or else you will be worthy of God's chastisements. I speak to you as a mother warning her children.

<u>*Comment*</u>
*Mary gives a clear picture of how God acts, according to various attributes.*

December 17, 2011
## 197. The Coming Destructive Events

## <u>Mary</u>

The events will begin, pouring out one after another. In the beginning, men will just see this as another difficulty to be grappled with. Then as a second and a third event happen, they will wonder how they can respond. Then as the events pour out more and more, all will realize that the state of the world is changing.

What do I mean by "the events"? These come from the hidden heart of Satan. Each event is touched by his demonic fire. They are human events, but they are not just human decisions. These decisions come from the hearts of people who are controlled by Satan. Their hearts are given over to hatred, anger and destruction. They are captured hearts. Unfortunately, they are not captured by love. They are not owned by my Son, Jesus. They are captured by the Evil One.

He will use the smallest first, to set a little fire of destruction (I do not just mean wars or violent destruction, but all manner of disturbances). Then other sources of his darkness will be poured forth. After that, seeing that each of these new problems has had its effect, he will reach deep within his bag and pull out unforeseen problems. These he will release upon a world that is already having difficulties coping with the previous problems.

At this point, he is not finished. He will hold his greatest powers in reserve. He will wait and he will rejoice in the destruction and confusion that he has stirred up through his minions, those whose hearts he controls. Yet, there are others. These still wait in the wings. It is not yet their time to go on stage. Satan wants to orchestrate everything. He wants it in his way and in his time.

But, I will not let this happen. This is what I am trying to teach mankind. Satan owns people. These people are destructive and he has armed them with every possible weapon. (Again, I am not just speaking about weapons of war. There are weapons of lies, of confusion, of political authority, of financial power. There are the weapons of mass communication and of the Internet. His weapons are everywhere and he owns people in every nation and in every walk of life.)

I know Satan's people, his weapons and his plan. I know his army and his legions of followers. I would have destroyed him long ago, but the human race has chosen to follow his darkness and to reject my light. So, it has walked into his trap and he is about to release his powers in all of their fury. I say this clearly. It will be released, step by step, always with increasing power and darkness. He will send forth many, but not all, of what he has accumulated over these centuries.

What can I do? I can protect all those who come to me. That is why the Father has sent me. This is the constant theme of the messages. The destructive events will pour forth but I can save those who trust in me. I do not say that I will save your lives. I will save your souls. Also, I will save you from much of the suffering (but not all). I will save your loved ones. You will see them return to the faith. Tell them not to despair. Tell them that all of this has been told to you ahead of time, so that all can believe that in these events, the Woman of Light stands in your midst calling all into the Noah's Ark of her Immaculate Heart.

*Locutions to the World* continues in *Volume Two* and *Volume Three*. *Volume Two* contains locutions from December 18, 2011 to October 28, 2012. *Volume Three* contains locutions from July 14, 2012 to January 30, 2014.